DIVERSITY, JUSTICE, and COMMUNITY

The **Canadian Scholars Series in Justice Studies** critically and creatively imagines how community and criminal justice approaches can contribute to more just and equitable communities. Packaging theory with application, the path-breaking volumes in this series will inform students, educators, academics, practitioners, policy-makers, and anyone interested in the pursuit of a more humane justice system.

DIVERSITY, JUSTICE, and COMMUNITY

The Canadian Context

EDITED BY
Beverly-Jean M. Daniel

Canadian Scholars' Press
Toronto

Diversity, Justice, and Community: The Canadian Context
Edited by Beverly-Jean M. Daniel

First published in 2016 by
Canadian Scholars' Press Inc.
425 Adelaide Street West, Suite 200
Toronto, Ontario
M5V 3C1

www.cspi.org

Library and Archives Canada Cataloguing in Publication

Diversity, justice, and community: the Canadian context / edited by Beverly-Jean M. Daniel.

(Series in social justice by Canadian scholars)
Includes bibliographical references.
Issued in print and electronic formats.
ISBN 978-1-55130-915-6 (paperback).--ISBN 978-1-55130-916-3 (pdf).--
ISBN 978-1-55130-917-0 (epub)

1. Crime--Canada--Sociological aspects. 2. Discrimination in criminal justice administration--Canada. 3. Racism in criminology--Canada.
4. Minorities--Canada--Social conditions. I. Daniel, Beverly-Jean M., 1967-, editor II. Title.

HV6197.C3D58 2016   364.089'00971   C2016-906062-4
                                                   C2016-906063-2

Cover and text design by Peggy & Co. Design Inc.

Printed and bound in Canada by Marquis

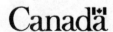

I chose the African symbol of the Siamese crocodiles, Funtunfunefu-Denkyemfunefu, to open this text because it truly represents the essence of this book. The crocodiles symbolize the importance of recognizing the extent to which we as people are interconnected and that when we do harm to others, we do harm to ourselves as well. In much the same way that the crocodiles are interdependent and the survival of one depends on the survival of the other, in this book we have attempted to highlight the relevance of balanced and equitable approaches to social justice, democracy, and anti-oppression to foster the growth of healthy global and local communities.

CONTENTS

INTRODUCTION

After years of teaching in the vast field of diversity studies, whether in the context of education, the justice system, or leadership development, there was one thing that was evident—Canadian-based content was lacking. Students, as a clear form of resistance to the examination of issues of diversity, consistently questioned the relevance of the American-based material, claiming that these issues did not apply to Canada. The United States was regarded as a space where varying forms of social evils occurred, leaving Canada as a land of innocence and inclusion, a multicultural paradise. Exposing students to the reality of oppression, marginalization, and everyday injustices in Canada often placed me on the frontlines of emotional crises in the classroom. Further to this, as a woman of colour addressing these issues in predominantly White classrooms, my credentials, my capacity, and the veracity of the information I presented were often questioned, at best, and my objectivity always critiqued. I was destroying the illusion of inclusion!

In spite of the challenges along the way, there were successes and learning opportunities. The idea for this text was based on those lessons learned. The decision to choose the chapters that are included in this text was based on observations about the gaps in the literature, the changing dynamics regarding which students were entering justice and diversity related fields, and the changing face of those who were involved in the justice system. Further to this, the need for Canadian content was also central to this exercise.

The reality is that the vast majority of offenders in the Canadian justice system and correctional institutions continue to be White men and women. However, because of exposure to messages from the media and society regarding who is the criminal, many of our students enter these programs and move into the field with stereotypes of racialized people as criminals intact. There is very limited understanding of the systemic and institutional factors that result in the production of criminality in marginalized and oppressed communities. The students and many average Canadians simply take the problematic messages as "truth." As such, one of the goals of this text is to attempt to examine, critique, and disrupt the taken-for-granted assumptions regarding who is a criminal. The majority of students, instructors, and administrators in these academic institutions are White, and people tend to be more willing and open to a broad range of explanations for behaviours within their own group. Therefore, crime and criminality among Whites is often analyzed through frames of familiarity and individualism, whereas there is a tendency to adopt frames of culture, religion, group norms, racial pathology, or biological determinism to explain the behaviours and actions of members of other groups.

For example, it is not uncommon to hear students say that Aboriginal people commit crimes because "that's just who they are" or that South Asians kill females in their community because that is "what they do in their culture." When there are acts of violence among Blacks, the term *Black-on-Black violence* is used. However, when White males kill their wives, children, partners, or other White males, there is no such term as *White-on-White violence*. There is no interrogation of "White people" as a group or a "race," nor are their actions regarded as culturally or biologically embedded. These acts are regarded as individual acts of pathology that can be explained by negative childhood experiences, improper parenting, and so on. Oppressed groups are seldom afforded such humanizing options and explanations.

The chapters in this reader seek to provide students with a historical context for understanding the factors that have promoted the development of crime in a range of communities. In addition, we attempt to facilitate students' understanding of the ways in which oppression is built into *all* social systems, which in turn negatively affects people's experience of the world, their opportunities, and their outcomes. It is also for this reason that there is limited focus on individualized understandings of issues, such as individual racism, because the reality is that individuals do what society gives them the option of doing. Individual racism exists because there are larger social, economic, and political structures that have embedded these patterns as a part of the fabric of the society. This text seeks to explore the existing patterns, rather than focusing on the acts of individuals. Many people adopt the stance of "I am not racist, sexist, homophobic, and so on, so it's not my problem!" In fact, we all need to recognize the impact of those patterns and the way that most of us in society contribute to the problem.

We have attempted to provide students with some level of insider knowledge of the issues that are covered in this text. We have tried to ensure that the authors are members of the represented community groups or have experience working with these populations. We have attempted to provide more than a theoretical exposition of the issues, but also to include the applied lenses. The text lends itself well to building linkages between the theories and the application of social justice practices. An applied lens allows students to put practices in place that are based on critical reflection and understanding.

We recognize that no one text can address the myriad issues connected to the field of justice and diversity studies, and that there will be limitations to what can be covered in this volume. There are populations in the justice system that are dealing with aging, mental health challenges, varying forms of addictions, and a range of intellectual disabilities. We have attempted to weave some of these issues, including social class, throughout the text. Understanding social class is a central aspect of understanding justice-related issues. The authors primarily focused on racial disparities, recognizing that the issue of class is intersectionally connected to all of these groups. One cannot, however, conflate race and class. People who are wealthy and racialized are often subjected to similar levels of scrutiny as members of their group who are poor. For example, a young racialized male driving an expensive car has a greater probability of being profiled by the police than one taking the bus. The assumption is often made that if a young, racialized male is driving an expensive car, that youth is probably involved in some sort of illegal activity. In a similar vein, if a young, racialized male is seen walking or riding a bike in a middle-class neighbourhood, that male has a high likelihood of being harassed by the police because he may be deemed to be out of place, the assumption being that he could not live in such an area. Therefore, whereas upper-class status may offer some long-term benefits to racialized youth, in the initial interaction or engagement with administrators of justice, the most visible characteristic is the one that would stand out, and that would be their racial markers.

The first chapter of this text focuses on the definitions of the many terms that are used when discussing issues of diversity. This decision was very purposeful. Over the years I have come to recognize that people assumed they knew the meanings of these terms; however, the ways in which they spoke and wrote about them indicated that their understanding was limited. Added to this, I had conducted some applied research in the classroom regarding the strategies that supported students in understanding and addressing these issues. Students indicated that when they were provided with a historical context for understanding the issues and the opportunity to learn about the terms, it gave them a solid starting point for challenging their knowledge base. Further to this, they came to recognize that their taken-for-granted assumptions about meaning and histories were addressed at the outset, thereby enabling them as a group to engage with the material rather than being stuck wrestling with multiple meanings of the terms. It is for this reason that the first chapter covers the meanings of terms, rather than this information being placed in a glossary at the end.

Chapter 2 introduces the reader to some critical discussions and debates related to concerns of justice and injustice and the ways in which it can influence people's worlds. It also pushes the reader to consider whether justice is as simple as guilt versus innocence, or whether the human circumstance has to be factored in when trying to understand human behaviour.

Chapter 3 provides a historical and contemporary look at the ways in which the use of jails and prisons has been connected to the application of justice. It forces us to question whether the methods that have been used historically, and in today's society, are the most effective ways to dispense justice and the role that social justice lenses may play in changing how we apply justice.

Chapter 4, on religion and rehabilitation, again asks the question of what is meant by justice, what strategies we have implemented to reintegrate people into society after they have paid for their crimes, and what role a person's belief system can play in reducing recidivism.

Chapter 5 provides a discussion of the ways in which practices evident within classrooms throughout Canada, but specifically in Ontario, become an entry-way to prisons for Black males. There is a recognition that these practices also affect Indigenous males; however, there is a need to examine this experience in a separate context to avoid assuming that the experiences of these two groups are the same. While Black males may have access to different levels of education in urban and suburban centres, the opportunity for schooling is limited on many reserves. We therefore examined the issue specifically in relation to Black males, given that (aside from Aboriginal males) they are the group that is most negatively affected by this destructive cradles to prisons pipeline, which also plays a significant role in destabilizing Black families and communities. It is this destabilization that has become central to the upkeep of the justice/injustice system.

Chapter 6 discusses the issue of violence against Indigenous women and girls in Canada. The chapter provides a historical look at the impact of colonization on Indigenous women and explores the governmental and social justice–based responses for accessing justice for these women.

Chapter 7 critically analyzes the response of the Canadian justice system to the deaths of Somali youth, primarily in Alberta. These youth, their families, and their communities are caught in multiple sites of oppression, including race, religion, class, and immigration status, and become an interesting example of the way in which intersectionality functions. It exposes the ways in which the agents of the system move between and within sites of oppression and illustrates that this strategy has led to limited success in solving these cases.

Chapter 8, on South Asian youth and the justice system, is framed within the discourse of changing demographic patterns and problematizes the notion of the "model minority" while simultaneously adopting a proactive stance to addressing the growing challenges of this population. The chapter initiates an exploration into issues related to cultural engagements, the benefits and limitations of collectivist cultures, and the ways in which silence becomes a barrier that needs to be addressed.

Chapter 9 explores the relationship between familial racism and gang involvement across several different groups and shows the ways in which racism, whether experienced as a victim or a perpetrator, can have extremely negative consequences for identity development and life choices. White gang members learn about racism in their families and the larger society, and this frames how they can engage with other groups in rather inhumane ways. For gang members from racialized groups, the authors demonstrate the ways in which the experience of racism diminishes their positive identity markers, pushes them to the fringes, and sets them up for recruitment into gangs.

Chapter 10, on LGBTQ issues in policing and prisons, discusses the treatment of members of this community in their engagements with the justice system. The chapter provides a historical and contemporary context for understanding these issues while providing students with several case studies to highlight the realities.

Chapter 11 again adopts an intersectional analysis, providing students with some insights into the experience of women and girls who become involved in the justice system. The chapter investigates some of the factors that have led to these groups' involvement in criminal activities while exploring community-based options available for working with women and girls.

Chapter 12 provides students with a brief introduction to some of the community-based options that have been used in attempting to address crime in communities. The discussion is not exhaustive; its aim is simply to provide students with some options they can research to enhance their understanding of what is available within a Canadian context.

There are many areas that are in need of ongoing theorization and research, including the involvement of Southeast Asians in the justice system and the experiences of the increasing number of immigrant and refugee families and the ways in which they are included and excluded from the system. In addition, there is a need to explore the experience of increasing migration from Eastern Europe, the growing problem of sex slavery, and the ongoing challenges of reducing the number of children who are victims of sexual violence.

The challenge of marginalized youth who are being drawn into fundamentalist religious sects is another area in need of exploration. Inasmuch as we can draw from American, British, and other global sources, the need for research based on the uniqueness of the Canadian context continues to grow. Research is fundamental to the development and implementation of effective, relevant, and culturally nuanced services.

Canada is uniquely positioned to harness and develop the potential of its increasingly diverse population. That requires an open and honest look at the existing challenges, limitations, and opportunities in our society. It requires us to move beyond limiting frames of individual analysis and explore the systemic patterns that affect people's lives. It requires us to move beyond the boundaries of our own personal worlds and experiences to recognize the extent to which all of our worlds are uniquely intertwined. What affects one community, eventually affects all of us. This idea connects directly to the symbol of the Siamese crocodiles, Funtunfunefu-Denkyemfunefu, described at the beginning of the book: We are interdependent beings.

Theories of Justice and Community Justice

CHAPTER 1

Critical Discussion of Terms

Beverly-Jean M. Daniel

Chapter Objectives

This chapter will help the reader develop an understanding of the major terms that are used in this collection and in relation to issues of diversity, justice, and difference. The aim of this chapter is to provide the reader with a basic introduction to the concepts, with the understanding that many of them are very complex. However, the complexity of the ideas can often confuse students who have not been exposed to them, and this chapter is aimed at initiating a conversation rather than being taken as the end point of these discussions.

Introduction

Today, Canada boasts one of the most cosmopolitan populations in the world. This means that Canada has a very diverse population, with people who have migrated from many parts of the world (Ash, 2004; Day, 2000; Salojee, 2004). The forms or sites of diversity in Canada include religion, ethnicity, race, culture, language, sexual identity, and ability, to name but a few. Prior to the arrival of Europeans (in 1491), Canada may be said to have been relatively monocultural— that is, having one primary culture, specifically the First Nations and other Aboriginal peoples—but the reality is that even within and among the Aboriginal peoples there existed multiple tribes, languages, and cultural practices. Drawing primarily from critical theoretical perspectives, including critical theory (Blum, 2012; Freire, 1996, 1999; Gillborn, 2007; Giroux, 1984, 2001; James, 2000), integrative anti-racism (Dei, 1996; Dei, Mazzuca, McIssac, & Zine, 1997; Rebello & Moras, 2006), critical race theory (Crenshaw, Gotanda, Peller, & Thomas, 1995; Delgado & Stefanic, 2001; Ladson-Billings, 1998), and post-colonial theory (Loomba, 1998), the following sections of this chapter will provide the reader with a brief history of Canada to show how differences emerged and how they are understood and experienced today. It will also discuss the primary terms related to notions of difference and justice. The examples used will be primarily based on Canadian situations and scenarios.

Context and Content—A Brief History of Oppression in Canada

Understanding many of the patterns in social relations today requires a look at how these interactions developed historically. We often believe that what we see today exists only in the present; however, Wallis, Sunseri, and Galabuzi (2010) argue that understanding modern-day relations in Canada requires a look at situations and circumstances in the past. The players in the game may change; the location may change; the context may change; but the patterns remain the same.

Europeans (specifically British and French populations) came to Canada in search of wealth and natural resources that could be collected and sent to Europe to build wealth (Mackey, 2010) and create new societies for the monarchies (Wallis et al., 2010). Although initially, as with most colonial ventures, only small groups of adventurers came, as time went by an increasing number of colonizers arrived on the shores of what is today referred to as Canada. In later years, other Europeans arrived in Canada and settled in different parts of the country, with the British controlling Upper Canada (which is in the southern part of Canada, but the upper part of the St. Lawrence River) and the French controlling Lower Canada. These groups used a wide range of strategies to control and oppress the Indigenous populations that resided in North America.

Through the use of British-developed legislation and laws, the colonizers seized land from the Aboriginal peoples, placed them on reservations (Lawrence, 2010), and curtailed their ability to hunt and gather as they had done for generations before the arrival of the colonizers. Containment on reserves resulted in the loss of trading opportunities, the limitation of their food supplies, and undermined their ability to care for and support the members of their communities. In addition, Aboriginal people were exposed to diseases such as smallpox, which resulted in the death of significant numbers of First Nations people (Cummins & Steckley, 2013) and limited their ability to resist the invasion of the Europeans (Lawrence, 2010). Along with these practices of containment (i.e., practices designed to control and limit the movement and growth of people), the Europeans implemented laws, specifically the Indian Act of 1876, which essentially gave them complete control over the lives of Aboriginal people (Cummins & Steckley, 2013). The Europeans determined where Aboriginal people could live, whom they could marry, whether they would be able to maintain their band status, and the quality of education they could get. According to Cummins and Steckley (2013), the Indian Act was "the tool with which the government controlled Native people [and] was not a new piece of legislation. Rather it was a consolidation of various pieces of existing federal and colonial statutes" (p. 128). The Indian Act was used as a way to exercise complete control over Canada's Aboriginal peoples.

Colonizers employed multiple practices to control Indigenous populations, including religious conversion, removal or expulsion, assimilation, and elimination or extermination (Hilberg, 2010; Joshi, 2010). Aboriginal people in Canada were subjected to every single one of these practices. The biggest national disaster that has been a part of Canada from its inception, and that continues to plague Canada today, is its treatment of Aboriginal peoples.

Oppression, and its modern-day forms, has a history. History helps us to understand that what we have come to accept as normal and unchangeable has been built by other human beings and as such can be changed. The Canada we know today has many positive features. We are a very diverse nation; the overall quality of life for the vast majority of us is quite good; we have a level of safety and security. We have not had to deal with significant experiences of civil or international war, natural disaster, or the ongoing instability that emerges when there are groups engaged in religious conflict. However, Canada has engaged and continues to engage in oppression, marginalization, exclusion, and other systemic forms of racism that have come to be regarded as normal. In the following sections, I will provide a very brief historical look at the experiences of inequality, oppression, and discrimination that have been evident in Canada's history. This information will help you as the reader to understand the historical background of many of the injustices evident in today's society. This chapter will focus primarily on the terms that are often used when we speak about issues of inequality or oppression, but are seldom defined or understood in their appropriate contexts. This will allow the reader to understand the terminology used in the text and the concepts that are being used, while providing concrete examples.

Definition of Terms

Oppression

Oppression and its practices result in treating people in a way that limits their access to full participation in society. When people are legally prevented from full participation in society, it has the potential to create significant social, educational, and economic deficits that span across generations. In order to understand oppression, one must recognize that individuals are part of a larger society, and that society is supported by a web of institutions that are connected and controlled by those in power. These institutions include every system that has been set up and supported by the government, including schools, the justice system, the medical system, the parliament, the media, and so on. (Although the media is usually controlled by private enterprises or corporations, these corporations still have to adhere to rules that are set in place by the government.) Each system was set up by and for the ruling classes. This means that those in power decided the rules and the laws of each system and designed them in such a way as to ensure that they and their heirs would continue to benefit from those systems. For example, the school system is set up in such a manner that the content that is included, the ideas that are promoted in the curriculum, and the version of history that is highlighted tends to identify those in power as the natural leaders of society (Doxtator, 2011). The curriculum that has been taught in Canadian classrooms has used images of European males as saviours and to represent people in positions of leadership. This includes politicians, scientists, engineers, professors, and doctors. What we learn from these images or subtle messages is who is expected to be the natural leaders in society and who is denied access to various forms of social reward (Doxtator, 2011), including leadership roles.

The power that colonizers or dominant groups held allowed them to exercise control over all public institutions and ensure that they received the vast majority of the benefits and privileges of the systems. They have access to the best places to live, the best quality of medical care, and the best quality of schooling. While the dominant groups receive the best that the system has to offer, those who are regarded as inferior—in other words, anyone who is not European or White, in the Canadian context—have benefits taken away from them. For example, the colonizers passed laws to justify their control of the lands while at the same time preventing anyone who was non-White, including the Aboriginal peoples who originally occupied these lands, from owning land (Henry & Tator, 2010). Because of the laws that were put in place, the dominant increased their benefits, wealth, and privilege, thus ensuring that each successive generation had a head start in life (education, wealth, property ownership, good neigbourhoods, etc.) while members of the subordinate groups were denied the same types of benefits. As such, each succeeding generation of the dominant group tends to outpace the members of the subordinate group, thus making it appear that members of the subordinate groups are not prepared to work as hard to be successful.

The term *meritocracy* means that people achieve or are compensated in direct relation to how hard they work and their capacity or intelligence (Young, 1994). The problem with this concept is that when people start off with different amounts of educational or economic capital or resources, some have to work much harder to achieve the same results. For example, a person who is a member of a family that has limited economic resources may have a more difficult time attending university simply because they do not have easy access to money to pay fees. By contrast, someone who is from a wealthy family that is willing to pay their fees can focus on their academics without having to worry about working while in school. The person with money is starting the race well ahead of the person who has limited economic resources, and as such, they seldom end up in the same place, potentially leading to educational, career, and lifelong inequality (Curtis, Grabb, & Guppy, 2004).

The experience of oppression has a major impact on a person's life. Every group in society is marked with a host of stereotypes that have been developed and imposed upon them by the dominant group, and this affects how people are treated. For example, women are stereotyped as being intellectually inferior to and more emotional than men. Women are often regarded as being incapable of leading major organizations and deserving of less pay than men. The result in terms of everyday life is that men continue to be the heads of most organizations (93 percent) and continue to be paid more than women for the same work (Kruth, 2014; Singh & Peng, 2010; Vincent, 2013). The Pay Equity Act was passed in 1987 in Canada; however, based on the 2014 report by the Canadian Centre for Policy Alternatives, there continues to be a 24 to 26 percent pay gap between men and women. The report also concluded that there was actually a

1 percent increase in the pay gap between 2010 and 2011 (Cornish, 2014). This pay gap means that throughout their entire lives, men will collect or amass more wealth than women. The amount of money a woman earns during her career is further reduced when we also factor in that women often take time off work if they have children and are more likely to take time off to care for sick or elderly relatives and added family responsibilities (Vincent, 2013). Added to the above factors, women tend to have the expense of caring for children in the event of divorce, and do live on average four years longer than men (the average lifespan is 79 years for men and 83 for women) (Statistics Canada, 2015). Therefore, women typically have higher expenses, but make less money than men. In the long term, this results in what is referred to as the feminization of poverty (Veeran, 2000), which means that women, particularly racialized women and those who are sole-support parents, tend to have a very high representation among people who are poor in Canada (Guppy & Luongo, 2015; Wallis & Kwok, 2008). These types of social practices allow wealth to remain in the hands of the dominant.

Stereotypes

One of the ways in which the dominant protects their resources is to create labels and stereotypes about subordinate groups, which, when these stereotypes are continually repeated in the media, members of society come to accept as truth. A *stereotype* can be defined as a belief or image of a person or group that is exaggerated and repeated in society to the point where people begin to assume that it is a true representation of a person or group. Stereotypes often function at an unconscious level as "pictures in our heads" (Isajiw, 1999), which means that we seldom have to think about them when we use these beliefs to make judgments about others. The dominant group can structure or control social relations and practices in such a way that the stereotypes can be made real. For example, Aboriginal people are often stereotyped as being alcoholics, when in reality, alcohol was introduced to Aboriginal people by the colonizers as a trading commodity (Cummins & Steckley, 2013). In Canada, the government plays a primary role in funding the food supply to Aboriginal communities (Palmater, 2011), and if the government does not provide subsidies for healthy food items, then the food options are limited. In such a situation, if people have easier access to alcohol, it is easy to understand why there would be higher rates of alcoholism in some communities. Added to this, there is a direct link between quality of food and quality of health; therefore, if Aboriginal people experience food insecurity, their quality of life and life expectancy are also lowered (Socha, Zahaf, Chabers, Abraham & Fiddler, 2012). According to Statistics Canada data, on average, a First Nations person is expected to live six to eight years less than the average

Canadian (73 years for men and 78 years for women, versus 79 years for men and 83 years for women in the population at large) (Statistics Canada, 2015).

The above patterns, processes, and outcomes (gender inequity and the oppression of Aboriginal people) are examples of the impact of the historical and contemporary oppression on people's entire lives that can then become intergenerational. Aboriginal people were colonized and laws were implemented to regulate where they lived, what they could do, and the quality of education they could receive (Fournier & Crey, 2011; St Denis, 2011). The government today consistently underfunds Aboriginal communities, resulting in lower rates of academic achievement, lower quality of health care, and less access to foods and quality housing (Baskin, 2011), in turn resulting in a lowered lifespan for Aboriginal people. These are mechanisms of control and domination that started in the past, but affect people's lives today. The belief that oppression is a thing of the past, which many Canadians have, is extremely troubling. Unless there is a recognition that these issues are relevant today, there will be no willingness or investment in changing society to ensure more equitable outcomes for all.

The dominant group has the power to shape how we understand and rank groups in society, and it is this power that is used to develop the stereotypes to oppress members of non-dominant groups (Ross, 1997). The individual is part of a family unit that is part of a larger social, cultural, or ethnic group. Each social marking is given a negative or a positive rating by the dominant group. To be male is positive, but to be female is negative. To be heterosexual is positive, but to be lesbian or gay, negative. Depending on the social status of the group to which the family and individual belong, their experience of oppression will differ. There is a direct relationship between a person's social status and the number of sites of oppression they occupy. Added to this, although people may share some sites of oppression (such as gender), the impact of the other sites that they occupy can affect their daily lives differently.

Intersection of oppression

The layering of oppressions, often referred to as *intersections of oppression* or *intersectionality* (Crenshaw, 1989, 1991; Hankivsky, 2014), best describes the way in which people occupy multiple social locations. For example, a woman who is White, has a learning disability, and is part of a lower socio-economic family group will experience life very differently from a woman who is White, does not have a disability, and is middle class. So, although they share the locations of gender and racial affiliation, the first woman has additional sites of oppression (ability/disability and class) and, as a result, her experience of her everyday world will be different. She may have a more difficult time accessing employment, finishing school, or being exposed to the social and career networks that will help her to get ahead in life. The intersection of oppressions plays a significant role in determining an individual's quality of life.

Privilege

Privilege is having access to forms of power and being afforded various types of social benefits without having worked for or earned it (Solomon, Portelli, Daniel, & Campbell, 2005; Solomon & Daniel, 2007). Height is an example of this. Men who are tall are regarded as being more attractive, competent, or capable. A tall man has the privilege of being regarded as a leader, although he may not have worked to prove his capacity. Other forms of privilege that people have access to but have not earned include socio-economic status, gender, sexuality, and skin colour, some of which will be discussed throughout this book.

Race

Race is a socially constructed marker (Carter, 2000). What this means is that "race" is a man-made categorization (Haney-Lopez, 1994; Smedley & Smedley, 2005) that is used to determine who gets access to social resources. Race is an ideological construct or system of beliefs that determines social relationships and interactions that have material or factual outcomes (Omi & Winant, 1993). Genetically and biologically, there is only one race of human beings (Fullerton, 2007); however, changing environmental conditions as well as the replication of groups of genes can account for external human variations such as skin colour, body shape, and facial features (Du Bois, 1995; Fullerton, 2007). Based on scientific and anthropological evidence, the earliest human beings were discovered in Africa (Gibbons, 2010; Shreeve, 2015), which means that we all came from the same African ancestors. As humans moved across the globe, they were exposed to differing environmental conditions, and our genes adapted to meet the demands of these conditions. This meant that some genetic combinations became more pronounced, while others were suppressed. Given that we are not able to see these internal genetic variations, we use the most visible markers to determine "racial" differences. In today's world, skin colour has come to be associated with racial difference, given that it is the most visible of all markers. Historically, in parts of the world such as Europe, India, or China, where skin colour markers were not evident because the populations looked quite similar, region, religion, and culture were used as markers of racial differences (Heng, 2011). Skin colour as the primary marker of racial difference emerged in the 1400s, when the colonial project began and Europeans began to explore the new world (Jablonski, 2012).

Based on outward skin colour presentations and other physical characteristics, such as eye shape, hair colour and texture, and so on, people are assigned to different racial groups, each of which is related to characteristics or behaviours that are presumed to be unique to that particular group. However, it is important to understand that there are no characteristics that are found in one group and not in another. The power amassed through the colonial project enabled Europeans to create these racial categories, assign people to those groups, and then identify sets of stereotypes that get attached to each socially constructed racial group.

The Europeans, who colonized various parts of the world, implemented markers of race based on observable skin colour or phenotypic differences. The visible marker of skin colour was used to create a hierarchy of races, which placed Europeans at the top and the groups they colonized at the bottom (Jablonski, 2012). Racial markers emerged as a binary, with positive characteristics assigned to Europeans and negative characterstics to those who were colonized. The binary of race meant, for example, that if Europeans marked themselves as cultured, they would mark the colonized populations as savage. If the colonizers marked themselves as intelligent, the colonized would be marked as unintelligent, thus creating this binary of superior versus inferior. In effect, what the colonizers did was produce or construct different racial groups. In each instance, the colonizers placed themselves at the top of the racial hierarchy and then engaged in racism as the strategy to ensure that they could continue to justify their position of dominance. Therefore, although there is no biological or scientific validity for race (Sapp, 2012), and race is not real, the *belief* that race is real significantly influences the way in which people experience life, or what has been referred to as the "materiality of race" (M'Charek, 2013). What this means is that although race is not real, it affects how people are treated and the opportunities that they have in society.

The replication of racial categories serves as a strategy for ensuring that the dominant remain in power, while those who are racially marked or racialized remain on the margins of society. Today it is not uncommon to see members of racialized groups in positions of power, and the election of US president Barack Obama is often used as a representation of racial inclusion or the existence of what has been termed a post-racial society (Cohen, 2011). However, if we were to take a closer look at the percentage of racialized people who are in positions of power in politics or in the media, we would recognize that they are not equitably represented. Their representation in positions of power is significantly lower than members of the dominant group.

When stereotypes are used to define a group of people as a racial group, the institutions that are set up by those in power repeat those stereotypes on a consistent basis. The media plays a primary role in repeating these stereotypes, and in so doing, those stereotypes become taken-for-granted markers of racial identity. A critical look at any stereotype will reveal how illogical they all are. Take, for example, the idea that one group of people is good at math. In order for that stereotype to be true, it would have to mean that there are no members of other groups that are also good at math. Another example would be that the members of one group are good at specific sports. Again, this stereotype can only be proven to be valid if there are no other members of another group that can be just as gifted at that particular sport if given the opportunity to learn the game.

Racism

Racism is a process and a strategy wherein markers of race are embedded in societal discourses and institutions, and then used to determine access to social resources, including education, justice, health care, jobs, and safe neighbour-hoods. Racism requires having the power to develop markers of race or to create racial groups and categories, which are then used to determine which group in a society is seen as dominant and which groups are seen as subordinate. Once these groups are marked, ideas about them are then repeated or replicated throughout society, and it is these markers that have been used to determine how people are treated based on the racial group to which they are assigned.

After generations, most people accept racial categories and stereotypes as natural and unchangeable. The colonizers, who in the Canadian context were the Europeans, structured society in such a way that their racial group would be afforded all forms of privileges and rewards, and that this unequal distribution of rewards would be legally, socially, and morally justified. Therefore, the colonizer received social rewards simply based on their membership in the White "race," while all other groups not considered to be White were legally prevented from accessing a similar quality of social reward.

The construction of race and the practice of racism are directly connected to power, which is the ability to control the political, economic, social, and cultural aspects of society and to influence or determine the beliefs or ideologies of a system. The processes and practices of colonialism were the strategies through which power was gained. In its simplest sense, *colonialism* refers to the migra-tion of a group of people into a new space or land where the migrating group takes control over the space, its inhabitants, and its entire system, including the economic, social, cultural, and political organizations. The new land is also exploited for its resources, which can sometimes include human resources—for example, the enslavement of Indigenous populations to work on plantations or mines—depending on the type of resources present in the environment.

The control of the people and resources of the space is what affords the colonizer power, and this power is used to produce racial categories and, as mentioned earlier, create laws that govern the entire functioning of the system. The colonizers legally entrenched their status as superior and that of the colonized as inferior by developing laws that supported their beliefs. In Canada, for example, Chinese people were legally considered to be valued at only one-fourth the value of a White man (Henry & Tator, 2010). What this meant in terms of everyday experience is that legally, a Chinese man could be paid much less than a White man; for every dollar a White man was paid, a company would only have to pay a Chinese worker 25 cents. Having control of all societal institutions, including religion, allows the colonizer to build these ideas about racial superiority and inferiority into all the systems, and the media becomes a primary source through which this information is given to the general public.

Building on the previous example of Chinese immigrants, the colonizers used the media during the early arrival of Chinese people in Canada during the 1800s to circulate stereotypes of Chinese people as dirty and diseased. Chinese people were referred to as the "Yellow Peril" (Deer, 2006), and these ideas allowed the colonizers to control the areas where Chinese migrants were allowed to live and work. A more recent resurfacing of this practice of producing racial categories was evident during the SARS (Severe Acute Respiratory Syndrome) outbreak in Canada in 2003. According to the Canadian Environmental Health Atlas, the origin of the disease was traced to China, where someone contracted the disease and returned to Canada, which resulted in many other infections and 44 deaths (Canadian Environmental Health Atlas, n.d.). This led to a sense of panic among people, particularly in Toronto, which experienced the highest number of infections. This panic caused people who were considered to be "Chinese" to be ostracized and avoided in public places, and also resulted in a significant reduction in the number of people who would shop in places like Chinatown (in the Dundas and Spadina area of downtown Toronto) that had a sizeable Chinese population (Leung, 2004). In this situation, the media reproduced the historical marking of Chinese people as dirty and the carriers of diseases (Tator & Henry, 2010).

Racism is not simply the act of one person calling another person derogatory names, which Henry and Tator (2010) term *individual racism*. The focus on individual racism limits the ability to focus on the structural and institutional foundations of the problem. Individuals engage in racist practices because society gives them permission to do so. Racism is a historically constructed, legally and institutionally embedded system of injustices that privilege one group over all other groups in a society, and "race" is used as the distinguishing feature that determines who gets rewards. These rewards or privileges multiply over generations. What we see in society today, where people of European descent possess the vast majority of the wealth and positions of power, is the result of generations of racial privilege that they afforded themselves. And it is this skin colour–based privilege that has come to be known as White privilege.

White Privilege

White privilege refers to the various benefits that members of society who are racially marked as "White" receive simply because they possess white skin (Levine-Rasky, 2000; McLaren, Carillo-Rowe, Clark, & Craft, 2001; Rodriguez & Villaverde, 2000; Solomon & Daniel, 2007). In the Canadian context, the Europeans colonized the land, controlled the Indigenous populations and the natural resources, and placed themselves at the top of the racial hierarchy. The Indigenous populations were placed at the bottom of the racial hierarchy and denied access to social rewards simply because they were not considered to be White. As mentioned above in the section on racism, the Europeans used race as the marker to determine who received social rewards and who did not. White skin, which was the most visible marker of racial difference, became the primary determinant of who was seen as being entitled to rewards (Jablonski, 2012).

Because these rewards have been built into society and all of its systems, those benefits and privileges are still in place today. Although Canada is "racially" diverse, the control of the country and its resources continues to be in the hands of European-descended males. According to the Canadian Board Diversity Council of Canada's 2014 report, 82.9 percent of heads of corporate boards were men, 17.1 percent women, and 2 percent members of racialized groups. The report states that "women, Aboriginal peoples, visible minorities and individuals with disabilities continue to be significantly under-represented on Boards of Directors in Canada" (Bloom, 2014). Therefore, if all else were equal, the representation in positions of power would approximate group representation in society. In reality, however, the binary of race assigns Europeans positive qualities while assigning negative qualities to those who are not White. Someone who is born with white skin is automatically given a set of privileges and positive social markers, including access to power, without having earned them. It is these benefits that are known as White privilege.

When conversations about White privilege emerge, many emotions are stirred up. People feel anger, guilt, frustration, and sometimes a sense of hopelessness (Kincheloe & Steinberg, 2000; Smith & Lander, 2012). Others feel a sense of vindication when their beliefs and experiences of being treated differently are recognized. And there are those who disagree with all of the ideas presented and feelings expressed. When this range of emotions emerges in the classroom, it can create unease among students when there are members of groups who have had privilege and of groups who have not been awarded privilege simply because of their "racial" grouping. Some White students may argue that White privilege does not exist; others may state that they did not cause the problems, so they should not be held responsible for them (McGrady & Reynolds, 2013). Others may argue that these issues do not happen in Canada because we are a multicultural society. However, remaining stuck in this emotional state does not improve equitable social outcomes for all. It is important to recognize these emotions, but also to recognize that people have differing realties that need to be addressed in order to create a more equitable society. It is also important to understand that the conversation around White privilege is not about blaming Whites for the privileges they have. Rather, the focus of the conversation is on recognizing that, like race, Whiteness is a system of beliefs that creates specific social outcomes (Dei, 2014). In addition, every institution in society has been set up to ensure that Whites have privilege, and those privileges that Whites take for granted are denied to other groups in society. Henry and Tator (2006) challenge claims that Canada is a liberal and democratic country in which every person is afforded the opportunity to be exceptional, irrespective of their race. A true investment in equality and equity requires that all members of society be aware of existing inequalities and contribute to making the society a safer place for all.

Culture versus Race, Ethnicity, and Geography

Many people tend to assume that race, culture, and ethnicity are one and the same. In addition, people often assume that geography tells you a person's "race." Historically, this assumption would have proven correct for the most part. For example, a person could make the assumption that someone who identified as European would most likely be racially marked as White. Today, however, with globalization, such assumptions need to be re-examined. To say that someone is Canadian has meant for many people that the person is White; however, it must be remembered that there have been Aboriginal, Black, Indian and Chinese Canadians, long before the arrival of many European groups. However, the Europeans, again because of White privilege that we spoke of above, tend to be regarded as true Canadians, whereas members of the other groups tend to be permanently marked as immigrants or outsiders (Ash, 2004; Bannerji, 2000). The assumption is that those who are marked as "people of colour" do not belong to or cannot be native to Canada, and as such are often asked, "Where are you from?" (Ash, 2004).

The movement of humans to and from different parts of the world has changed our understanding of who belongs in which spaces. This is most evident among the children of immigrants who are born in the country to which their parents migrated. These second- and third-generation children of immigrants are Canadian and have more of an affiliation to Canadian culture than to the land where their parents were born. Although in the past we may have been able to make a connection between people's assigned race and a geographical location, those assumptions do not hold true today. Canadians today represent a wide range of cultural, social, and racial histories.

Another assumption that people often make is that race and culture are the same. The reality is that the racial group to which a person is assigned today has no relationship to her or his culture or ethnicity. In a recent conversation I was having with a group of educators about racial identity and image, a group member, who was White, indicated that the father of her children was Jamaican. I asked the participant several times to tell me what racial category her husband belonged to, given that simply telling me he was Jamaican only spoke to his nationality. She had a difficult time separating geography from "race." I had to be very specific in my questioning, asking, "Is he White Jamaican, Black Jamaican, Chinese Jamaican, or biracial?" She gave me a rather perplexed look and stated that he was Black Jamaican, at which point I indicated to her that nationality and region of birth cannot provide definitive markers of race. Clearly, for her, like so many others, geography, culture, and race had been conflated into one site of meaning.

Culture refers to the practices that a group of people engages in that can be used as markers of identity, such as foods, dances, modes of dress, and language. For example, people may refer to "Japanese culture," which may give us a sense of the customs, food, dances, and so on that Japanese people as a nationality partake in. Culture can be influenced by religion, and vice versa. The environment can also influence both culture and religion. Food, for example, is a marker of culture. The foods that are available in a particular environment determine the culinary fares of a particular group. Nationality, as evidenced by place of birth, can provide some markers of cultural practices and norms; however, level of adherence to religious norms and social class status also influence these practices.

In Canada, for example, we have markers of the dominant culture. The piano and violin are musical instruments that are associated with members of the dominant class. Although Whites form the dominant power group in Canada, Whites who are poor seldom play those instruments simply because they cannot afford to. All cultural practices therefore cannot be used as markers for all members of a given society. There are cultural groups that form outside of, or on the fringes of, society, some of which can emerge as a form of resistance. The hippies of the 60s, the punk rock movement, and skinheads are all examples of marginal cultural groups. Even rap music, which has become one of the fastest-growing forms of musical performance in the world, emerged as a form of resistance to mainstream cultural norms among Black urban youth. Today there are Chinese, Japanese, Aboriginal, and Hispanic people who perform rap music that is relevant to their particular cultural context, but they are not Black. Therefore, in much the same way that geography cannot be conflated with race, neither can culture or cultural performances. Understanding identities and experiences in this global world requires a more in-depth analysis of people's lives.

Sexism

Women in Canada have not fared much better in terms of their experience of life than women in other parts of the world. As mentioned earlier, women continue to be paid less than men and are still often relegated to jobs that most closely mirror the role of nurturer, such as nurses and teachers. Although there has been a significant increase in the number of women attending universities, and in some cases their rate of attendance is higher than that of men (Frenette & Zeman, 2007), the fields are still rather stereotypical, resulting in more males being in the fields of engineering, science, and technology (Hango, 2013).

Sexism can be defined as the systemic and institutional process of regarding and treating women as though they are inferior to men. For example, women are regarded as being more emotional than men and less qualified to undertake roles or positions in society that require them to think. These ideas are promoted at all levels of the society, including the family, many of whom prepare and expect their female children to marry and have children rather than pursue careers. It is evident at the institutional level—for example, at schools, where female students are pushed toward the helping professions and male students are pushed toward math and sciences (Blickenstaff, 2005). And it is also experienced at the systemic level; although it is not legal to treat women differently, the ideas are so embedded in the systems that women are denied equal pay (Cornish, 2014). Women are often prevented from accessing positions of power, and the wage gap and other forms of gender-based discrimination are worse for racialized women, who earn less than White women (Zamon, 2015).

Women's options for upward mobility are limited by the relationships that males have with each other. These relationships between men result in males deciding who should be the heads of political parties and corporations, and using the "old boys' network" to support the advancement of their male counterparts. Therefore, although women may be qualified for these positions, the possibility of them getting the position is severely limited by perceptions that they are not as capable as men. In North America today, although women compose a little more than 50 percent of the population, they make up about 4.6 percent of the heads of major corporations (Catalyst, 2015). A 2013 CBC report indicated that the heads of major Canadian corporations included only three women (CBC News, 2013). About 25 percent of elected politicians in Canada are female, which is significantly lower than in countries such as Nepal, Mexico, and Cuba (Inter-Parliamentary Union, 2016), all of which could be considered developing countries. If all were equal, we would expect to see women equitably represented at all levels of society.

When women do enter what has historically been considered to be male spaces, their experience in those positions can often be fraught with violence. Women experience sexual harassment and other demeaning behaviours. Female members of the Canadian military, the RCMP, and various police units across the country have reported long-standing and ongoing experiences of sexual harassment and rape by their male counterparts. In a recent *Maclean's* magazine article by McDonald and Gillis (2015), the authors discussed the ongoing and troubling experience of sexual harassment of female officers. In a June 2015 CBC interview regarding the sexual harassment allegations against the Canadian Armed Forces, General Tom Lawson, at that time chief of defence for the organization, indicated that males are "biologically wired in a certain way" to engage in those types of practices (Levitz, 2015). He was pressured to resign his position soon after those comments were made public. This statement is problematic because the understanding is that the abuse that women suffer is not a result of the poor socialization of males in our society; it is simply because men are biologically programmed to rape and harass women. If it is based on biology, there should be no expectation that the behaviour will change. The other side of that argument would be that women are biologically destined to be raped and to accept being raped. It is the result of ideas and beliefs such as this that women across all cultural and social groups continue to experience extremely high levels of physical, sexual, and psychological violence at the hands of men (Hunnicutt, 2009). In Canada today, we need to examine and challenge the historical and contemporary patterns of sexist targeting of women. We also need to explore the different conceptions regarding the role of women that are emerging as there are more groups that are migrating to Canada who also have ideas about the way in which women should be treated, some of which can significantly limit women's equitable participation in society.

LGBTQQ2

As members of Canadian society become more aware of the multiple markers of identity, people who are part of the LGBTQQ2 (lesbian, gay, bisexual, transgender, queer, questioning, two-spirited) community are increasingly exposed to opportunities where they can safely make their sexual identities public. This is not to say that the situation is ideal, given that LGBTQQ2 youth have one of the highest levels of suicide and suicide ideation of any group in Canada (Canadian Mental Health Association, 2016) and that racialized members of the trans community experience one of the highest levels of violence in the justice system (Opatut, 2014). According to a 2014 report by the Gay and Lesbian Alliance Against Defamation (GLAAD), 89 percent of homicides against trans people were against people of colour (Opatut, 2014). However, the very fact that we can have more public dialogue regarding these issues and lived realities is a step in the right direction. In addition, the removal of homosexuality from the DSM (Diagnostic and Statistical Manual of Psychological Disorders) as a mental health condition, and in some cases, one that could be cured through the use of medicine, therapy or prayer, is also indicative of growth.

This section will briefly discuss some of the primary terms associated with sexual identity and orientation. It is important to state that many of these terms are emerging and fluid, and that people can inhabit multiple categories at any given time. It is also important to recognize the impact that factors such as class, race, religion, and culture play in mitigating the experiences of members of the LGBTQQ2 community. As well, one always has to remain cognizant or aware that the intersections of oppression that we discussed previously inform the lived reality of these members. For example, a White male who is gay and middle class will experience and live his sexual identity in ways that may be significantly different from a male who is South Asian and Muslim, both at the broader societal levels and within their respective communities.

In order to explain sexual identity and orientation, one must first understand the difference between sex and gender. At its most simple level, sex is related to biology, while gender is about behaviour. In other words, *sex* tells you whether you will be categorized as male or female simply based on your genitalia. *Gender* is about how you are expected to behave or perform based on your assigned sex.

Sex and gender categories need to be understood on a spectrum, rather than as a binary. If one were to imagine a long line, the spectrum of sex and gender means that people can be located anywhere along the line. The binary of sex and gender is based on the idea that people should "naturally" or "biologically" fall at either one end of the line or the other, with one end representing male and the other end representing female. "Normal" (which is an extremely troubling term) males and females are expected to occupy either end of the binary, and their biological sex and their gender are expected to be in alignment. The modern term for people whose sex and gender align is *cisgender*. The use of the term *normal*, however, marks people who fall along the spectrum as *abnormal*. In order to understand sex and gender identities and categories, one must recognize the existence of the spectrum and the reality that people can "naturally" and "normally" fall anywhere on the spectrum.

A *heterosexual* is defined as someone who is male or female and has a primary sexual attraction to members of the opposite sex. *Lesbian* is most easily defined as a person who identifies as female and whose primary sexual attraction is to other people who also identify as female. To be *gay* is to be a person who identifies as male and whose primary sexual attraction is to other male-identified people. *Heteronormativity* refers to the social practice and assumption that male/female sexual attractions and relationships are the norm. There are multiple ways in which heteronormativity is evident in our everyday language and interactions. For example, most heterosexual couples are afforded the privilege of putting pictures of their spouses in their workspaces without being questioned about it, while a gay or lesbian person might feel uncomfortable doing the same thing. In addition, our everyday language reinforces these ideas through the pairing of words such as husband and wife, father and mother, man and woman. Even in the fields of plumbing and electricity, for example, there are parts that are referred to as the male and female couplings.

Someone who is *bisexual* has sexual attraction to both males and females, and someone who is *asexual* has no sexual attraction to either males or females. The terms *trans* and *queer* have emerged as umbrella terms to describe a range of sexual and gender identities that fall along the spectrum. Inherent in the use of these terms is the notion of agency and power; members of the community retain the right to define themselves when and where they choose, rather than having fixed labels imposed upon them. The term *transgender* has at times been used interchangeably with the term *transvestite*, which, though related, is not the same. For someone who is transgender, their biological sex and their gender presentation do not align. Some people have described it as simply being in the wrong body. This has been referred to in the psychological literature as *gender dimorphism*. There are people who live with this duality of identities and may dress to match their gender, but do not use surgery or hormones to make the change permanent. A transvestite is someone who dresses as the opposite sex/gender. For example, a heterosexual male may enjoy dressing in women's clothing, but his primary sexual attraction is to females.

A *transsexual* is someone who has surgery or takes hormones to permanently align their sex to their gender. This is a much more intrusive, expensive, and long-term process than simply presenting as their gender through dress and behaviour. In Canada, a person seeking sex reassignment surgery has to be supervised by a doctor and a psychologist who will monitor their physical and mental condition. They have to live as their sex/gender for a minimum of one year before getting "permission" to have the surgery to permanently change their sexual organs. Sex change operations can be extremely expensive, and as such, most transgender people are unable to afford the cost of having their identities integrated in terms of their outward appearance, their inner experiences, and their cognitive experiences. A person who is a transsexual can also legally change their name and personal identification; however, there continue to be debates regarding the legitimacy of forcing people to change their identification to ensure that it matches what society expects.

An analysis of history reveals that variations along the sex, gender, and sexual attraction spectrum have always been in existence in one form or another, even though they may appear to be a recent phenomenon. *Two-spirited* is a modern term that is used to refer to the ability of some people within First Nations communities to connect with and manifest or present both female and male aspects of their identity. In some cultures and among some Indigenous groups, being two-spirited was regarded as a gift. Two-spirited people could present multiple forms of sexual attraction (University of Toronto and Centre for Addiction and Mental Health, 2016). Another example of a culture that includes the ability to change genders is Hinduism, and the figure of Lord Shiva. Lord Shiva was revered as a god that could change his appearance to meet the needs of a given situation. The Hijras in India, also known as the third gender, were historically regarded as positive members of the community (Khaleeli, 2014). In ancient Greece, same-sex attractions between younger and older men were not always regarded as negative, and in some cases, those interactions were seen as transitory and a way of preparing the younger males for adulthood (ReligionFacts, 2015). The attitude that people have regarding sexual and gender identity is clearly influenced by context. All humans occupy multiple identity locations, and those locations are both imposed and chosen.

Ableism

Ableism refers to the idea that society makes the assumption that people do not have disabilities or that they are able-bodied. This results in discrimination in favour of people who do not have disabilities and discrimination against people who do. For example, a building that can only be accessed using stairs is built on the assumption that everyone has the ability to use stairs. However, for a person who is in a wheelchair or has a physical impediment, being able to get into such a building may be impossible. Imagine, then, that this is the building where employment or education offices are located. What this means then is that a person who is able to walk will automatically have easier access to the supports they may need to advance. However, for the person who is denied access, their options for advancement are limited. This reality plays out in many places every day in our society. Things that many of us take for granted, such as being able to eat in a restaurant, sit at a booth, or go to the movies, may be activities that require additional planning or provide unnecessary barriers to people who have both visible and invisible physical challenges.

In addition, people with physical, emotional, or mental challenges are often seen as being less competent, intelligent, or valuable in society than those who are regarded as "normal." In much the same way that we have discussed the multiple sites of discrimination, exclusion, and marginalization in our society, people with disabilities or limitations experience many of the same challenges. If a person is born with a disability (for example, missing a limb), they will face a host of challenges in life simply because we do not ensure that the necessary supports to facilitate their growth are in place. This often results in lowered academic options and expectations and limited employment and personal growth opportunities, which can also result in higher levels of poverty. According to a report by the Council of Canadians with Disabilities (2013), approximately 31 percent of people with disabilities live in poverty, compared to 21 percent of the general population. Factors such as gender, race, and geography can of course further increase the experience of marginalization for people living with disabilities, thus reinforcing the intersectional nature of identity.

Social Class Inequality

Throughout the chapter we have examined various sites of inequality. Class is yet another of these sites. Social class is linked to economic wealth (income and actual assets)—the more money you possess, the higher up the social class ladder you are placed. The less money you and your family have, the lower on the social class ladder you are placed. Canada, like most developed countries, experiences significant class distinctions. According to Statistics Canada data, 20 percent of the wealthiest families saw a 107 percent increase in wealth from 1999 to 2012, while families at the bottom 20 percent of the scale saw only a 15 percent increase in wealth. What this means is that the rich get richer and the poor get poorer, given that the cost of living continues to increase (Statistics Canada, 2014). Families with little or no wealth were not factored in this analysis.

Social class and wealth play a significant role in determining a person's quality of life. A person with money can have greater access to education, jobs, housing options, and so on, thus giving them the opportunity for a better overall quality of life. Quality of life is linked to lifespan, or how long a person may live. Social class also plays a central role in the way in which the justice system treats people—people with wealth have better access to better lawyers, reduced sentencing options, and the willingness of administrators of justice to explain their behaviour as a temporary character flaw. Those who experience economic deprivation are socially marked as inferior, less intelligent, and more prone to criminality. Therefore, when that person is placed before a judge, their social class is linked to their moral character, and the judges are often inclined to give higher sentences (Reiman & Leighton, 2013).

When other sites of difference, such as race, ability, and even gender, are layered onto social class, the reality of intersectionality is again brought to bear. In Canada, Black and Aboriginal males from economically deprived environments continue to receive the harshest sentences in the Canadian court system (Wortley, 2003).

Summary

The primary aim of this chapter was to provide the reader with a brief discussion of some of the terms that will be used throughout the book. The discussion is not comprehensive, and readers should explore a variety of resources to provide more in-depth information.

Discussion Questions

1. How does an understanding of the theory and application of inter-sectionality foster an understanding of people's everyday lives?
2. What is the relationship between class, poverty, and gender discrimination?
3. What are the factors that can help us to explain the continued marginalization of so many people in our society, including women, LGBTQQ2 people, and people with disabilities?

Additional Resources

Adelman, L. (Executive Producer). (2003). *Race: The Power of an Illusion* [Film]. United States: California Newsreel: http://www.pbs.org/race/000_General/000_00-Home.htm.

Townsley, G. (Producer & Director). (2015). *Dawn of Humanity* [Film]. United States: NOVA and National Geographic Studios: http://www.pbs.org/wgbh/nova/evolution/dawn-of-humanity.html.

References

Ash, M. C. T. (2004). But where are you REALLY from? Reflections on immigration, multiculturalism and Canadian identity. In C. A. Nelson & C. A. Nelson (Eds.), *Racism eh? A critical inter-disciplinary anthology of race and racism in Canada* (pp. 398–409). Concord, ON: Captus Press.

Bannerji, H. (2000). *The dark side of the nation: Essays on multiculturalism, nationalism and gender.* Toronto: Canadian Scholars' Press.

Baskin, C. (2011). Aboriginal youth talk about structural determinants as the causes of their homelessness. In M. J. Cannon & L. Sunseri (Eds.), *Racism, colonialism and indigeneity in Canada* (pp. 192–202). Toronto: Oxford University Press.

Blickenstaff, J. C. (2005). Women and science careers: Leaky pipeline or gender filter? *Gender and Education, 17*(4), 369–386.

Bloom, M. (2014). *2014 annual report card: Canadian Board Diversity Council.* Retrieved from https://www.boarddiversity.ca/sites/default/files/ARC-2014-Final-ENG.pdf

Blum, L. A. (2012). *High schools, race, and America's future: What students can teach us about morality, diversity, and community.* Cambridge, MA: Harvard Education Press.

Canadian Environmental Health Atlas. (n.d.). SARS outbreak in Canada. Retrieved from www.ehatlas.ca

Canadian Mental Health Association (CMHA), Ontario. (2016). *Lesbian, gay, bisexual, trans and queer identified people and mental health.* Toronto: CMHA Ontario. Online at ontario.cmha.ca

Carter, B. (2000). *Realism and race: Concepts of race in sociological research.* New York: Routledge.

Catalyst. (2015). *Women CEO's of the S&P 500.* Retrieved August 7, 2015, from www.catalyst.org

CBC News. (2013, March 8). Canada falling behind on women on corporate boards. Online at www.cbc.ca

Cohen, C. J. (2011). Millennials and the myth of the post-racial society: Black youth, intra-generational divisions and the continuing racial divide in American Politics. *Daedalus, 140*(2), 197–205. Retrieved from: http://www.mitpressjournals.org/doi/abs/10.1162/DAED_a_00087#.VcQWFRNViko doi:10.1162/DAED_a_00087

Cornish, M. (2014). *A growing concern: Ontario's gender pay equity gap.* Toronto: Canadian Centre for Policy Alternatives.

Council of Canadians with Disabilities. (2013). *As a matter of fact: Poverty and disability in Canada.* Winnipeg: Council of Canadians with Disabilities. Retrieved from www.ccdonline.ca

Crenshaw, K. (1989). Demarginalizing the intersection of race and sex: A Black feminist critique of antidiscrimination doctrine, feminist theory and antiracist politics. *University of Chicago Legal Forum, 99*(1), 139–167.

Crenshaw, K. (1991). Mapping the margins: Intersectionality, identity politics and violence against women of color. *Stanford Law Review, 43*, 1241–1299.

Crenshaw, K., Gotanda, N., Peller, G., & Thomas, K. (1995). *Critical race theory: The key writings that formed the movement.* New York: The New Press.

Cummins, B., & Steckley, J. (2013). *Full circle: First Nations of Canada.* Toronto: Prentice Hall.

Curtis, J., Grabb, E., & Guppy, N. (2004). *Social inequality in Canada: Patterns, problems and policies* (4th ed.). Toronto: Pearson.

Day, R. J. F. (2000). *Multiculturalism and the history of Canadian diversity.* Toronto: University of Toronto Press.

Deer, G. (2006). The new yellow peril: The rhetorical construction of Asian Canadian identity and cultural anxiety in Richmond. In C. Teelucksingh (Ed.), *Claiming space: Racialization in Canadian cities* (pp. 19–40). Waterloo, ON: Wilfrid Laurier Press.

Dei, G. S. (1996). *Anti-racism education: Theory and practice.* Halifax: Fernwood Publishers.

Dei, G. S. (2014). Foreword to the second edition. In D. E. Lund & P. R. Carr (Eds.), *Revisiting the Great White North: Reframing Whiteness, privilege and identity in education* (2nd ed.). Netherlands: Sense Publishers.

Dei, G. S., Mazzuca, J., McIssac, E., & Zine, J. (1997). *Reconstructing dropout: A critical ethnography of the dynamics of Black students' disengagement from school.* Toronto: University of Toronto Press.

Delgado, R. A., & Stefanic, J. (2001). *Critical race theory: An introduction.* New York: New York University Press.

Doxtator, D. (2011). "The idea of Indianness" and once upon a time: The role of Indians in history. In M. J. Cannon & L. Sunseri (Eds.), *Racism, colonialism and indigenity in Canada* (pp. 31–36). Toronto: Oxford Univerrsity Press.

Du Bois, W. E. B. (1995). The conservation of races. In D. L. Lewis (Ed.), *W.E.B. Du Bois* (pp. 20–27). New York: Henry Holt and Company.

Fournier, S., & Crey, E. (2011). "Killing the Indian in the child": Four centuries of church run schools. In M. J. Cannon & L. Sunseri (Eds.), *Racism, colonialism, and indigeneity in Canada* (pp. 173–177). Toronto: Oxford University Press.

Freire, P. (1996). *Education for critical consciousness.* New York: Continuum.

Freire, P. (1999). *Pedagogy of the oppressed.* New York: Continuum.

Frenette, M., & Zeman, K. (2007). Why are most university students women? Evidence based on academic performance, study habits and parental influences. Analytical Studies Branch Research Paper Series. Catalogue no. 11F0019MIE, no. 303. Ottawa: Statistics Canada. Retrieved from http://www.statcan.gc.ca/pub/81-004-x/2008001/article/10561-eng.htm

Fullerton, S. M. (2007). On the absence of biology in the philosophical considerations of race. In S. Sullivan & N. Tuana (Eds.), *Race and epistemologies of ignorance* (pp. 241–258). New York: SUNY Press.

Gibbons, A. (2010). Our earliest ancestors. *Smithsonian, 40*(12), 34–41.

Gillborn, D. (2007). Combating racism in schooling: A critical perspective on contemporary policy and practice. In W. T. Pink & G. W. Noblit (Eds.), *International handbook of urban education* (pp. 979–1006). New York: Springer.

Giroux, H. (1984). *Critical theory and educational practice.* Waurn Ponds, VIC: Deakin University.

Giroux, H. (2001). *Theory and resistance in education: Towards a pedagogy for the opposition.* Westport, CT: Bergin & Garvey.

Guppy, N., & Luongo, N. (2015). The rise and stall of Canada's gender-equity revolution. *Canadian Sociological Association, 52*(2), 241–265.

Haney-Lopez, I. F. (1994). Social construction of race: Some observations on illusion, fabrication and choice. *Harvard Civil Rights-Civil Liberties Law Review, 29*, 1–62.

Hango, D. (2013). *Gender differences in science, technology, engineering, mathematics and computer science (STEM) programs at university.* Catalogue no. 75-006-X. Ottawa: Statistics Canada. Retrieved from http://www.statcan.gc.ca/pub/75-006-x/2013001/article/11874-eng.pdf

Hankivsky, O. (2014). *Intersectionality 101.* Vancouver: Institute for Intersectionality Research and Policy, Simon Fraser University.

Heng, G. (2011). The invention of race in the European Middle Ages 1: Race studies, modernity and the middle ages. *Literature Compass.* Retrieved from www.academia.edu

Henry, F., & Tator, C. (2006). *The colour of democracy: Racism in Canadian society* (3rd ed.). Toronto: Thomas-Nelson.

Henry, F., & Tator, C. (2010). *The colour of democracy: Racism in Canadian society* (4th ed.). Toronto: Thomson Nelson Publishing.

Hilberg, R. (2010). Precedents: The destruction of the European Jews. In M. Adams, D. Blumenfeld, C. Castaneda, H. W. Hackman, M. L. Peters, & X. Zuniga (Eds.), *Readings for diversity and social justice* (pp. 258–273). New York: Routledge.

Hunnicutt, G. (2009). Varieties of patriarchy and violence against women: Resurrecting "patriarchy" as a theoretical tool. *Violence Against Women, 15*(5), 553–573.

Inter-Parliamentary Union (IPU). (2016, February 1). *Women in parliaments: World classification.* Geneva: IPU. Retrieved from www.ipu.org

Isajiw, W. (1999). *Understanding diversity: Ethnicity and race in the Canadian context.* Toronto: Thompson Educational Publishing.

Jablonski, N. G. (2012). *Living color: The biological and social meaning of skin color.* Berkeley: University of California Press.

James, C. E. (2000). Rethinking access: The challenge of living with difficult knowledge. In G. J. S. Dei & A. Calliste (Eds.), *Power, knowledge and anti-racism education.* Halifax: Fernwood.

Joshi, K. (2010). Religious oppression of American Indians in the contemporary United States. In M. Adams, D. Blumenfeld, C. Castaneda, H. W. Hackman, M. L. Peters, & X. Zuniga (Eds.), *Readings for diversity and social justice* (2nd ed., pp. 254–261). New York: Routledge.

Khaleeli, H. (2014, April 16). Hijra: India's third gender claims its place in law. *The Guardian.* Retrieved from www.theguardian.com

Kincheloe, J. L., & Steinberg, S. R. (2000). Constructing a pedagogy of Whiteness for angry White students. In N. M. Rodriguez & L. E. Villaverde (Eds.), *Dismantling White privilege: Pedagogy, politics and Whiteness* (pp. 178–197). New York: Peter Lang Publishers.

Kruth, S. (2014). A case for Canadian pay equity reform. *Western Journal of Legal Studies, 5*(2), 1–22.

Ladson-Billings, G. (1998). Just what is critical race theory and what's it doing in a nice field like education? *International Journal of Qualitative Studies in Education, 11*(1), 7–24.

Lawrence, B. (2010). Rewriting histories of the land. In M. Wallis, L. Sunseri, & G.-E. Galabuzi (Eds.), *Colonialism and racism in Canada: Historical traces and contemporary issues* (pp. 38–60). Toronto: Nelson Education.

Leung, C. (2004). *Yellow Peril revisited: Impact of SARS on the Chinese and Southeast Asian communities.* Chinese Canadian National Council. Retrieved from www.ccnc.ca/sars/SARSReport.pdf

Levine-Rasky, C. (2000). Framing Whiteness: Working through the tensions in introducing Whiteness to educators. *Race and Ethnicity in Education, 3*(3), 272–292.

Levitz, S. (2015, June 17). Gen. Tom Lawson's harassment comments "inexplicable": Harper. *The Huffington Post.* Retrieved from www.huffingtonpost.ca

Loomba, A. (1998). *Colonialism/postcolonialism.* New York: Routledge.

Mackey, E. (2010). Settling differences: Managing and representing people and land in the Canadian nation building project. In M. Wallis, L. Sunseri, & G.-E. Galabuzi (Eds.), *Colonialism and racism in Canada: Historical traces and contemporary issues* (pp. 17–37). Toronto: Nelson Education.

McDonald, N., & Gillis, C. (2015, February 27). Inside the RCMP's biggest crisis. *Maclean's*. Retrieved from www.macleans.ca

McGrady, P. B., & Reynolds, J. R. (2013). Racial mismatch in the classroom: Beyond Black-White differences. *Sociology of Education, 86*(1), 3–17.

M'Charek, A. (2013). Beyond fact or fiction: On the materiality of race. *Cultural Anthropology, 28*(3), 420–442. doi: 10.1111/cuan.12012

McLaren, P., Carillo-Rowe, A. M., Clark, R. L., & Craft, P. A. (2001). Labeling Whiteness: Decentering strategies of White racial domination. In G. M. Hudak & P. Kihn (Eds.), *Labeling: Pedagogy and politics* (pp. 203–224). New York: Routledge Falmer.

Omi, M., & Winant, H. (1993). On the theoretical concept of race. In C. McCarthy & W. Crichlow (Eds.), *Race, identity and representation in education* (pp. 3–10). New York: Routledge.

Opatut, K. (2014). *Anti-LGBTQ & HIV-affected hate violence in 2013* [Blog post]. Retrieved from www.glaad.org/blog

Palmater, P. D. (2011). Stretched beyond human limits: Death by poverty in First Nations. *Canadian Review of Social Policy, 65*(66), 112–127.

Rebello, G., & Moras, A. (2006). Defining an "anti" stance: Key pedagogical questions about engaging antiracism in college classrooms. *Race, Ethnicity and Education, 9*(4), 381–394.

Reiman, J., & Leighton, P. (2013). *The rich get richer and the poor get prison: Ideology, class and criminal justice*. New York: Routledge.

ReligionFacts. (2015, November 15). Homosexuality in ancient Greece. *ReligionFacts.com*. Retrieved from www.religionfacts.com/homosexuality/greek-religion.

Rodriguez, N. M., & Villaverde, L. E. (2000). *Dismantling white privilege: Pedagogy, politics and Whiteness*. New York: Peter Lang Publishers.

Ross, T. (1997). The rhetorical tapestry of race. In R. Delgado & J. Stefanic (Eds.), *Critical White studies: Looking behind the mirror* (pp. 90–97). Philadelphia: Temple University Press.

Salojee, A. (2004). Social cohesion and the limits of multiculturalism in Canada. In C. A. Nelson & C. A. Nelson (Eds.), *Racism eh? A critical inter-disciplinary anthology of race and racism in Canada* (pp. 410–428). Concord, ON: Captus Press.

Sapp, J. (2012). Race finished. *American Scientist*. Retrieved from www.americanscientist.org

Shreeve, J. (2015, March 5). Oldest human fossil found, redrawing the family tree. *National Geographic*. Retrieved from http://news.nationalgeographic.com/news/2015/03/150304-homo-habilis-evolution-fossil-jaw-ethiopia-olduvai-gorge/

Singh, P., & Peng, P. (2010). Canada's bold experiment with pay equity (pp. 1–16). Toronto: School of Human Resource Management, York University.

Smedley, A., & Smedley, B. D. (2005). Race as biology is fiction, racism as a social problem is real: Anthropological and historical perspectives on the social construction of race. *American Psychologist, 60*(1), 16–26. http://dx.doi.org/10.1037/0003-066X.60.1.16

Smith, H. J., & Lander, V. (2012). Collusion or collision: Effects of teacher ethnicity in the teaching of critical Whiteness. *Race and Ethnicity in Education, 15*(3), 331–351.

Socha, T., Zahaf, M., Chabers, L., Abraham, R., & Fiddler, T. (2012). Food security in a Northern First Nation community: An exploratory study on food availability and accessibility. *Journal of Aboriginal Health* (March 2012), 5–14. Retrieved from www.naho.ca

Solomon, R. P., & Daniel, B. M. (2007). Discourses on race and "White privilege" in the next generation of teachers. In P. R. Carr & D. E. Lund (Eds.), *The great White north? Exploring Whiteness, privilege and identity in education* (pp. 161–172). Rotterdam: Sense Publishers.

Solomon, P., Portelli, J., Daniel, B.-J., & Campbell, A. (2005). The discourse of denial: How White teacher candidates construct race, racism and "White privilege." *Race, Ethnicity and Education, 8*(2), 147–169.

Statistics Canada. (2014, February 25). Survey of financial security, 2012. *The Daily.* Catalogue no. 11-001-X. Retrieved from http://www.statcan.gc.ca/daily-quotidien/140225/dq140225b-eng.htm

Statistics Canada. (2015). Life expectancy. Retrieved from www.statcan.gc.ca/pub/89-645-x/2010001/life-expectancy-esperance-vie-eng.htm

St Denis, V. (2011). Rethinking culture theory in Aboriginal education. In M. J. Cannon & L. Sunseri (Eds.), *Racism, colonialism and indigeneity in Canada* (pp. 177–157). Toronto: Oxford University Press.

University of Toronto and Centre for Addiction and Mental Health. (2016). Two-spirit community. *Researching for LGBTQ Health.* Retrieved from lgbtqhealth.ca

Veeran, V. (2000). Feminization of poverty. Paper published in proceedings of the Conference of the International Association of the Schools of Social Work, Montreal, Quebec, vol. 29 (pp. 1–12).

Vincent, C. (2013). *Why do women earn less than men? A synthesis of findings from Canadian Microdata.* Hamilton, ON: The Canadian Research Data Centre Network.

Wallis, M. A., & Kwok, S.-m. (2008). *Daily struggles: The deepening racialization and feminization of poverty in Canada.* Toronto: Canadian Scholars' Press.

Wallis, M., Sunseri, L., & Galabuzi, G.-E. (2010). Introduction: Tracking colonial and contemporary racialization patterns. In M. Wallis, L. Sunseri, & G.-E. Galabuzi (Eds.), *Colonialism and racism in Canada: Historical traces and contemporary issues* (pp. 1–12). Toronto: Nelson Education.

Wortley, S. (2003). Hidden intersections: Research on race, crime, and criminal justice in Canada. *Canadian Ethnic Studies Journal, 35*(3), 99–117.

Young, M. (1994). *The rise of the meritocracy.* Piscataway, NJ: Transaction Publishers.

Zamon, R. (2015, May 6). The gender gap in Canada is twice the global average. *Huffington Post.* Retrieved from www.huffingtonpost.ca

CHAPTER 2

Explorations of Justice and Injustice: A Canadian Perspective

Beverly-Jean M. Daniel and *Greg McElligott*

Chapter Objectives

This chapter will discuss multiple conceptions of justice and its links to morality and ethics, which in turn control people's behaviour. It will highlight the connections between theories and applications of justice and the ways in which conceptions of justice can be compromised and lead to unjust outcomes. Students will also be re-introduced to the theory of intersectionality to examine the ways in which being located within multiple sites of diversity or oppression can affect a person's everyday lived reality.

Conceptions of Justice

There are multiple ways to explore notions of justice. Justice can be understood in the context of the legal system, which would include the application of laws that members of society are expected to obey. In its most basic form, a person's innocence or guilt is based on whether or not they obeyed the law. The person's sentence is then based on the type of crime they committed and the rules for punishment that are set out in the legal system.

Another conception of justice is based on principles of morality and ethics. Ethics can most easily be understood as the values or beliefs that determine ideas of "good" and "bad" and that guide the behaviours of the members of society, but it is not necessarily based on legal principles. Morality is related to one's ability to adhere to the values or expectations of society. At its most basic, therefore, ethics is about beliefs, and morality is about behaviour. All forms and conceptions of justice should be built on the foundation that all people should have equal rights and recognition before the law and that their experience of the system should result in equal outcomes, irrespective of their status in society. However, we are far from that ideal notion of the equal dispensation of justice. Instead, our human frailties, preconceptions, and biases significantly inform the way in which members of society experience the systems of justice. When we refer to systems of justice, we are including all bodies and organizations that create and apply laws, including the police, lawyers, court workers, and judges, as well as law and policy-makers. An applied notion of justice is justice from a community perspective, which recognizes that the idea of "equality before the law" is an illusion. At its foundation, community justice seeks to lay bare and challenge stereotypes, and provide a more nuanced and intersectional framework for critically analyzing and applying notions of justice, fairness, equity, and access.[3]

Notions of justice remain complex and abstract. Justice can sometimes be most evident when it is not present; in other words, we can easily tell what is wrong in a given situation or context, but it can be challenging to identify what is the right or just course of action. If, for example, we were to witness a crime being committed, we could easily determine that the act of committing the crime is unjust. If, however, we were given an understandable rationale for the act, our ability to easily identify the appropriate course of action would become more complicated. The act of a woman stealing makeup, for example, can be easily identified as wrong, because in our society it is a crime to steal. If, however, we were to find out that the woman had a facial disfigurement and had an upcoming job interview but could not afford to purchase makeup to cover up her blemishes, would our response to her situation be as simple and logical? What if we also added that she had two small children in her care and that she had received the scars while trying to protect one of the children from being hurt and had lost her job because of the length of time it took her to recover? It is for reasons such as these that it is difficult for society to identify one rigid and immovable conception or application of justice. And it is for these same reasons that it becomes almost an impossible feat to work with just one frame of justice when the reality of the human condition is complex and fluid. The capacity to equitably address the complex needs of human beings requires a more applied concept of social justice and demands the application and integration of intersectional analyses.

Intersectionality

According to Crenshaw (1989), most theoretical frames of reference examine experiences as individual acts of oppression, which only provide a partial view of the actual experience or the impact. Building on critical race theory (Crenshaw, Gotanda, Peller, & Thomas, 1995; Delgado & Stefanic, 2001; Ladson-Billings, 1998), which critiques the manner in which race is taken up within or excluded from systems of justice, Crenshaw used discrimination cases against Black women as her primary site of analysis. She argued that the legal system looked at either the race or the gender of the claimants, but failed to explore the ways in which Black women experience discrimination that is affected by race, gender, and class, along with other sites of oppression such as sexual orientation and ability/disability, to name a few. This results in Black women's unique experiences being lost within the folds of gender or race. Although Crenshaw's work specifically looked at the issue in relation to Black women, the theory of intersectionality can be and has been adopted as essential to understanding the lived experiences of people who are located within multiple sites of oppression, or the "multidimensionality" (Crenshaw, 1989) of people's lives. An intersectional perspective states that "inequities are never the result of single, distinct factors. Rather, they are the outcome of intersections of different social locations, power relations and experiences" (Hankivsky, 2014, p. 2).

An intersectional analytical framework refers to the analysis of information, which recognizes that human beings occupy multiple identity locations at any given time, and as such, any decision, whether legal or values based, regarding that person, has to incorporate an understanding of those realities. For example, a person can be a woman, mother, friend, daughter, and worker all at the same time, while also being poor and having an identifiable disability. Each of these identities is understood and responded to differently at a societal level. Therefore, in order to understand the complexity of a person's world, the analysis has to integrate these multiple locations and societal perceptions and recognize the ways in which these identities can also be sites of oppression that at times compete with each other. Being poor, being female, being racialized, and being lesbian are all identifiable sites of oppression in a Western context. However, these sites can at times be set up to compete for funding and other social resources. In such circumstances a woman may be expected to decide whether she wants to put her support behind her racialized identity, her identity as a woman, or her identity as a lesbian woman. For example, a Black woman falls within the categories of gender and race. Feminism would ask that she support the battle for gender equality; however, in reality, she may experience racism more regularly than she does gender-based discrimination. In addition, her husband or sons may be heavily targeted because they are Black males. Therefore, she may be more likely to focus on issues of racism than gender. The site of oppression that she may support can in large part be based on what is most difficult to endure. Being forced to make such decisions can result in significant social and mental distress for a person who is then left to straddle but never completely occupy any of their multiple identities. An intersectional analysis examines the realities of life from all identity locations, while at the same time highlighting each of their social impacts. Therefore, any analysis or programmatic suggestion would attempt to address the majority and the most pressing of the sites as identified by those who occupy the sites, rather than simply imposing programming options from a top-down perspective.

In the context of justice, an intersectional analysis examines the experiences of marginalized women with the justice system and its representatives. For example, Aboriginal women have the highest rate of incarceration of all women in Canada (see chapters 6 and 11 in this text), and their historical experiences of colonialism within Canada create a unique set of circumstances that frame their everyday world. Therefore, an equitable distribution of justice requires that these histories and their contemporary impact be factored in when making sentencing and probationary decisions. Ensuring that there are educational, training, and programmatic options for justice staff, along with an appropriate understanding of the impact of intersectionality, will enhance the decision-making options that staff can employ. All of these factors, when applied in real-world contexts, can significantly improve the quality of life for Aboriginal women, families, and communities.

Basic Laws of Nature and Justice

According to Jacobs (2005), when we speak of justice we are speaking about the most basic rights that people have, whether based on the legal system or natural laws—that is, laws of nature and ideas of morality (good or bad). What complicates these conversations, however, is when ideas about justice are also based on ideas of merit. In other words, who deserves what? Nussbaum's (1997) theory of capabilities indicates that all human beings need an equitable distribution of "core social entitlements" to enable them to live a full life, and that society (i.e., the state and system of governments) should be responsible for these. These capabilities include life, bodily integrity, imagination, thought, and control over their social environment. However, recognizing that morality and ethics are culturally and historically embedded concepts means that these capabilities will look different in different contexts. Added to this, as contemporary societies experience significant social changes facilitated by transnational migration patterns, people move to new regions with morals and values that they developed in their countries of origin. How then do we determine what is just when there are so many ideas that come together in the same place? And further, how do we dispense justice when those charged with dispensing it are often also the ones who play a role in determining which people are the most valuable? As well, how is the application of justice compromised when those who dispense justice also distribute social entitlements?

According to Aristotle's theories, justice is determined based on that which is just or lawful and fair, recognizing that something that is unfair is not necessarily unlawful. Therefore, justice has to be understood through differing and at times seemingly competing lenses. However, the conversations, by necessity, should be grounded in a specific context, because the context frames the actions, analyses, and options. It is on this basis that we examine the issues in this book from a Canadian context, recognizing that the laws that guide legal decisions are different from those in other parts of the world, even if there may be similarities; Canadian and American laws, for example, have the same historical British foundation. The everyday reality of life informs and influences what we understand as "just" and "unjust." When we begin to examine and critique the application of power, social injustices, discriminatory practices based on gender, sexual orientation, race, social class status, and so on, people's actual quality of life and their interactions with the justice system can change when appropriate policies and practices are implemented.

Building on John Rawls's (1971) principles of justice, which speak to the importance of equal liberties and access to social resources, what are the safety nets that should be put in place when existing social conditions violate principles of fairness? Both Aristotle and Rawls state that 'all human beings should have equal levels of access to social resources' when they possess the required natural endowments. For example, all people who have the ability to play music well should have access to the resources that will allow them to develop those talents. However, the reality is that laws, social policies, and economic barriers have been put in place that limit people's options to develop their natural endowments. For example, a child with budding musical talents whose parents are financially secure will be afforded the privilege of being enrolled in music classes and having access to resources that can help them develop their skill set. By comparison, a child who has a strong natural musical ability but is living in an environment or attending a school in a neighbourhood that is economically deprived will not usually have access to the resources that may allow them to fine-tune their skills. In this example, a social policy (the use of geographical boundaries to determine which schools students attend) is applied in ways that limit the full and complete development of people's talents. In such situations, these practices can be said to be unjust, and Aristotle would argue that fair practices should be considered to foster a more complete engagement and development of one's talents. In other words, the child with musical talents should be provided with opportunities to develop those talents, irrespective of their family's economic background, particularly given that the development of those skills can improve the circumstances of the family in the long run. This would be a fair and just distribution of social resources.

To understand the application of just and fair rewards, it is important to draw a distinction between equality and equity. The term *equality* relates to giving each person the exact same amount of resources, irrespective of their specific needs. *Equity* is based on the distribution of resources based on a critical analysis of each person's situation and context. When Group A already has more access to resources or has amassed more resources (money, cultural capital, access to education, and so on) than Group B, to give Group A the same amount of resources as Group B simply ensures that the members of Group A will continue to outpace the members of Group B on a host of social and economic outcomes. An equitable distribution of outcomes would dictate that the members of Group B would be given increased access to resources and rewards to improve their chances of success in life. That would be considered just and would support John Rawls's principles of justice. If we connect the principles of justice back to the previous example of the child with musical talents, an example of an equitable distribution of justice and resources would allow the child with the most talent to go to the school district where he or she would get the level of support needed to develop their skills. This scenario would allow for the child to develop their talents regardless of their family's economic background, which is one of the goals of a fair, just, and democratic society.

The Reality of Justice Today

Today, a mountain of evidence shows that the principles of justice as advanced by Rawls and Aristotle have been violated on multiple levels. Women are paid less than men; poor people have less access to quality legal representation; and Aboriginal people in Canada are afforded a lower quality of education than the dominant group (Mendelson, 2006; Statistics Canada, 2011). The lists of social inequalities are endless, and our conceptions of justice and injustice are based on our experiences of the system. In spite of the multiple examples of injustice and unjust acts that are visible on a daily basis, an illusion of liberal equality continues to exist. The vast majority of the Canadian population continues to invest in the idea that all people in our society have the same level of access to social resources. What they fail to recognize is the existence of an array of obstacles that limit the level and quality of access that people actually have. For example, everyone theoretically has access to education; however, the reality is that not everyone has the financial resources that would allow them to access those educational options.

People with money can afford to send their kids to the best schools, which would then allow them to access to the best jobs. Families that experience economic instability have a much more difficult time sending their children to post-secondary schools, even with access to student loans. The person whose parents can support their educational growth will be able to start their career without debt, while the person who has had to borrow money will start their career with approximately $28,000 debt for a bachelor's degree and $100,000 for a medical degree (Burley & Awad, 2014). A person's social class is a significant predictor of levels of access to education. Simply having access in theory does not guarantee equitable outcomes in real life.

The Western Un-Justice System?

The theoretical concepts of justice are often quite wordy and complex, but become quite messy and muddy when we attempt to examine them in their everyday interactions, intersections, and deployment. It is not enough just to think seriously about these complexities. In order to deliver something closer to real justice, our justice system must be able to respond to situations in meaningful ways, which would require judges to consider offender history, context, and current circumstances when making sentencing decisions. When aggravating factors (which tend to involve links to drugs, guns, or organized crime) are seen to be present, the penalties rise still further. So every time Ottawa adds more of these factors to the Criminal Code, it binds judges' hands a little tighter, and limits their discretion to shape sentences to fit the specific circumstances surrounding a crime. More people go to jail, sentences are longer, communities are further disrupted, and there is even less room to develop alternative approaches.

At a community level, these measures have far-reaching consequences when we look at the impact of incarceration as a result of the inequitable application of justice measures. There is the impact on a family's structure, economic stability, and viability, the impact on the children of incarcerated individuals, the collateral victims, and the larger structural instability of the communities to which these individuals belong. The majority of incarcerated individuals do return to the community. However, with the limited rehabilitative, employment, and educational support services available in prison, in some ways they are more of a burden to the community than when they were initially incarcerated. Once home, they have to deal with the emotional scarring of imprisonment; with a criminal record that limits their ability to access viable employment; with strain on their marital and familial relationships; and with the shame that accompanies criminal involvement.

Along with all of the aforementioned challenges, the releasees are still expected to support their families, but now have an increasingly limited range of options. Scenarios such as these provide the perfect environment in which to create cycles and patterns of criminality. Such problems still tend to be understood only in individualistic terms, without any real critical analysis of the structural and institutional factors that help produce criminality in some communities. These communities experience multiple, overlapping forms of marginalization based on race, class, perceived immigration and citizenship status, limited access to social, economic, and educational capital, and extremely negative social perceptions and stereotypes. As Weinrath, Murchison, and Markesteyn (2012) argue, conceptions of justice will shape people's attitudes: some believe in punishing people for bad behaviour, while others believe in "offering help and assistance to offenders, particularly those historically disadvantaged through racial discrimination, class bias or both" (p. 32). And the unfortunate reality is that justice will be dispensed based on the beliefs of those in positions of power.

Increasingly, Canadian governments have not appeared to be concerned with the discretionary power of other actors in the justice system, like prosecutors and police. In the United States, the prospect of longer sentences due to minimum mandatory sentences and other factors have boosted the power of prosecutors when negotiating plea bargains. They have generally used this power to put more people in jail, and innocent suspects often confess to lesser crimes just to avoid longer sentences. We are then caught in a problematic cycle of subjecting people to unjust practices and calling it justice, whether we are looking at justice in terms of access to social supports and entitlements or as specifically related to the application of laws. The ultimate question that then emerges is who benefits from the miscarriage of justice that is aimed at communities that are already marginalized. What is the resulting impact on these communities and society and who are the primary beneficiaries of these unjust practices? Such questions lead community justice research toward issues related to power, politics, and social control. Some of these will be addressed in chapter 3 of this book. Miscarriages of justice can affect people as individuals and the communities to which they belong.

The situation with police discretion is more complex. Theoretically, most North American police departments are committed to community policing, which means that police officers try to spend more time out of their patrol cars in an attempt to get in touch with the community. This could lead to more sensitive use of police discretion, and less frequently resorting to formal charges. But, in practice, community policing has often opened the door to more intrusive face-to-face surveillance of minority groups, as with carding in Toronto or stop-and-frisk in New York. The application of social justice and anti-oppression theories and practices provides an alternative lens for us to understand applications of justice.

Social Justice and Anti-Oppression

There are multiple social justice and anti-oppression theories including feminist theory (Frankenberg, 2004; hooks, 2000; Mohammed, 1998), critical race theory (Crenshaw et al., 1995; Delgado & Stefanic, 2001; Ladson-Billings, 1998), critical theory (Apple, 2007; Foucault, 1980; Freire, 1976; Giroux, 1984, 2001), queer theory (Butler, 1990), anti-racism (Dei, 1996; Kailin, 2002; Scheurich, 2002), and anti-racist feminism (Calliste & Dei, 2000). Social justice and anti-oppression theories are foundationally built on the premise that those with wealth and power control the society, which results in an imbalance in the distribution of social rewards; therefore, the application of true justice requires a redistribution of social resources and entitlements to ensure that all members of society, irrespective of gender, race, citizenship, language status, and so on, have full and equitable access to the resources.

Social justice has been seen as a process or set of steps that guides the way in which something is done. It is also regarded as a goal or something to be achieved (Bell, 2010). According to Bell (2010),

> the goal of social justice is full and equal participation of all groups in a society that is mutually shaped to meet their needs. Social justice includes a vision of society in which the distribution of resources is equitable and all members are physically and psychologically safe and secure …. Social justice involves social actors who have a sense of their own agency as well as a sense of social responsibility toward and with others, their society, and the broader world in which we live. (p. 21)

Bell goes on to say that the practices we enact are based on the theoretical frame that we use; in other words, actions will be guided by beliefs. If someone believes that we live in a society in which oppression does not exist or, at the very least, is minimal, that person would be reluctant to examine or partake in conversations related to challenging oppressions.

Social justice theoretical frameworks focus on critiquing larger historical, systemic, and institutional practices that protect those with wealth and power while simultaneously limiting access to social resources for those who are less privileged. Social justice and anti-oppression theories, therefore, analyze and critique colonial practices and projects that put laws in place that allowed the European colonizers to own land (which historically was regarded as foundational to the development of wealth), while at the same time enacting laws that prevented non-White groups from owning land. The resulting impact of this was that Whites were afforded a host of privileges and opportunities for wealth, and political, social, and economic advancement, thus resulting in what is referred to today as "White privilege." Therefore, social justice and anti-oppression approaches examine the ways in which Whites as a group have afforded themselves the opportunities to advance in society while at the same time using the "justice" system to limit the advancement of other groups. Although this divide is evident today, many mainstream theories such as liberalism and structural functionalism use individualistic analyses to explain the success or failure of members of society. This is known as *meritocracy*—the idea being that people get what they deserve or work for.

Social justice and anti-oppression theories and theorists would argue that the opportunities made available to an individual are primarily grounded in the broader systems and institutions that are at work, which can limit options for advancement. Further to this, success or failure can be intergenerational. In other words, Western societies are set up in such a way that, in most cases, where you start in life is directly related to how far you will climb. And this is not because of particular capacities such as intelligence, effort, or desire. Instead, it is because the society has been built to ensure that those who have power are supported in keeping that power; those who have been raised in economically deprived environments will continue to experience varying forms of deprivation (related to education, health, justice, career, etc.) simply because of where their parents were positioned on the economic spectrum. Difference and diversity in capacities are often offered as explanations for differential levels of achievement in society. Social justice and anti-oppression theories reject these explanations. It is important to understand that people seldom choose their social location. Those locations (sex, class, religion, race), along with value judgments about those locations, are imposed by those in power.

To explore the concept of social justice, it is also important to understand issues of difference and diversity. Understanding diversity means recognizing the ways in which these differences have had meanings assigned to them and the way in which a person's everyday life is lived based on those meanings. Within Canadian society, the concept of diversity tends to be related to visible differences. It is not uncommon to hear people say things like "I grew up in a very homogeneous community and we had no difference there." The problem with this statement is the assumption that diversity is based on the visible or phenotypic differences between groups of people.

Diversity refers to the multiple sites and experiences that make one person experience life differently from someone else—these can include gender, ability/disability, religion, family patterns, social class, race, and sexual orientation. For example, being male or female, in reality, is based on minor biological differences that are related to internal and external genitalia and hormones. In our society, many people have learned to attach meaning to these biological differences according to which we believe that males are biologically and intellectually superior to females, although there is no evidence to prove this difference. When meaning is attached to different categories, we assign positive and or negative values to those meanings, and it is based on those values that we determine how people are treated. This means that much of what we have come to expect is based on ideas that have been created or socially constructed. The way in which people are treated in our society is based on what we think about the varying sites of difference rather than who people really are. The above example referred specifically to biological sex-based differences; however, these values and judgments are attached to every site of human difference, including height, the shape of one's body, and the colour of one's hair.

Broadening the Concept of Social Justice

Another extension of the concept of social justice is *applied social justice*, which is based on the understanding that justice must include both theoretical analyses and applied practices. One of the challenges that has been noted with many philosophical approaches is the gap between theory and application. Applied social justice aims to build a bridge from the philosophical foundations of justice to examine, embed, and activate the ideas in everyday practical applications. Students in the justice field must be made aware of the existence of oppression to develop a more comprehensive understanding of the world, which can then propel them to engage with and support their clients in ways that are socially just. If, however, we leave the conversations regarding social justice at the theoretical level without providing students with clear examples of what social justice looks like when it is applied, we are simply contributing to the development of theory, rather than working toward challenging the status quo.

Applied social justice seeks to highlight the varying ways in which differently located concrete examples can foster an understanding of the lives that people live. By doing so, people will be positioned to work with diverse social groups and can develop a more comprehensive picture that will enable them to dispense justice based on more communal and distributive principles of justice and fairness. Applied social justice further allows for the identification and development of specific services and supports to meet the needs of different groups of people, with an understanding that people have differing needs that cannot be met by the one-size-fits-all model.

Another social justice theory is *community justice*, which is regarded as a theory and philosophical orientation; it continues to grow as a field both at a global and national level (Clear & Karp, 1998; Karp & Clear, 2000). It is important to note that community justice as a theoretical framework and an applied theory borrows from Aboriginal and Indigenous Australian models of dealing with crime. These models are based on the importance of healing and providing supports to the offender, rather than ostracizing them from the community. It is only in very rare cases that an offender would be cast out of the community, which is in direct contrast to Western models that remove individuals from the community for even petty criminal acts that do not warrant incarceration, such as thefts, threats, and minor assaults. Canada and the United States have historically adopted retributive forms of justice, which means the offender is punished for their crimes (see chapter 3 in this text for a discussion on the history of prisons and imprisonment). The negative and long-standing impacts of imprisonment on the offender and community for these types of crimes are much greater than any identifiable benefit. Lanni (2005) indicates that the improper and unfair application of justice in the criminal justice system and the over-incarceration of community members have contributed to increasing the commission of crime in already compromised communities, given that an ex-offender with a criminal record has a much more difficult time accessing employment.

To date there have been limited research-based projects that examine the efficacy of the application of theories related to community justice; however, within a Canadian context, Statistics Canada clearly shows that Aboriginal, Black, and poor White people are the groups that have been most negatively affected by retributive conceptions and applications of justice. Aboriginals and Blacks are more likely than their White counterparts to be denied bail, more likely to be sentenced to longer prison terms, and they wait longer to be paroled (Canadian Civil Liberties Association, 2014; Fine, 2015; Public Safety Canada, 2015). This pattern of incarceration is applied regardless of the gender of the person before the courts. The resulting impact of retributive justice at an individual level is the reduced capacity for full adult participation in society. These realities dictate that the theory and application of community justice principles be much more empirically based or grounded in research if there is to be any real change to the practices of injustice in the name of justice.

Community justice adopts rehabilitative and reintegrative approaches to justice, rather than focusing on punishment. This approach recognizes that crime happens when there is dysfunction within a community, and that the primary way to reduce or repair harm to communities is to support the viable development of those communities. Retributive justice programs, as discussed above, have the opposite impact and lead to the further destabilization and destruction of communities. It is important to state that any analysis of incidences of crime in communities requires a systemic and institutional approach that includes an understanding of the historical experiences of the community and the application of justice in the community, as well as quality of life indicators. These indicators include access to viable employment, rather than precarious or unstable jobs; quality of schooling; availability of necessary social supports; and economic viability of the community, rather than individual pathology.

Community justice programs such as restorative and transformative justice programs seek the involvement of the offender, the victim, and the broader community to help reduce the incidence of crime and repair the damage done. This model centralizes the role of community members to identify the strategies and requirements for their individual community rather than relying on one-size-fits-all models that have limited applicability. Lanni (2005) indicates that there are four main practices of community justice initiatives: community prosecution, community courts, sentencing circles, and citizen involvement in determining sentencing and probation requirements. He argues that although community justice initiatives have been primarily used for dealing with less serious cases, there should be some exploration of their applicability in more serious cases.

According to Karp and Clear (2000),

> community justice broadly refers to all variants of crime prevention and justice activities that explicitly include the community in their processes ... [and] is rooted in the actions that citizens, community organizations, and the criminal justice system can take to control crime and social disorder. Its central focus is community-level outcomes, shifting the emphasis from individual incidents to systemic patterns, from individual conscience to social mores, and from individual goods to common good. (p. 324)

Community justice initiatives, as a form of social justice, primarily seek to involve the community in reducing crime. This may mean having members of the community participate in restorative justice programs or identify the types of supports that are needed within their community to facilitate development. Specifically, with regard to community members who have been involved in the justice system either as victims or offenders (and in many cases both), community justice–based initiatives ensure that the input of those who have committed crimes is taken into account when determining the types of supports they need to be effectively reintegrated (see chapters 5, 6, and 11 in this text).

McCold and Wachtel (1997) argue that one challenge of effectively implementing community justice initiatives is the continually shifting conception of community, and, I would argue, the meanings of ideals such as "justice," which also remain in flux. For some, community refers to a geographically contained area. For others, community may refer to a group of people who share racial, ethnic, or cultural histories and characteristics. This shared history may indicate a more romanticized notion of community than one that exists in the real world. These conceptions of community are problematic and limiting for several reasons. In Canadian society today, most urban centres are inhabited by people who have multiple histories and languages, although they reside in the same geographical area. If, however, a crime occurs in that area, most community members will be affected although the crime may not have been committed by someone who resides in the area or who shares a racial, cultural, or ethnic history with the majority of people within that community.

As I have argued elsewhere (Daniel, 2007), the idea of community needs to be extended to include the concept of networks in which people may simultaneously inhabit multiple communities and broader communal networks. For example, an individual may be a member of the Jewish community, which has local and global connections and shared histories, but may also be a member of a communal network, which will consist of members who share common goals. In this case, the development of a safer community would be one of the common goals that links the communal networks. McCold and Wachtel (1997) suggest that consideration also be given to using the term *neighbourhood* as a marker of community, while Lanni (2005) suggests employing the term *community of interest*, which speaks to the involvement of the local residents in justice initiatives. Employing the idea of neighbourhood allows for the shared response to safety within the area that does not rely on the development of personal relationships, or the assumption of shared points of connection such as ethnicity, religion, culture, or language.

Notwithstanding these challenges, community justice still remains a viable option for effecting change in the conceptions and practices of justice both in its legal and everyday interactions and engagements. If justice is expected to be blind both in its practice and administration, the racially coded application of injustice is a clear violation of human rights. The current justice system—within which Aboriginal and Black defendants are fighting to remain innocent until proven guilty—is inconsistent with the precepts of justice. Perhaps using community-based justice imperatives is a more equitable way of claiming basic human rights. Along with practices of community justice, social justice and anti-oppression and applied social justice initiatives can also be considered important theoretical and practical orientations for supporting the development of healthier communities.

Summary

This chapter provided a brief introduction to the notions of justice, community justice, social justice, and anti-oppression frameworks. These are the major theoretical frameworks that foreground the writing throughout this book. The criminal justice system, through the inequitable application of principles of justice, has had a significant destructive impact on marginalized communities. The rebuilding and stabilizing of these communities requires a different way of understanding, conceptualizing, and working with communities.

Discussion Questions

1. Discuss how intersectionality theory allows for a more comprehensive discussion of the ways in which class, gender, and justice intersect.
2. What is the difference between morality and ethics? How do they inform or affect how people behave?
3. What are the central tenets of social justice approaches and how do they help us understand larger social and systemic processes that lead to injustice?

Additional Resources

It Gets Better Project: www.itgetsbetter.org

O'Reilly, H. B. (n.d.). Guide to Social Justice Resources. Kingston: Queen's University: http://library.queensu.ca/webedu/grad/Social_Justice_Resources.pdf.

References

Apple, M. W. (2007). Are markets in education democratic? Neoliberal globalism, vouchers and the politics of choice. In M. W. Apple, J. Kenway, & M. Singh (Eds.), *Globalizing education: Policies, pedagogies and politics* (pp. 209–230). New York: Peter Lang.

Bell, L. A. (2010). Theoretical foundations. In M. Adams, W. J. Blumenfeld, C. Castaneda, H. W. Wickman, M. L. Peters, & X. Zuniga (Eds.), *Readings for diversity and social justice* (2nd ed., pp. 21–35). New York: Routledge.

Burley, G., & Awad, A. (2014). *The impact of student debt*. Ottawa: Canadian Federation of Students. Retrieved from http://cfs-fcee.ca/wp-content/uploads/sites/2/2015/03/Report-Impact-of-Student-Debt-2015-Final.pdf

Butler, J. (1990). *Gender trouble: Feminism and the subversions of identity*. New York: Routledge.

Calliste, A., & Dei, G. (2000). *Anti-racist feminism*. Halifax: Fernwood Publishing.

Canadian Civil Liberties Association. (2014). By the numbers: Crime, bail and pre-trial detention in Canada. Retrieved from https://ccla.org/cclanewsite/wp-content/uploads/2015/02/2014-07-23-By-the-numbers1.pdf

Clear, T. R., & Karp, D. R. (1998). The community justice movement. In D. R. Karp (Ed.), *Community justice: An emerging field* (pp. 3–30). Lanham, MD: Rowman & Littlefield.

Crenshaw, K. (1989). Demarginalizing the intersection of race and sex: A Black feminist critique of antidiscrimination doctrine, feminist theory and antiracist politics. *University of Chicago Legal Forum, 99*(1), 139–167.

Crenshaw, K., Gotanda, N., Peller, G., & Thomas, K. (1995). *Critical race theory: The key writings that formed the movement*. New York: The New Press.

Daniel, B.-J. (2007). Developing educational collectives and networks: Moving beyond the boundaries of "community" in urban education. In R. P. Solomon & D. N. R. Sekayi (Eds.), *Urban teacher education and teaching: Innovative practices for diversity and social justice* (pp. 31–48). Mawah, NJ: Lawrence Erlbaum Publishers.

Dei, G. S. (1996). *Anti-racism education: Theory and practice*. Halifax: Fernwood Publishers.

Delgado, R.A., & Stefanic, J. (2001). *Critical race theory: An introduction*. New York: New York University Press.

Fine, S. (2015, June 14). Longer waits for parole disadvantage Aboriginal offenders: Report. *Globe and Mail*. Retrieved from http://www.theglobeandmail.com/news/national/longer-waits-for-parole-disadvantage-aboriginal-offenders-report/article24954998/

Foucault, M. (1980). *Power/knowledge*. L. M. Colin Gordon, John Mephan, & Kate Soper (Trans.). New York: Pantheon Books.

Frankenberg, R. (2004). Growing up White: Feminism, racism and the social geography of childhood. In A. Prince & S. Silva-Wayne (Eds.), *Feminisms and womanisms: A women's studies reader* (pp. 139–165). Toronto: Women's Press.

Freire, P. (1976). *Education: The practice of freedom*. London: Writers and Readers Publishing Cooperative.

Giroux, H. (1984). *Critical theory and educational practice*. Warun Ponds, VIC: Deakin University.

Giroux, H. (2001). *Theory and resistance in education: Towards a pedagogy for the opposition*. Westport, CT: Bergin & Garvey.

Hankivsky, O. (2014). *Intersectionality 101*. Vancouver: Institute for Intersectionality Research and Policy, Simon Fraser University.

hooks, b. (2000). *Feminist theory: From margin to center* (2nd ed.). Cambridge, MA: South End Press.

Jacobs, J. (2005). *Ethics A–Z*. Edinburgh: Edinburgh University Press.

Kailin, J. (2002). *Antiracist education: From theory to practice*. New York: Rowman & Littlefield.

Karp, D. R., & Clear, T. R. (2000). Community justice: A conceptual framework. In C. M. Friel (Ed.), *Boundary changes in criminal justice organizations* (Vol. 2, pp. 323–368): Washington, DC: US Department of Justice.

Ladson-Billings, G. (1998). Just what is critical race theory and what's it doing in a nice field like education? *International Journal of Qualitative Studies in Education, 11*(1), 7–24.

Lanni, A. (2005). The future of community justice. *Harvard Civil Rights–Civil Liberties Law Review, 40*, 359–405.

McCold, P., & Wachtel, B. (1997). *Community is not a place: A new look at community justice initiatives*. Paper presented at the International Conference on Justice without Violence: Views from Peacemaking Criminology and Restorative Justice, Albany, NY.

Mendelson, M. (2006). Aboriginal peoples and postsecondary education in Canada. Ottawa: Caledon Institute of Social Policy. Retrieved from http://www.caledoninst.org/Publications/PDF/595ENG.pdf

Mohammed, P. (1998). Towards Indigenous feminist theorizing in the Caribbean. *Feminist Review, 59*, 6–33.

Nussbaum, M. (1997). Capabilities and human rights. *Fordham Law Review, 66*(2), 273–300.

Public Safety Canada. (2015). Corrections and conditional release: Statistical overview; 2014 annual report. Ottawa: Public Works and Government Services Canada. Retrieved from https://s3.amazonaws.com/s3.documentcloud.org/documents/2110762/ps-sp-1483284-v1-corrections-and-conditional.pdf

Rawls, J. (1971). *A theory of justice*. Cambridge, MA: Harvard University Press.

Scheurich, J. J. (Ed.). (2002). *Anti-racist scholarship: An advocacy*. New York: State University of New York Press.

Statistics Canada. (2011). The educational attainment of Aboriginal peoples in Canada. Retrieved from https://www12.statcan.gc.ca/nhs-enm/2011/as-sa/99-012-x/99-012-x2011003_3-eng.cfm

Weinrath, M., Murchison, M., & Markesteyn, T. (2012). Measuring success of corrections programs: The evaluation of the Minobimasdiziwin prison gang intervention program. In K. Gorkoff & R. Jochelson (Eds.), *Thinking about justice: A book of readings*. Halifax: Fernwood Publishing.

CHAPTER 3

Upgrading Fear: The Politics of Prisons in Canada

Greg McElligott

Chapter Objectives

This chapter will help the reader develop an understanding of the role and purposes of prisons. Since governments have traditionally used prisons to control oppressed populations, issues related to justice and criminal justice are often closely connected to political concerns and ruling strategies. In turn, governments have historically relied heavily on force and fear to secure obedience, and to safeguard systems that exploit poor and marginalized people. Clarifying the place of prisons in these larger ruling strategies will help to show how class, gender, and race shape prison populations. Because American approaches have often set the pace for those used in Canada (and elsewhere), they will be given what is perhaps a surprising amount of attention in the pages below.

Introduction

It is commonly assumed that prisons are an essential and inevitable part of social life; however, many scholars see them as relatively recent inventions that began to take their present form only in the 1830s (Foucault, 1995; Ignatieff, 1978; Rothman, 2002). This would mean that for all prior human history, societies managed to exist without prisons as we now know them. If indeed prisons are not permanent social fixtures, but inventions produced to meet the needs of a society during a particular time, then we can imagine a much greater range of possibilities for changing or even abolishing them. At the very least we can ask ourselves whether an institution designed in the midst of the Industrial Revolution is still appropriate to 21st-century needs and conditions.

This chapter considers this latter question in two parts. The first tries to establish the purposes that prisons were initially designed to serve. The second places prisons in their modern Canadian context, and assesses the needs they now serve. The chapter concludes with a brief consideration of the prison's future prospects.

Origins

Hiding Punishment, Threatening Harm

The advent of the prison is often said to have made punishment more rational and humane, allowing states to do away with the more horrific practices used in the past. Canadian governments, for example, no longer lock people in the pillory, nail their ears to the wood, and allow crowds to pelt them with rotten fruit, dead animals, or bricks. Punishment in Canada today is less overtly brutal, and the decline of grisly public tortures (many much worse than the pillory) is undoubtedly a step forward for civilization. Progress on this front should not be overstated, however. On one hand, the situation remains grim at a global level: most of the world's population is still potentially subject to the death penalty; execution is still frequently public; and ancient tortures like crucifixion and stoning remain legal, and, in fact, are enjoying a resurgence, in some parts of the world (Shahidullah, 2014; Zimring & Johnston, 2008). On the other hand, even in countries like Canada the delivery of pain and fear remain central functions of the state.

The prison allowed many countries to hide—not abolish—punishments that involve outright physical violence (Garland, 1993).[1] Thus Kingston Penitentiary, one of the earliest modern prisons, was supposed to reform criminals through its innovative "moral architecture," but in fact relied heavily on beatings, whippings, and various forms of water torture throughout much of its history (Oliver, 1998). Practices like flogging were officially sanctioned in Canadian prisons until the 1970s,[2] and vigorously defended by officials like the aptly named Headley Basher, who saw them as indispensable for maintaining prison discipline (Corpun, n.d.).[3]

Even after corporal punishment was outlawed, brutality could still be a kind of unofficial state policy. Candidates rarely win elections by promising to improve prison conditions. In fact, "tough-on-crime" politicians often compete with one another to make conditions worse. Nevertheless, failure to safeguard prisoners' basic human rights is a form of state crime, according to Ross (2009/10), and it allows other crimes to flourish.

This is particularly clear with respect to prisoners' right to be safe from violence. Rape, for example, is one among many crimes considered appalling when it happens in the outside world, but taken for granted behind bars. So even though rape is at epidemic levels in US prisons, it remains fodder for jokes made by those on the outside (National Prison Rape Elimination Commission, 2009; Parenti, 2000). As Gopnik notes, TV cops who threaten suspects with prison rape are engaged in a practice that is portrayed as "an ordinary and rather lovable bit of policing" (2012, p. 73).

Although judges never explicitly sentence anyone to be raped, officially approved programs like Scared Straight highlight this possibility when trying to frighten young delinquents. Despite the trend toward hiding violence, prisons' role in threatening harm clearly remains important. Prison authorities seem willing to allow such threats, even though doing so really means advertising their own incompetence at maintaining prison safety. And this is not a minor matter. Crime rates for the whole United States have been declining for some time. But one estimate suggests that this is only because official rates do not count crimes that occur inside of prisons, including hundreds of thousands of rapes each year (Voorhees, 2014).

Delivering Pain

Prisons have also hidden violence in a much more profound way. Even apart from the very personal, and perhaps unplanned, forms of brutality described above, confinement by its very nature delivers pain, theoretically in a carefully measured form.

Early modern prisons were partly a product of legal changes meant to make punishment less random and more certain. Physical punishments had been uncontrollable in many respects, and this made them risky when performed in public. Using sentences marked off in units of time—days or years behind bars—seemed less excessive, and more responsive to "rational" control from above. But this crucial switch sparked debate about what exactly constituted a "just measure of pain" for any particular crime (Ignatieff, 1978).

Today, prisons go by many names. In Canada, people serving sentences of two years or longer are in placed in penitentiaries or institutions run by the federal government. Those serving shorter terms, or awaiting trial, are held in provincial/territorial facilities that are called jails, correctional centres, and detention centres, among other names. But in no case are they waiting to be flogged or mutilated in public by the authorities.

This is what sets modern (Canadian) prisons apart from the jails and dungeons that came before, which were essentially holding cells where prisoners awaited punishment—whipping, branding, execution, transportation, and so on. In the modern prison, incarceration itself is the punishment, handed out in distinct periods of time (sentences) that are supposed to be proportional to the crime (Foucault, 1995).[4] The point, however, is that incarceration—even in its cleanest, best-managed form—is designed to deliver pain (Christie, 2000).

At this it clearly succeeds, even if debates continue about appropriate amounts. Gresham Sykes's classic study of the "pains of imprisonment" highlights how the basic features of even the best prisons hurt those inside them. All prisoners endure losses—of liberty, personal possessions, heterosexual relationships, autonomy and security—that attack them "at the deepest layers of personality," according to Sykes (1958, p. 69).

Those who doubt this assessment might consider the analogy often used by guards and prisoners to describe the experience. Incarceration, they say, is like being locked in your bathroom for years on end. Exercise and time outside are rare. Inside, cellphones, cigarettes, and alcohol are prohibited, as are most personal possessions. Deprived of basic life choices like what and when to eat, and when to shower, prisoners spend their days and all of their most intimate moments with a cellmate chosen by someone else. Those placed in solitary confinement escape the cellmate, but only at the cost of mind-warping isolation and solitude.

Spectacle and Terror

Michel Foucault (1995) argues that, for reasons such as these, prisons are not, in fact, less painful and more humanitarian than the tortures that preceded them. Instead, they simply entail another form of torture that is aimed primarily at the mind rather than the body. But why are governments engaged in torture of any kind? Foucault suggests that this is a legacy of punishment's history. His account stresses how strategies for controlling crime have historically overlapped with those aimed at controlling whole populations (Foucault, 1995).

Pre-modern royals had no means of mass communication to spread the word about crimes committed, and no police forces to hunt down criminals. Instead they relied on "the spectacle of the scaffold" (Foucault, 1995, p. 32)—the ritualistic performance of public executions—to keep both crime and rebellion at bay. If all went according to plan, the condemned would be brought before a crowd, admit their guilt, and be dispatched efficiently (or slowly) by the royal executioner. This spectacle, which became increasingly elaborate, was designed to drive home the message that the king's (or queen's) power was awesome and overwhelming. Anyone who defied royal law or royal wishes, it promised, would be crushed.

This message would be delivered in support of undemocratic governments and tiny ruling elites who assumed that some lives were much less important than others. Commoners—men, women, and children—were subject to public torture or execution for crimes as minor as petty theft, unless they had friends in high places (Hay, 1975). Actual guilt was often hard to determine, and it was not really necessary to prove it if the point was to make an example of someone.

Flawed Performances

Things did not always go according to plan. As with any performance, there was much room in these events for mistake and miscalculation. Hanging in particular was a tricky business that left much room for error. If the executioner misjudged his victim's weight or the length of rope required, the condemned could be slowly strangled or gruesomely beheaded. Either result risked undermining confidence in the authorities and/or antagonizing a restless crowd, which might attack the executioner or attempt to free his victim. Unseemly scenes of a different sort broke out under the Tyburn gallows in 18th-century London, where relatives and barber-surgeons battled over whether the bodies of the hanged should be buried or dissected (Linebaugh, 1975).

Brief "gallows speeches" that the condemned were allowed to give in their final moments could also vary from the script and disrupt the proceedings. From the perspective of the authorities, such speeches would ideally be remorseful, exhorting the crowd not to choose the wicked path that led to the scaffold. But these speeches also gave those with nothing to lose a rare opportunity to air dissenting views. One condemned pirate in colonial Virginia called for "Damnation to the Governour and Confustion to the Colony" (cited in Palmer, 2000, p. 190). Variations on this theme ran directly counter to the message that the elaborate execution ceremony was designed to convey.

If the whole point of the spectacle was to suppress disorder and crime, then the attending crowds needed to be tightly controlled. This became increasingly difficult as execution days grew to be public holidays. Surrounding businesses lost customers as rowdy merrymakers (and opportunistic criminals) were drawn into the streets. To many observers, such scenes of carnival and wickedness were inconsistent with the image of awe-inspiring majesty that the spectacle of terror was meant to convey.

The transition to prisons may have been aided by legal reforms and by more humanitarian notions of punishment. But it seems also to have been pushed by the gradual collapse of traditional ruling practices based on spectacle and physical torture. Like flogging and other bodily assaults, executions were not abolished at first, but were brought inside. There, conditions were easier to control and only vestiges of the old crowd remained as witnesses. But by this point prisons were already well-developed, due in part to the efforts of what Feeley (2002) calls the "entrepreneurs of punishment."

Planning the Panopticon

Feeley uses the term *entrepreneurs of punishment* to highlight the role of profit-seeking private operators in developing public punishments. One of the most influential of these was British philosopher and politician Jeremy Bentham, who, in the late 18th century, promoted a design he called the "panopticon" to government officials in England and elsewhere (1786/1995). The panopticon embodied many elements central to the modern prison, and while Bentham never convinced a sponsor to fund his own plan, many later designs followed its precepts.

As the name suggests, the panopticon relied on "all-seeing" surveillance to control those inside. A central observation tower would be surrounded by banks of backlit cells arranged in cylindrical formation like a silo. Inmates were to be confined alone and, because of the lighting, would be visible at all times to those in the tower. Occupants of the tower, on the other hand, would be shaded so that prisoners could never tell whether they were being watched, or indeed if any guards were present at all. Bentham claimed that this arrangement would give the keepers "apparent omnipresence"—essentially god-like powers—and apologized for the potential sacrilege involved in such a claim (1786/1995, Letter VI).

Because Bentham provided blueprints and considered the workings of the panopticon in extraordinary detail, its essential elements are clear: inmates were to be classified and separated (to prevent collective resistance or criminal conspiracies); they were to be controlled by unseen surveillance (not direct violence or spectacle); and the sense of "conscious and permanent visibility" delivered through these measures would cause inmates to control themselves

(Foucault, 1995, p. 201). To Foucault, Bentham's plan symbolizes the beginning of an entirely new way of ruling that would prove much more powerful than the old spectacles of terror.

This new way was the "exact reverse" of the old (Foucault, 1995, p. 216). While the public spectacles were performed by a select few to be seen by a large crowd, panoptic surveillance makes a large population continuously and intensely visible to a select few. And its reach extends beyond prisons. Bentham had pitched his design as a model for other institutions, including workplaces, hospitals, and schools (1786/1995). Foucault argued that by the late 20th century, most institutions—in fact, most human relations—had been decisively shaped by panoptic principles, if not Bentham's detailed plans (1995). Setting aside the larger implications here—that modern society itself is essentially a prison—we might still wonder what motivated such a dramatic shift in ruling practices.

Crisis and Disorder

As noted above, humanitarian considerations, legal reforms, and a gradual loss of confidence in the spectacle all played a part in this transition. But prisons spread across North America and Western Europe very quickly in the early part of the 19th century. This timing led historians to debate the role of social crisis—or perceived social crisis—in prompting the move to incarceration as the dominant form of punishment. David Rothman, in *The Discovery of the Asylum* (2002), argues that modern prisons sprang into existence alongside mental institutions and poorhouses (and later, public schools) to create a whole new layer of state-directed control over the population. These versions of the asylum shared an emphasis on "order and regularity, the insistence on uniformity and punctuality, [and] the devotion to steady labor and habits of discipline" (2002, p. xxxviii). And all responded to heightened fears of social and moral disorder expressed by privileged groups of various kinds, and directed primarily at the behaviour of the poor (2002).

In many places, it should be noted, the poor had grown more plentiful and more desperate, as displaced farming families surged into cities to find work in the factories driving the Industrial Revolution. Rothman (2002) and Ignatieff (1978), among others, see the prison as the product of efforts by middle-class reformers to restore "morality" and discipline to this group in particular. But the gradual transition from an agricultural to an industrial economy (first in England, later elsewhere) would continue to produce disruption and fear. And the developing capitalist economy had a low tolerance for disorder.

Time, Work, and "Idleness"

Employers in a capitalist economy have a crucial interest in controlling how workers spend their time (Thompson, 1967). To maximize profits, workers must be available, ready, and willing to work hard whenever, and for as long as, employers need them. In the early days, few workers entered into such arrangements voluntarily, and only the desperation brought on by the destruction of rural economies forced them to do so.

For those used to supporting themselves at their own pace on a farm, or perhaps for humans in general, wage work drew a strange distinction "between their employer's time and their 'own' time" (Thompson, 1967, p. 61). Employers would continually press to lengthen and/or intensify the working day, and workers would resist to the best of their ability. And because workers might spend what time remained to them in activities (like drinking) that affected their ability to work, early capitalists often felt they had a crucial interest in regulating behaviour outside work as well. As Thompson says, "in mature capitalist society all time must be consumed, marketed, put to use; it is offensive for the labour force merely to 'pass the time'" (1967, pp. 90–91).

Thus it is not surprising that by the 19th century, "idleness" was seen as the root of crime (and many other social ills) and punishment became increasingly focused on using hard labour to remedy it. This was the era of the tread wheel, the crank, and other exhausting but pointless punishments that were supposed to instill better work habits (Ignatieff, 1978). In fact, the whole range of new asylums and prisons fit into this agenda, since those who could not, or would not, absorb the proper attitudes in the new public schools might be targeted for confinement of some sort later on.

It is important to remember, however, that the exact meaning of "proper work ethic" has always been a relative and contested term. Is it "proper" for children or anyone else to work 16-hour days, seven days a week, as they once did? When labour is divided, weak, and easily replaceable (due to high unemployment or workplaces changes), employers will push for longer hours, lower wages, and less job security. At other points, when labour is strong (because workers have enough unity and leverage to demand more), it can win victories like weekends off, shorter hours, and minimum wages. (In our time, decades of high unemployment and declining state support have made workers—especially young workers—increasingly insecure, and forced them into work conditions that previous generations could afford to refuse.)

Thompson (1967) observes that pre-capitalist ways of working reflected the "seasonal rhythms of the countryside, with its festivals and religious holidays" (p. 92). Where people were free to choose how they worked, the pattern often included "alternate bouts of intense labour and idleness" (p. 73). That pattern persists among certain groups today—small farmers, culture workers, and perhaps students, he says—and Thompson wonders whether, in fact, it is a "natural" rhythm for human work (1967, p. 73). Nonetheless, neither the seasons nor that peculiar human trait were compatible with the increasingly mechanized routines of factory production. These demanded a steady and consistent pace of work, each and every day. It would become the task of schools, and (as a last resort) asylums and prisons, to transform human nature so that it fit the needs of the factories.

Prisons and Industry

Much has been made of the differences between two early approaches to incarceration. The "Pennsylvania System" embodied in Philadelphia's Eastern State Penitentiary, enforced almost total solitary confinement. This was intended to exclude bad social influences, encourage penitence, and prevent prison from becoming a "school for crime." The "Auburn System," on the other hand, kept prisoners physically apart only at night, whereas by day they would live under canvas hoods and enforced silence in New York State's Auburn Prison.[5] Despite these differences, however, both systems attempted to reform and/or punish prisoners by forcing them to work—at individual crafts in Pennsylvania and at factory production in New York. And both systems traded in what Thompson calls the "currency" of time (1967, p. 61), as prisoners gave over their "own" time to satisfy judges and benefit their prison employers.

These methods were not particularly useful in combatting crime, and Pennsylvania's solitary system proved much more successful at producing madness, rather than penitence, in inmates. Later critics found themselves trying to explain the persistence of the prison even as it continued to fail to reduce crime. Michael Ignatieff says the prison survived "despite its evident failure to reform or deter" (1978, p. 215) because it operated like a factory: "Its order was the order of industry .... By 1850 to challenge its logic was to challenge not just one discrete institution, but the interlocked structure of a whole encircling industrial order" (1978, p. 215).

The link between prisons and the emerging industrial economy is clear in the case of Kingston Penitentiary (the Pen), which opened in 1835. Convicts built the prison, and were forced to contribute to its upkeep in an "unceasing routine of slave labour" inspired by "lash and fear of the lash" (Oliver, 1998, pp. 124, 126–127). Kingston's prison was constructed on the Auburn model, and was designed by that prison's deputy warden. He promised that its hidden observation corridors (a panoptic feature) would maintain perfect discipline even if all of the guards were to leave (Oliver, 1998, p. 113). The Pen was built just as tensions were mounting over demands for democracy in the Canadian colonies, and this imposing structure was meant to reassert royal power outside its gates as well (McElligott, 2008).

Both hopes proved illusory, since resistance, floggings, and water torture continued inside the Pen, and open rebellion broke out in the colonies in 1837. Plans to finance the prison through the sale of convict-made goods also produced dashed hopes. As elsewhere, producers on the outside resisted what they saw as unfair competition, and the prison soon became a major drain on the public purse. Overall, however, the apparent potential for profit, and its consistency with the form and needs of the industrial economy, gave Auburn a consider-able advantage over the Philadelphia model. As the link between Philadelphia's solitary confinement and madness became clearer, the preference for Auburn's factory-like system became even more widespread.

Prisons and Slavery

Kingston Pen was hardly the first institution to use convicts as slaves. Even today, this practice spans the globe, and it has been traced back at least to the Roman Empire (Sellin, 1967). The use of convict labour in the former slave states of the American South has, however, had particularly important consequences for prison systems there and elsewhere.

The South emerged from the US Civil War (1861–1865) with shattered cities, razed farms, and no captive labour force to aid in the massive reconstruction effort required to rebuild them. The 13th Amendment (to the US Constitution) had abolished slavery in 1865, but it explicitly allowed for exceptions "as a pun-ishment for crime whereof the party shall have been duly convicted" (National Archives, n.d.). Many Southern governments seized on this loophole to recreate something that looked very much like the old slave economy. In fact, critics like Angela Davis (2003) argue that American slavery was never actually abolished—it just moved to prison.

Although they were legally free, most former slaves had very little on which to live. In the aftermath of the war, loosely defined vagrancy laws—which were enforced only on the Black population—and the more explicitly racist "Jim Crow" segregation laws brought more and more former slaves before the courts. There, faced with fines they could not pay, and "fees" levied on top of those, former slaves found themselves sentenced to long prison terms of hard labour. In some states the prison population shifted from mostly White to mostly Black in just a few years (Davis, 2003).

Many Southern convicts spent little time in prison, however. Instead they were "leased" to private overseers for a small fee, and worked in chain gangs, often to death, on projects for which they were never paid. Conditions were appalling, whether in mines, on farms, or building roads and railways. Convicts were easily replaced, so employers who leased their labour had little stake in their survival, and corruption, abuse, and brutality were rampant (Mancini, 1996). Former slaves filled the prisons, former slave owners leased their labour, and many of the latter made a fortune rebuilding the infrastructure that had sustained the old South. According to Davis, for example, many railroads and most of Atlanta's main streets were rebuilt by leased convict labour after the war (2003).

Prisons and Colonialism

Canadian authorities never had to deal with the sudden freeing of such a large captive population. But the destruction of Aboriginal communities by treaty, law, and encroaching settlement would prove to be as important to prisons in Canada as the (apparent) abolition of slavery had been in the United States. Joan Sangster (1999), for example, documents the almost direct connection between the advance of the White frontier in Northern Ontario, and the overrepresentation of First Nations women in Toronto's Mercer Reformatory (one of Canada's first prisons for women).

In her account, as in many others, the reserve system created by the Indian Act comes across as a system that enforced racial segregation and poverty. It was administered by unaccountable government agents who felt they could intervene in every aspect of reserve life.[6] The biases of the Indian agents, sometimes supported by those of male band leaders, sent many "troublesome" First Nations women to Mercer for confinement. Mercer itself was bigger than many Aboriginal communities, and once there, culture shock and cultural misunderstandings often lengthened a woman's stay in the institution. Silence, for example, was considered among many First Nations to be a polite and respectful response to unfamiliar situations. To the White staff at Mercer, however, silence often came across as resistance and/or "idiocy," and either diagnosis might prolong confinement (Sangster, 1999).

Observers like Loïc Wacquant (2010) argue that Black Americans were contained first by slavery, then by Jim Crow segregation in the South, then by urban ghettoes in the North, and finally by today's expanding prison system. Aboriginal people in Canada now live mostly off reserve, but if the ghetto is indeed a form of containment, they experience it as well. As Carol La Prairie (2002) has shown, those who flee poverty and despair on the reserves frequently end up in the poorest areas of a few Canadian inner cities. Often young and with few marketable skills, these new arrivals join thousands of others who, it seems, the economy does not need. And in cities, they are heavily policed. La Prairie shows that while crime rates are higher on the reserves, crimes committed by Aboriginal people in cities are much more likely to get them jail time. In fact, the burgeoning Aboriginal population in Canadian prisons comes mostly from four inner cities: Saskatoon, Regina, Winnipeg, and Thunder Bay (2002). For the country as a whole, Aboriginal people now comprise about 3 percent of the total population. But so many are incarcerated that they fill 20 percent of all federal prisons spaces, and 26 percent of provincial/territorial ones (Correctional Services Program, 2015, p. 7; Dauvergne, 2012, p. 11).

Summary

The picture painted above suggests that modern prisons were part of a larger response to: (a) problems with the old ways of governing; (b) apparent crises of order; and (c) the demands of a new and disruptive capitalist economy. Early prisons were essentially machines built to contain potentially unruly populations, and to train them in the industrial work ethic—perhaps making money in the process. Somehow all of this was supposed to prevent crime. But none of these efforts altered the disruptive path of economic change, which continued to create more crises, more victims, and more fear. Prisons might hide these symptoms, but they could not cure the disease.

Ironically, there was a long period in the mid-1900s when a "medical model" of crime was popular. Those convicted of crimes were seen as sick and needing treatment, rather than as immoral and needing punishment. But that model was built around prison's four central pillars of pain, order, obedience, and work. Today the "softer" features have melted away, and the pillars are visible once again.

Prisons Today

The historical examples cited by Davis are relevant to critics because they seem to echo current trends. In this more recent American scenario, young Black men have been corralled into prison by the "war on drugs," which has targeted them selectively and punished them far more severely than other groups. New drug offences and tougher punishments have boosted America's prison population by over 400 percent since 1970 (Austin & Irwin, 2012, p. 2).

Canada has yet to experience such a dramatic surge, but it has recently adopted many of the same policies that produced the American prison boom: a renewed war on drugs, mandatory minimum sentences for many crimes, longer sentences in general, and a tougher approach to bail and parole. Taken together, these measures make it easier to get into prison and harder to get out—which means that prison populations are very likely to grow (Story & Yalkin, 2013).

And similar populations are targeted here. Canada has historically imprisoned Aboriginal people at a much higher rate than other citizens (see above), so they will feel more than their share of pain from the new measures (Fine, 2015). American-inspired police practices such as carding (collecting personal information without laying charges or having probable cause) have been used against urban Black youth more than other groups, and so they too are more likely to be imprisoned (Known to police, 2013).

In the United States, the prison boom has again allowed many private interests to make huge fortunes from supplying, building, or even running prisons on contract to state governments. More money can be made by exploiting prison labour. Chain gangs (for both men and women) have returned in some states, but the more common pattern is for captive labour to stay in prison while doing work for an outside company. For a fee, governments will organize prisoners to do the necessary work, and absorb overhead costs, including security and housing (LeBaron, 2008). In exchange, companies like IBM, Toys"R"Us, Starbucks, and even Victoria's Secret, get easy access to low-cost, well-disciplined workers (LeBaron, 2008, p. 72).

Companies pay prisoners as little as 5 percent of what outside workers get, and these meagre gains are reduced further by deductions that make prisoners help pay for their own incarceration (Wright, 2003, p. 116). Yet many prisoners are eager to be exploited, because other prison jobs (in the kitchen, etc.) pay substantially less. Moreover, in some states prisoners can rack up a debt for room and board that follows them even when they leave prison. As Wright notes, this is a "Third World labour model in the heart of America" (2003, p. 116).

Meanwhile, conditions within prison get worse and worse, as inmates are "warehoused" within increasingly stark, harsh, and impersonal institutions. And the worst part is that in the cells, prison work looks more attractive—even if it threatens your life, as it does in the annual convict rodeo at Louisiana's Angola prison, where inexperienced inmates ride bulls, which may result in serious injury or death (see Smith, Bordelon, & Jackson, 2008).

Selectivity and Containment in America

Incarceration in the United States is a notoriously selective process. In 2006, only 1 in every 365 White women aged 35 to 39 was in prison. Comparable figures for Black men aged 20 to 24 were 1 in 9 (Warren, 2008, p. 6). This means that young Black men were over 40 times more likely to be in jail at that time. Figures for Hispanic Americans show that they too were overrepresented in prison, but not to the same degree as African Americans (Warren, 2008, p. 6).

America is not unique in incarcerating men much more than women—the Canadian prison population is about 90 percent male (Dauvergne, 2012, p. 11). So part of the disparity noted above can be accounted for by a "normal" gender imbalance. There are also some obvious connections to the demographics of crime, because young people, especially young men, commit more crime than other groups.

The disparity is not just a matter of demographics, however, as it raises larger issues about how crime is defined, and how laws are enforced. The American war on drugs made it much more likely that minor possession would result in jail time, and used changes to conspiracy laws and "three strikes" rules to increase penalties even more. The laws were particularly harsh if crack cocaine was involved. Until 2010, possession of 500 grams of powder cocaine could result in a jail term of five years without parole, but possession of only 5 grams of crack cocaine led to the same sentence. Because crack users tended to be poor and Black, and powder users were often White and wealthier, this 100 to 1 sentencing difference was much more likely to send Blacks to prison (American Civil Liberties Union, n.d.; Sterling, n.d.).

The net effect of biases like this throughout the system was to force huge numbers of young Black men off the streets and into the burgeoning prison population. David Garland suggests that the "mass imprisonment" of this particular group was historically unprecedented in its scope and speed, and it made prison "a shaping institution for whole sectors of the population" (2001, p. 6). African Americans now have a presence in prison that is about four to five times greater than their share of the US population as a whole (Smith & Hattery, 2007, p. 277).

While imprisoned, this group is also disproportionately absent from their home communities. Thus their families, friends, and neighbourhoods are deprived of whatever positive contributions they made as parents or breadwinners, and their children are more likely to go to jail themselves. So the "coercive mobility" that cycles young Black men in and out of prison also helps to destabilize their communities. As a result, both are more prone to poverty, despair, and crime (Frost & Gross, 2012).

Selectivity and Containment in Canada

If African Americans take up about four or five times more prison places than their share of the outside population, the problem is even worse for Aboriginal Canadians, whose presence in our prisons is seven to eight times greater than their share of the population outside (Correctional Services Program, 2015, p. 7; Dauvergne, 2012, p. 11). Rates of overrepresentation vary by jurisdiction. Aboriginals are represented in Ontario's provincial prisons at a rate that is about five times higher than their proportion in its outside population. In Alberta's provincial prisons and in Canada's federal prisons (where the longest sentences are served) the rate is seven times higher (Perrault, 2009). The most severe over-representation occurs in Saskatchewan's provincial prisons, where Aboriginals are represented at rates eight times greater than their share of the outside population would predict (Perrault, 2009). So if prison is a "shaping institution" in the United States, it very likely serves a similar function with regard to Aboriginal communities in Canada.

Overall incarceration rates in Canadian prisons have not grown nearly as much as they have in the United States. This says little, though, because American rates are by far the highest in the world (with 698 of every 100,000 people in prison in 2015). Canadian rates are lower than this (at 118/100,000), but only slightly lower than those reported for China (119/100,000) (International Centre for Prison Studies, 2015). However, trial delays and increasingly onerous bail conditions have pushed up remand populations (those in jail awaiting trial or sentencing) across the country (Deshman & Myers, 2014). And new tough-on-crime measures (like longer mandatory sentences and reduced credits for time served) have convinced Ottawa and the provinces to initiate multi-billion dollar programs to expand their prison capacity. Both the legal changes and the vast new spending in this area have been influenced by developments in the United States, which has always been a world leader in this field.

Those filling the new prison spaces will continue to be drawn selectively from the rest of the population. In Canada, as elsewhere, the vast majority of prisoners come from the poorest 10 percent of our population. Besides being overwhelmingly male and relatively young, about 80 percent of them have substance abuse problems. This group has not done well at school—on average, Canadian prisoners begin their sentences with somewhere between a Grade 7 and a Grade 8 education (Correctional Services Canada, 2012; Maher & Berzins, 2011, p. 5). In the United States, and increasingly in Canada, there is growing concern that this last fact is due to the operations of a "school to prison pipeline." Vaguely defined zero-tolerance policies, combined with racial bias in the authorities that interpret them, have forced many young men of colour out of school and more or less directly into prison (Heitzeg, 2009). (The school to prison pipeline is taken up more comprehensively in chapter 5 of this text.) Prisoners also tend to be unemployed on entry—a fact no doubt related to the disappearance of the low-skilled manufacturing jobs that used to employ much of this part of the population (Maher & Berzins, 2011, p. 5; Tiessen, 2014).

Of course, most people who experience the disadvantages listed above do not commit crimes or end up in jail. But if social conditions that produce desperation and despair are neglected, more people will be pushed in the direction of crime and prison. Even if rehabilitation is possible in prison, people who experience these disadvantages can do nothing but play eternal catch-up when the social causes of crime are ignored. For every criminal "cured," two more may be in production. And although prisons may try to prepare inmates for their return to society, these efforts can be undermined by what awaits outside. One article that highlights the difficulties faced by released prisoners in time of high unemployment asks "reentry to what?" (Hallett, 2012).

The Penal Management of Poverty

Unfortunately, neglecting the causes of crime, and treating just its symptoms, is precisely what has been happening in most of the Western world since at least the 1970s. As Garland notes, the loss of "entry-level jobs for young underclass males," along with related damage to their families and communities, "has meant that the prison and parole now lack the social supports upon which their rehabilitative efforts had previously relied" (cited in Hallett, 2012, p. 213).

The story of why those jobs disappeared, and why many communities have been allowed to decay, is essentially the story of (a) declining faith in old ways of governing (the postwar welfare state); (b) a perceived crisis of order highlighted by neoconservative politicians; and (c) the new demands of a globalized capitalist economy. These are the same sort of factors that led to the creation of the modern prison in the 19th century. In the late 20th century, they produced bigger, tougher prisons, and sidelined other approaches (like rehabilitation and welfare) that were seen as weak, futile, and expensive.

As noted above, early efforts at reforming or rehabilitating prisoners centred almost entirely on reinstilling a proper work ethic and a willingness to obey higher powers. Serious efforts at other sorts of rehabilitation (treatment for addictions, anger management, and so on), involved help from the medical and social sciences. But these did not begin on a wide scale until after the Second World War ended in 1945 (Garland, 1993).

The rise of rehabilitation programs in prison and elsewhere was part of a broader expansion of the public sector. States now took responsibility for meeting social needs that had previously been ignored, or covered only in a haphazard way by private charities. The welfare states that emerged at this time committed themselves to keeping unemployment low, and to providing safety nets like unemployment insurance, welfare, pensions, and disability payments for those unable to work. These expensive new programs were sustained by, and helped to sustain, a long economic boom that lasted until the 1970s.

Support for the welfare state was founded on a broad consensus that states had done far too little to ease suffering during the Great Depression of the 1930s. Experience during the Second World War seemed to show that democratic governments had the expertise and power to mobilize society for a great cause—like the defeat of Fascism. But by the 1970s, faith in governments' social/economic interventions, and in expertise of all kinds, had been seriously eroded. The economic boom was slowing, government deficits were rising, and an influential study by Robert Martinson (1974) seemed to argue that "nothing works" in rehabilitation. This criticism paralleled similar ones aimed at welfare, where a "war on poverty" was widely seen to have failed.

Influential neoconservatives (such as British Prime Minister Margaret Thatcher, and US President Ronald Reagan) argued that the welfare state had "coddled" many of those who relied on it—the poor, students, prisoners, and so on. It was time, they said, for more discipline, more self-reliance, and fewer expensive social programs. These governments claimed they were reducing the size of the state, and allowing free markets and corporations to tackle problems that it had failed to solve. But, in fact, it was usually programs for the poor and marginalized that were cut. Meanwhile more coercive agencies—the police, prisons, courts, and armed forces—experienced explosive growth.

This pattern leads Hallett (2002) to suggest that governments now engage in the "penal management of poverty"—using police and prisons, rather than social supports, to keep the poor in line. Thus crime is portrayed as a problem of irresponsible individuals, rather than degraded communities, and every discussion of social problems seems to lead to calls for tougher sentences and more prison time.

Within prisons, rehabilitation programs continue to fall far short of what is needed, and programming in Canada and elsewhere is increasingly focused on making prisoners "employable." In practice, this means instilling a new, tougher work ethic that will make ex-prisoners happy to accept any job in the lower ranks of the labour market (McElligott, 2007). But "freer" markets have included higher levels of unemployment, and globalization has exposed workers to competition from cheap labour abroad. Canadian workers have been forced to work longer and harder at jobs that are increasingly precarious (insecure, part-time, and benefit-free), and stifle their hopes for something better (Tiessen, 2014).

This general degradation of work, if left unchecked, will make it increasingly difficult for ex-prisoners and other marginalized people to succeed in the legitimate economy. In fact, as job quality declines, crime becomes a more attractive option, especially for those whose addictions and mental health needs were never treated in prison. Canadian governments, rather than fighting the trend toward precarious work, have instead ignored or enabled it. In this context it seems reasonable to ask whether prison work programs have now become part of a larger government effort to lower Canadians' expectations, and get them to accept the degradation of work.

Conclusion: Prisons Tomorrow

Although prison critics are often accused of idealism, those who support prison expansion indulge in a fair bit of magical thinking themselves. Despite much historical evidence to the contrary, the latter insist that better work ethics can reform prisoners, and that the latest prison designs can reduce crime, lower costs, and perhaps even allow prisons to pay for themselves (McElligott, 2008). The US "supermax" prison (short for super-maximum security), which has influenced recent jail designs all over Canada, is one more example here. Its reliance on high-tech surveillance, centrally controlled doors, minimal inmate movement, and video "visits" has made prisons increasingly impersonal and alienating for everyone involved. In this model, according to Nils Christie, "the possibilities of monster-creating are considerable" (2000, p. 185). So while cash may be saved, other costs are likely to rise.

Perhaps the central metaphor explaining where we stand with prisons today is the prison-industrial complex. This concept, which has its origins in the United States (Schlosser, 1998), suggests that prison building develops a momentum of its own, independent of any crime-related needs. Private interests make money from supplying, building, or running prisons on contract to the state. Politicians win elections by constantly talking about crime, and promising to be tougher than their competitors. Bureaucrats find it easier to go with the flow and con-tract out, rather than come up with new ideas. Crime dominates the political agenda to the point where other programs that might limit crime, like education, are slashed in even the most crime-prone communities. And once the prisons are built and the contracts are flowing, corporate lobbyists press for longer and longer sentences, to keep the "clients" coming back.

At the time of this writing (2015), Canada sits in the early stages of this vicious cycle. Many provinces are building new prisons using the supermax model, and the federal government, which, under the Harper Conservatives, used the same tough-on-crime slogans pioneered in the United States, is making substantial additions to most of its existing prisons (Piché, n.d.). Ontario has experimented with a privately run prison, and entered into long-term agreements with private companies to build and lease back new ones (Buitenhuis, 2013). There are some indications that Ottawa may be prepared to increase private involvement as well. Multinational prison companies actively lobbied the Harper government, presumably to push privatization (Tencer, 2012). It is not yet clear whether popular support has reached the critical mass necessary to perpetuate the cycle, but Harper's defeat in 2015 has probably slowed down that process.

What ultimately may derail the rise of a prison-industrial complex in Canada are the immense costs involved in feeding it. This is perhaps the central contradiction of the tough-on-crime position for conservatives who also believe in balanced budgets. The experience of California, which started one of the earliest and biggest prison booms, shows that prison expenditure can quickly grow large enough to imperil the whole state's finances. California may now be reaching the end of this road, and politicians there have begun to back off the tough-on-crime measures that helped to flood their prisons.

What Canada needs to do at this stage is make a decisive break with the cycle that creates perpetual prison growth. That means freezing prison construction and thinking seriously about whether so many minor crimes need to result in prison time, and whether some crimes (like cannabis possession) need to be crimes at all. Alternative measures, such as probation, are substantially cheaper than prison, and do less damage to convicts' job prospects, their families, and their communities.

Breaking the cycle also means finding innovative ways to take the profit out of prisons, so that no one will have a material interest in expanding punishment. This means redirecting the billions of dollars now planned for prison construction into something more socially useful, and reclaiming the space that prisons now occupy. There are indications that this is already beginning to happen in the United States, where 15 prisons closed in 2011–2012. Some business leaders abandoned the usual argument that prisons were good for economic growth, and instead called for the conversion of more old prison sites into condominiums, shopping malls, and other lucrative developments (Lawrence, 2013). While these may not be the most socially useful alternatives, it is encouraging to see even mainstream groups looking beyond prison-based local economies.

The emphasis on labour market conditions above suggests that we might take a real bite out of crime if governments were to legislate better working conditions for entry-level jobs. Rather than pushing released prisoners toward bad jobs, we could then pull them toward good ones. What this means ultimately is that to avoid a society increasingly dominated by prison's values—pain, order, obedience, and work—we need to move toward a more supportive, self-governing society that does not need prisons at all. Such a society would decouple punishment from economic self-interest, and reclaim prisons as public spaces.

Discussion Questions

1. Is it fair to talk about prisons mostly in terms of fear, work, and social control? What about crime, justice, and the law?
2. Don't prisons do at least some good? If you worked in one, would you be able to make a difference in someone else's life?
3. What is so wrong about making money off of prisons? People need to have jobs, and do prisons really do any more damage than, for example, tobacco companies or the arms industry?

Additional Resources

Hemmati, T. (2006). *The nature of Canadian urban gangs and their use of firearms: A review of the literature and police survey.* Ottawa: Department of Justice Canada, Research and Statistics Division: http://www.justice.gc.ca/eng/rp-pr/csj-sjc/crime/rr07_1/rr07_1.pdf

Mellor, B., MacRae, L., Pauls, M., & Hornick, J. P. (Canadian Research Institute for Law and the Family). (2005). *Youth gangs in Canada: A preliminary review of programs and services.* Calgary: Public Safety and Emergency Preparedness Canada: http://www.turtleisland.org/resources/youthgangs.pdf

Public Safety Canada. *Youth gangs in Canada: What do we know?* Ottawa: National Crime Prevention Centre: http://www.publicsafety.gc.ca/cnt/rsrcs/pblctns/gngs-cnd/index-en.aspx

Notes

1. Garland's (1993) chapter 10 provides a useful summary of the work of Norbert Elias and Peter Spierenburg. They focus on the role of changing cultural values to explain the need to hide punishment.
2. Similarly, a decades-long pattern of physical and sexual abuse was officially sanctioned or officially tolerated in Canada's residential school system, as we are now discovering (see Truth and Reconciliation Commission of Canada, 2015).
3. For Headley's testimony to the Joint Committee of the Senate and House of Commons on Capital and Corporal Punishment and Lotteries, 1953–55, see http://www.corpun.com/cajur3.htm.
4. A minority tradition, represented by Thorsten Sellin, argues that penitentiaries were not such a radical break from the past, and were essentially elaborations of previous forms of organized forced labour going back at least to Roman times. See Sellin (1967).
5. The Pennsylvania System was also called the "Separate System" versus Auburn's "Congregate System" for this reason.
6. Not coincidentally, Canada's Indian Act was used as the model for South Africa's vicious apartheid system of racial segregation. See Saul (2010).

References

American Civil Liberties Union. (n.d.). *Fair sentencing act*. Retrieved from https://www.aclu.org/fair-sentencing-act

Austin, J., & Irwin, J. (2012). *It's about time: America's imprisonment binge* (4th ed.). Belmont, CA: Wadsworth.

Bentham, J. (1995). *The Panopticon writings*. M. Bozovic (Ed.). London: Verso. (Original work published 1787)

Buitenhuis, A. (2013). *Public-private partnerships and prison expansion in Ontario: Shifts in governance, 1995 to 2012*. Unpublished master's thesis, Department of Geography and Program in Planning, University of Toronto. Retrieved from https://tspace.library.utoronto.ca/bitstream/1807/42694/6/Buitenhuis_Amy_J_201311_MA_thesis.pdf

Christie, N. (2000). Dangerous states. In M. Brown & J. Pratt (Eds.), *Dangerous offenders* (pp. 181–193). Abingdon, UK: Taylor & Francis.

Corpun (World Corporal Punishment Research). (n.d.). The Canadian prison strap. Retrieved from http://www.corpun.com/canada.htm

Correctional Services Canada. (2012). 2012 corrections and conditional release statistical overview. Retrieved from http://www.publicsafety.gc.ca/cnt/rsrcs/pblctns/2012-ccrs/index-eng.aspx

Correctional Services Program. (2015). Adult correctional services in Canada, 2013/2014. *Juristat*. Statistics Canada. Retrieved from http://www.statcan.gc.ca/pub/85-002-x/2015001/article/14163-eng.htm

Dauvergne, M. (2012). Adult correctional statistics in Canada, 2010/2011. *Juristat*. Statistics Canada Catalogue no. 85-002-X. Retrieved from http://www.statcan.gc.ca/pub/85-002-x/2012001/article/11715-eng.pdf

Davis, A. (2003). *Are prisons obsolete?* New York: Seven Stories Press.

Deshman, A., & Myers, N. (2014). *Set up to fail: Bail and the revolving door of pre-trial detention*. Toronto: Canadian Civil Liberties Association and Education Trust. Retrieved from https://ccla.org/dev/v5/_doc/CCLA_set_up_to_fail.pdf

Feeley, M. (2002). Entrepreneurs of punishment. *Punishment and Society, 4*(3), 321–344.

Fine, S. (2015, June 15). Longer waits for parole disadvantage Aboriginal offenders. *Globe and Mail*. Retrieved from http://www.theglobeandmail.com/news/national/longer-waits-for-parole-disadvantage-aboriginal-offenders-report/article24954998/

Foucault, M. (1995). *Discipline and punish*. New York: Vintage.

Frost, N., & Gross, L. (2012). Coercive mobility and the impact of prison-cycling on communities. *Crime, Law and Social Change, 57*, 459–474.

Garland, D. (1993). *Punishment and modern society*. Chicago: University of Chicago Press.

Garland, D. (2001). Introduction: The meaning of mass imprisonment. *Punishment and Society, 3*(1), 5–7.

Gopnik, A. (2012, January 30). The caging of America. *New Yorker, 87*(46), 72–77.

Hallett, M. (2002). Race, crime and for-profit imprisonment. *Punishment and Society, 4*(3), 369–393.

Hallett, M. (2012). Reentry to what? Theorizing prisoner reentry in the jobless future. *Critical Criminology, 20*(12), 213–228.

Hay, D. (1975). Property, authority and the criminal law. In D. Hay, P. Linebaugh, J. G. Rule, E. P. Thompson, & C. Winslow (Eds.), *Albion's fatal tree: Crime and society in eighteenth-century England* (pp. 17–63). New York: Pantheon.

Heitzeg, N. (2009). Education or incarceration: Zero tolerance policies and the school to prison pipeline. *Forum on Public Policy Online, 2*, 1–21. Retrieved from http://files.eric.ed.gov/fulltext/EJ870076.pdf

Ignatieff, M. (1978). *A just measure of pain: The penitentiary in the Industrial Revolution 1750–1850*. New York: Columbia University Press.

International Centre for Prison Studies. (2015). Highest to lowest: Prison population rate. In World Prison Brief. Retrieved from http://www.prisonstudies.org/highest-to-lowest/prison_population_rate?field_region_taxonomy_tid=All

Known to police 2013: A Toronto Star investigation into race, policing and crime (2013). *Toronto Star* (various dates). Retrieved from http://www.thestar.com/news/gta/knowntopolice2013.html

La Prairie, C. (2002). Aboriginal over-representation in the criminal justice system: A tale of nine cities. *Canadian Journal of Criminology, 44*(2), 181–208.

Lawrence, A. (2013). Shrinking prisons. *State Legislatures, 39*(1), 26–27.

LeBaron, G. (2008). Captive labour and the free market: Prisoners and production in the USA. *Capital & Class, 32*(95), 59–81.

Linebaugh, P. (1975). The Tyburn riot against the surgeons. In D. Hay, P. Linebaugh, J. G. Rule, E. P. Thompson, & C. Winslow (Eds.), *Albion's fatal tree: Crime and society in eighteenth-century England* (pp. 65–117). New York: Pantheon.

Maher, M., & Berzins, L. (2011). Open the doors to smarter justice. Smart Justice Network. Retrieved from http://www.johnhoward.mb.ca/wp/wp-content/uploads/2013/08/Open-Doors-to-Smarter-Justice-Smart-Justice-Network-Report.pdf

Mancini, M. (1996). *One dies, get another: Convict leasing in the American South, 1866–1928.* Columbia: University of South Carolina Press.

Martinson, R. (1974). What works? Questions and answers about prison reform. *Public Interest, 35,* 22–54.

McElligott, G. (2007). Negotiating a coercive turn: Work discipline and prison reform in Ontario. *Capital and Class, 9,* 31–53.

McElligott, G. (2008). A Tory high modernism? Grand plans and visions of order in neoconservative Ontario. *Critical Criminology, 16*(2), 123–144.

National Archives (US). (n.d.). *America's historical documents: 13th Amendment to the US Constitution; Abolition of slavery.* Retrieved from http://www.archives.gov/historical-docs/document.html?doc=9&title.raw=13th+Amendment+to+the+U.S.+Constitution%3A+Abolition+of+Slavery

National Prison Rape Elimination Commission. (2009). *National Prison Rape Elimination Commission report.* Retrieved from https://www.ncjrs.gov/pdffiles1/226680.pdf

Oliver, P. (1998). *"Terror to evil-doers": Prisons and punishments in nineteenth-century Ontario.* Toronto: University of Toronto Press.

Palmer, B. (2000). *Cultures of darkness: Night travels in the histories of transgressions (from medieval to modern).* New York: Monthly Review Press.

Parenti, C. (2000). *Lockdown America.* New York: Verso.

Perrault, S. (2009). The incarceration of Aboriginal people in adult correctional services. *Juristat.* Statistics Canada Catalogue no. 85-002-X. Retrieved from http://www.statcan.gc.ca/pub/85-002-x/2009003/article/10903-eng.pdf

Piché, J. (n.d.) Tracking the politics of "crime" and punishment in Canada. Retrieved from http://www.tpcp-canada.blogspot.ca/

Ross, S. (2009/10). Resisting the carceral state: Prisoner resistance from the bottom up. *Social Justice, 36*(3), 28–45.

Rothman, D. J. (2002). *The discovery of the asylum* (revised edition). New York: Aldine de Gruyter.

Sangster, J. (1999). Criminalizing the colonized: Ontario women confront the criminal justice system, 1920–60. *The Canadian Historical Review, 80*(1), 32–60.

Saul, J. S. (2010). Two fronts of anti-apartheid struggle: South Africa and Canada. *Transformation, 74,* 135–151.

Schlosser, E. (1998). The prison-industrial complex. *Atlantic Monthly* (December), 51–77.

Sellin, T. (1967). A look at prison history. *Federal Probation, 31*(3), 18–23.

Shahidullah, S. (2014). *Comparative criminal justice systems: Global and local perspectives.* Burlington, MA: Jones & Bartlett.

Smith, E., & Hattery, A. (2007). If we build it they will come: Human rights violations and the prison-industrial complex. *Societies Without Borders, 2,* 273–288.

Smith, J., Bordelon, J., & Jackson, J. (Directors). (2008). *Six seconds of freedom: The Angola Prison rodeo story* [Film]. United States: Oasis Films. Retrieved from https://vimeo.com/18428560

Sterling, E. (n.d.). Drug laws and snitching: A primer. *PBS Frontline*. Retrieved from http://www.pbs.org/wgbh/pages/frontline/shows/snitch/primer/

Story, R., & Yalkin, T. (2013). Expenditure analysis of criminal justice in Canada. Ottawa: Parliamentary Budget Office of Canada. Retrieved from http://www.pbo-dpb.gc.ca/files/files/Crime_Cost_EN.pdf

Sykes, G. (1958). *The society of captives*. Princeton, NJ: Princeton University Press.

Tencer, D. (2012, July 13). Prison privatization: Canada mulls contracting services to companies lobbying for correctional work. *Huffington Post*. Retrieved from http://www.huffingtonpost.ca/2012/07/13/prison-privatization-canada_n_1670755.html?view=print&comm_re%E2%80%A6

Thompson, E. P. (1967). Time, work-discipline and industrial capitalism. *Past and Present, 38*, 56–97.

Tiessen, K. (2014). *Seismic shift: Ontario's changing labour market*. Ottawa: Canadian Centre for Policy Alternatives. Retrieved from https://www.policyalternatives.ca/publications/reports/seismic-shift

Truth and Reconciliation Commission of Canada. (2015). Honouring the truth, reconciling for the future: Summary of the final report of the Truth and Reconciliation Commission of Canada. Ottawa: Truth and Reconciliation Commission of Canada. Retrieved from http://www.trc.ca/websites/trcinstitution/File/2015/Findings/Exec_Summary_2015_05_31_web_o.pdf

Voorhees, J. (2014, June 30). A city of convicts: The statistical sleight of hand that makes the US crime rate seem lower than it really is. *Slate*. Retrieved from http://www.slate.com/articles/news_and_politics/politics/2014/06/prison_crime_rate_the_u_s_violent_crime_rate_is_falling_partly_because_the.html

Wacquant, L. (2010). Class, race & hyperincarceration in revanchist America. *Daedalus, 139*(3), 74–86.

Warren, J. (2008). One in 100: Behind bars in America 2008. The Pew Center on the States. Retrieved from http://www.pewtrusts.org/en/research-and-analysis/reports/2008/02/28/one-in-100-behind-bars-in-america-2008

Wright, P. (2003). Making slave labour fly: Boeing goes to prison. In T. Herivel & P. Wright (Eds.), *Prison nation* (pp. 112–119). New York: Routledge.

Zimring, F. E., & Johnston, D. T. (2008). Law, society and capital punishment in Asia. *Punishment & Society, 10*(2), 103–115.

CHAPTER 4

Religion and Rehabilitation

Aqeel Saeid

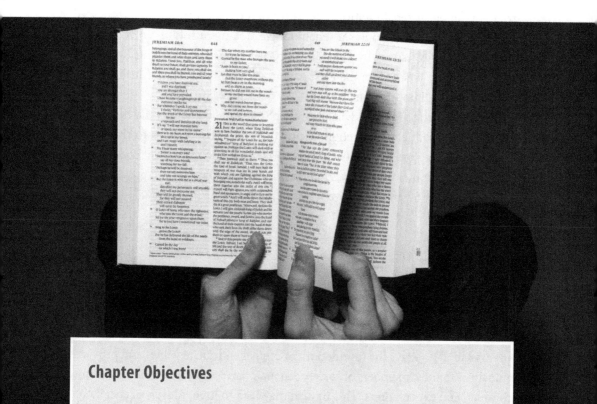

Chapter Objectives

This chapter will help the reader develop an understanding of the relationship between religion and rehabilitation by conducting a review of existing literature to identify the primary role of religion in rehabilitation programs. The discussion will explore the goals of those interventions and the outcomes for participants. Given the limited research on the role of religion in Canada's penal system today, the American literature was reviewed to evaluate the role of religion in a penitentiary setting. Much of the existing literature is based on data from qualitative research studies, many of which admittedly have flaws in their research and analysis; however, the available research evidence shows a positive association between religion and rehabilitation.

Introduction

Canada continues to experience significant demographic shifts, including an increase in the diversity of religious groups with varying religious expectations and practices. This changing demographic requires a greater focus on the role of religion in Canadian society today.

Religion was commonly used as a form of treatment programming in correctional settings in the 19th century, but the emphasis on the secular ethics, which are mainly based on social and psychological adjustment, minimized the role of religion in rehabilitation. The latter half of the 20th century witnessed a re-emergence of religion as a rehabilitative treatment tool in corrections in the United States, especially after the emphasis on prisoners' rights, including religious rights, as based on the First Amendment in 1960. Black Muslims were granted their religious rights in 1962 (Clear & Sumter, 2005).

In the following sections I will briefly explore religion and identify the rationale for the introduction of religious practices and observances to the justice system. I will explore the relationship between religion and social control, and discuss the outcomes of religious intervention with offenders and provide some indications for how we can move forward as a society.

What Is Religion?

Religion is a vital social phenomenon in both simple and complex industrial societies, as it provides information about the meaning of life and answers to some eternal questions related to God, supernatural power, spirits, and life after death. It also lays the foundation for ethical and social values and provides guidelines for how members of society can maintain society's behavioural norms, conduct, and expectations. This in turn may lead to higher levels of social harmony and social cohesion in most societies, especially homogeneous societies. In complex societies,[1] religion helps to build harmony among social systems through its institutional role in society as it provides the ethical foundation for other systems, such as family, economics, politics, education, and health care. According to sociologists such as Emile Durkheim, Max Weber, and Auguste Comte, religion plays an important role in maintaining social order and social control.[2] Durkheim believed that religion was the basic root of civilizations and the basic form of social life (LaCapra, 1972, p. 246). Furthermore, laws and morals and daily social interactions were based on religious ideals, which makes religion an essential social phenomenon in providing societies with the basic foundation of rules to guide human behaviour. Comte emphasized that religion and religious socialization are the main strategies for maintaining social order in simple and complex societies by passing religious values and norms from one generation to the next. Based on the prevalence of these religious socializing practices, Comte defined religion as "the state of complete harmony to human life" (Wernick, 2004, p. 102).

Religion, as a social fact, refers to patterns of thinking, feeling, and acting that are external to individuals and are endowed with a power of coercion over them (see Durkheim 1895/1982). It is also a set of beliefs, observances, and rituals that are connected to certain beliefs in God/gods or supernatural power. Those beliefs help groups and individuals to answer some questions related to the meaning and purpose of life and to unify believers into a community (Durkheim, 1895, as cited in Murray, Linden, & Kendall, 2012, p. 468).

Theoretically, most religions are composed of three fundamental components that guide groups and individuals in their daily lives. These components are: (1) spiritual and sacred components; (2) social components; and (3) symbolic components. The spiritual and sacred components refer to the relationship between individuals and God/supernatural power that aims at explaining and answering some fundamental questions, including questions about life and death, life after death, Day of Judgment, prayer, fasting, and certain types of observances and rituals that vary based on religion. It also provides answers for some eternal questions: What is the purpose of life? Is there life after death? And where does the world come from? In certain religions, such as Christianity, Islam, Judaism, and Buddhism, the spiritual and sacred component is facilitated through specific institutions, such as churches, mosques, temples, and synagogues. Some rituals and observances require the facilitation and guidance of a religious leader. Such institutional activities can promote social bonds by engaging individuals in similar spiritual activities, such as prayers or meditation. Social bonds refer to the level of integration of individuals in their society. Travis Hirschi (1969) focused on four social bonds that uphold conformity and protect social order. These four bonds are attachment, commitment, involvement, and moral beliefs. When individuals are attached to parents, teachers, and peers; committed to the conventional lines of life; involved in social activities; and accept the value system in their society, they are less likely to be involved in delinquent behaviour.

The social components of most religions provide the foundation for developing social relationships among individuals within society. Religion outlines or identifies some important aspects of social life, including family, marriage, politics, and education, although the specific type of involvement can vary. In Christianity, Islam, and Judaism, religion plays an important role in delineating multiple aspects of social life, such as defining marriage and its purposes as a social institution; providing details about family values; and describing social roles for parents, including how they should interact with and raise their children, and how children should deal with their parents; and they highlight the ethical foundation of politics, the economy, and many other aspects of life. Below are some examples from the Bible and the Quran:

> Fathers, do not provoke your children to anger, but bring them up in the discipline and instruction of the Lord. (Ephesians 6:4)

> And treat your parents with kindness. If one or both of them attain old age in your care, never say to them a word (suggesting) disgust, nor reproach them, but address them with reverent speech. And humble yourself out of mercy before them, and pray: "My Lord! Be merciful to them for having cared for me in my childhood." (Quran 17:23–24).

The symbolic component of religion can be explained by using symbolic interactionism theory; it refers to the subjective meanings of objects, events, social actions, and life in general (Anderson & Taylor, 2013, p. 19). Subjective means that individuals and groups behave based on what they have faith in and not just on what could be objectively true. Subjectivity of religion is related to how individuals, who believe in certain faiths, interpret and attach meaning to objects, events, and actions. It is also relevant to how they perceive themselves and others according to their own religious thoughts and guidelines. Religions have certain symbols that are deeply embodied in the collective consciousness of most individuals and groups who identify themselves based on their beliefs, such as the cross in Christianity, the Star of David in Judaism, the dharma wheel in Buddhism, the Sikh coat of arms or "Khalsa Crest," and totem poles for the First Nations of the Pacific Northwest, which represent honour, ancestry, historical events, and people (Goodwin & Scimecca, 2006, p. 130). These types of symbols strengthen the collective consciousness of society's members, as they are connected with core religious and cultural values or norms.

In general, religion refers to an integrated system of beliefs, symbols, and actions relating to sacred and supernatural powers that unite individuals or believers into a moral community (LaCapra, 1972, p. 250; Murray, Linden, & Kendall, 2011). Building on Durkheim's interpretation of social phenomena, religion refers to patterns of thinking, feeling, and acting that are external to individuals (Durkheim, 1895/1982, pp. 51–59). They are external to the individual as they were created and practiced by previous generations and became fundamental aspects of values in the collective consciousness. Although these patterns are considered external, they are also internal as they are embodied in the collective consciousness[3] of members of society through socialization, learning, and social control. The fact that religion is intergenerational and embedded in the collective mind and milieu of a people could explain its coercive power and its capacity for relatively strong social control.

Functions of Religion

There is a debate among sociologists about the role of religion in social life. Structural functionalists such as Emile Durkheim and Max Weber believed that religion plays an important role in social life and provides the fundamental function of maintaining social solidarity and social order in human societies. Marxist theorists believe that religion promotes social inequality and justifies a miserable life for the poor, and increases the possibility of social clashes among religious groups or communities based on the spiritual and ethical differences between religions and sects. Karl Marx also believed that the capitalist class uses religion to hinder social change and to keep workers at a lower status. Feminists view religion as a backbone for patriarchal systems that justifies the separation between men and women and places women at a lower social status (Murray, Linden, & Kendall, 2011, pp. 472–473).

Religion is also regarded as having important psychological and sociological functions. For example, a psychological component of religion is that it helps individuals and groups find meaning and purpose in life. Even in this scientific era, the death a loved one remains a mystery to many people in terms of understanding what happens after death and what it means to lose a person. Such challenges cause psychological and social stress for the majority of human beings. Most religions help individuals and groups find relief from such challenges to the human mind. Religion provides explanations for many of these unknown challenges—such as whether there is life after death, spirits, and the Day of Judgment—although the explanations may differ from one religion to the next. The belief in life after death, the idea of a Day of Judgment, paradise, heaven, and repentance can provide satisfaction for individuals in this life as the promise of justice, equality, and fairness in the afterlife. These promises could provide incentives for believers to engage in positive behaviour during their lifetimes.

Religion and Its Influence on Social Control and Deterrence

Weber and Durkheim predicted that religion would have significant effects on human behaviour in general, and on conformity and deviance in particular. Religion has what Durkheim calls a "dynamogenic" quality (Jones, 2005). In other words, religion has the capacity not only to dominate individuals but also to elevate them above their abilities and capacities (Ritzer, 2000). Through this dominance, religion controls individuals and imposes its symbols on them. Durkheim believed that religious life constituted the chief element in any social order. A community lacking a religious life would be atomized and character- ized by anti-social behaviour (Stark, Kent, & Doyle, 1980). Religion has received renewed interest as a social control variable that potentially reduces crime. For example, in his 1990 study titled "Crime and Religion: A Denominational and Community Analysis," John Olson's investigation provided evidence linking church membership and belief with reduced crime.

Hirschi and Stark (1969) proposed that religiosity deters crime through a system of rewards and punishments (e.g., paradise for believers and hellfire for sinners and unbelievers), which promotes adherence to religious and social values, norms, and ethics. Similarly, rational choice theory indicates that the possibility of experiencing shame and embarrassment tends to deter religious individuals from committing crimes.

There are still some researchers who doubt religion's effectiveness in preventing crimes and controlling criminality. For example, Hirschi and Stark did not find a correlation between church attendance and the moral attitudes related to the social behaviour of northern California high school students (Olson, 1990). However, one cannot rely on such results in evaluating the role of religion in controlling human behaviour because church attendance is a limited criterion for evaluating this role. Religion and its impact on human behaviour cannot be limited to such institutionalized forms of social action. In religions such as Islam, Judaism, and Christianity, religiosity influences different forms of social phenomena, including family, the economy, and political and judicial systems, as indicated earlier.

Michael Cretacci (2003) studied the relationship between social bonds and deviance by using a series of subsamples and a modified version of the social bond scale developed by Hirschi (1969). Social bond theory is based on the idea that the bonds or relationships that we have, play a central role in reducing a person's involvement in crime and delinquent behaviour. The main objective of Cretacci's study was to determine whether social bonds, including religion, are associated with lower levels of violence. The study did not indicate significant correlation between a person's engagement with religion or religious commitment[4] and lowered levels of involvement in violence. However, Cretacci assumed that taking a sample from agricultural or homogeneous societies would probably bring different results due to the involvement of religion in many aspects of life in such societies in comparison to industrial and complex societies such as the United States where the study was conducted. He also thought the definition of religion and religious commitment would probably affect the result of the study, which is expected as the definition of religious commitment varies between religions and cultures (Cretacci, 2003). He indicated that the literature is inconsistent in terms of looking at the role of religion in reducing violence. He followed Durkheim in emphasizing that in mechanical or simple societies, religion increases social bonds and decreases deviance; however, this impact was not as clearly evidenced in complex or heterogeneous societies.

The role of religion in deterring crime depends on the principle of reward and punishment in the present life and in life after death. The social status of criminals and deviants could be reduced in their community if they were labelled as sinners, and could be threatened by a higher level of punishment in life after death (e.g., paradise versus hellfire). Religions rely on socialization as a mechanism to support their values and norms and to transfer them from generation to generation, which allows religion to maintain itself and support the social order. In some religions, such as Islam and Judaism, the threat of harsh punishment in both lives is thought to be a key element in preventing anti-socio-religious actions.

Religion and Rehabilitation

In general, rehabilitation refers to reintegration efforts to prepare inmates for social life after their release from prison. Religious programs suggest that inmates could be morally changed after attending certain faith- and spiritual-based sessions (Camp, Klein-Saffran, Kwon, Daggett, & Joseph, 2006). Religious programs in correctional settings have been used widely in the United States as a form of institutional programming for inmates. Despite this important role for religion in the rehabilitative process, the criminological literature identifies very few studies that examine this correlation (Camp et al., 2006).

Some studies that have been identified above indicate that religion plays a profound role in maintaining social control, social cohesion, deterrence, and brings psychological comfort and satisfaction for individuals. Building on these studies, is it safe to say that religion has a positive influence on rehabilitating offenders?

Answering such a question requires some significant empirical results. Statistics from the United States indicate that almost every prison has a chaplain who provides incarcerated individuals with religious accommodations (O'Connor & Perreyclear, 2002). Chaplaincy services are also available for all offenders in federal penitentiaries across Canada (Correctional Service Canada, 2013). The purpose of religious accommodation for offenders in Canadian correctional settings is to help them explore questions related to spirituality, religion, and life purpose. It is a collaborative effort for chaplains and volunteers to help offenders examine their behaviour and make better decisions for their future.

The presence of these chaplaincy services may provide opportunities to conduct research on the effectiveness of religious accommodation in prison and how religion can have a positive impact on the rehabilitation process. O'Connor and Perreyclear (2002) conducted a small study that emphasized that religious practice could have an extensive effect on prisoners. They estimated that about 50 percent of inmates attend religious services, which might indicate that some level of involvement in faith-based activities may have a positive influence on offenders. According to the same study, the involvement of significant numbers of volunteers signals that religious programming can be regarded as a source of social modelling, as those volunteers may inspire inmates to reduce their involvement in crime. It may bring the sense of hope needed for inmates to change their lives and search for social and religious forgiveness. Those volunteers could break the barrier between inmates and the community, and ease the reintegration process after leaving the institution. The researchers acknowledge the methodological limitation of their study, recognizing that because of the small size of the study's sample population, the results are preliminary and cannot be generalized.

Another study was conducted by Clear, Hardyman, Stout, Lucken, and Dammer (2000) to understand the meaning of religion for inmates and its effectiveness as a form of rehabilitation. Individual and group interviews with inmates were conducted in prisons in Delaware, Texas, Indiana, Missouri, and Mississippi in order to evaluate the connection between religion and rehabilitation. In their study, the researchers divided the meaning of religion into individual (or subjective) meaning, which focused on how each participant interpreted the role of religion in prison. Researchers also looked at how religion could be used to develop faith-based groups that practice religious observances on a daily basis.

The analysis of the data collected from the interviews indicated that imprisonment for many inmates promotes negative images about the world and the possibility of rehabilitation. One inmate said that "being incarcerated makes you bitter toward the world. They think it is going to make you better, but it does not"

(Clear, Hardyman, Stout, Lucken, & Dammer, 2000, p. 57). On the other hand, religion, for some prisoners, "holds possible routes out of the dilemma," as it could explain the causes of their failure and provide some possible solutions. According to one prisoner, "the true religious, they become stronger. They can deal with the ills that affect them and they can ease the ills that affect you, and [they can] cause you to be able to avoid more crimes" (p. 58).

Religion could help prisoners reduce their feeling of guilt, given that incarceration becomes an indication of moral faults and is associated with public shaming. It could also be a reminder of the person's previous rejection of their belief. The practice of religion offers internal discipline for battling individual's urges for criminality. Some inmates indicated that religion reduced their feelings of guilt and that being Christian would allow them to ask Jesus for forgiveness (Clear et al., 2000).

Another important theme generated from the interviews is that their faith provided inmates with a new way of life as they showed greater commitment to their religion and felt an active role for God in their journey. Some inmates indicated that their faith provided them with a sense of freedom although they were confined within the prison walls (Clear et al., 2000).

Participating in religious groups and services also provided material comforts, given that the participants were paid minimal wages and provided with basic needs. In other words, religious involvement served to reduce financial strain. An additional benefit was that the interactions with volunteers in the religious programs provided them with access to outsiders, especially women. This was a consistent theme in the interviews (Clear et al., 2000). The qualitative results indicated above show how religion and religious programs are important for inmates' life in prison; however, these themes need to be tested on a larger scale by conducting quantitative studies to confirm the validity of these themes.

Thomas and Zaitzow (2006) indicated that religious programing directly or indirectly enhances the rehabilitation process and successful integration for individuals after leaving the penitentiary. The study also showed that administrators in prisons view rehabilitation programming, including religious programs, as helpful in dealing with problems that occur in prison, such as the possibility of involvement in violence. Religious organizations help inmates channel their energy and actions in meaningful ways, which can also reduce the level of hostility in prison. Informally, religious activities help prisoners take advantage of the available supports to form groups that could provide them with opportunities to use their time productively (Thomas & Zaitzow, 2006).

Elisha, Idisis, and Ronel (2012) conducted a qualitative study about social acceptance and life transformation in the rehabilitation of imprisoned sex offenders. In two prisons in Israel, 38 male prisoners who had been convicted of sex offences participated in semi-structured interviews. The main objective of the study was to "identify the internal strengths and the external forces" (p. 323) that could correct and transform the behaviour and lifestyle of imprisoned sex offenders. Several participants indicated that religion presented a significant support in their rehabilitative process. Some described their offences as moral weaknesses because of their inability to cope with challenges in life. Their attachment to religion increased while in prison and they described themselves as converted ultra-orthodox believers. Those who were not religious decided to become religious in order to cope with the challenges and difficulties they faced in prison. Those participants with a non-religious background indicated that religion and spirituality helped them discover the spiritual meaning of their suffering (Elisha, Idisis, & Ronel, 2012).

Camp and colleagues (2006) conducted a survey to evaluate a faith-based program known as the Life Connection Program (LCP), which was initiated by the Federal Bureau of Prisons (BOP) in the United States. The survey was designed mainly to identify the characteristics of inmates who were likely candidates for participation in LCP, rather than to evaluate the effectiveness of religious rehabilitation programs. Surveys were collected from 407 inmates who participated voluntarily in LCP at five treatment prisons. The results showed that program participants were motivated to make changes in their life, which was indicated in their score on the motivation for change. The program created a good atmosphere for participants to practice their own beliefs. The study also showed that inmates who scored high on the motivation scale were more likely to be involved in LCP, meaning that religiosity or faith could motivate inmates to change since religion and spirituality are important components of LCP.

Sundt, Dammer, and Cullen (2002) focused on the role of prison chaplains in rehabilitation and the effectiveness of religious rehabilitation as viewed by chaplains themselves. They also sought to determine whether chaplains view their counselling sessions as rehabilitative or mainly spiritual. Of the original sample size of 500 participants identified by the American Correctional Association, 232 chaplains participated in the first survey. The second sample was selected to explore the content of chaplains' counselling sessions. Of the 45 chaplains attending a conference at Niagara University in New York, 32 returned their questionnaires. About 60.2 percent of participants emphasized that conducting religious services and coordinating religious programs and religious education were the best methods of rehabilitation and treatment. Chaplains also indicated that teaching inmates skills that they could use to get jobs in the future was an important rehabilitative point.

The majority of chaplains rejected the claim that rehabilitation does not work and instead indicated that treatment programs could be enhanced by obtaining better funding. To examine the content of the counselling sessions, Sundt, Dammer, and Cullen (2002) employed Worthington's (1986) theoretical framework to guide their interpretation of the responses of the second sample. Worthington identified three types of religious counselling techniques. The first one uses secular- or non-religious-based theoretical techniques to positively influence religious inmates. The second counselling technique focuses on the inclusion of religious practices such as prayers and meditation, and the third is a combination of secular and religious techniques. The responses of the 32 participants identified patterns that indicate that the majority of chaplains did not describe their sessions with inmates as typical religious sessions. About 64 percent of them indicated that their counselling sessions did not have a clear focus on religious or spiritual techniques. Nine participants indicated that they included religious counselling in their sessions but that they did not use secular theories to influence inmates' religious behaviour and spirituality (Sundt et al., 2002).

The results showed that chaplains utilize some established secular counselling methods, such as reality therapy, group counselling, client-centred therapy, and behavioural treatment methods. However, it was also indicated that they place a significant emphasis on religious and spiritual values in their counselling sessions. The mean level of emphasis on religion and spirituality was nine out of ten, which clearly indicates the emphasis on religious rehabilitation regardless of the method used in counselling. The results of the research indicate that there is a significant emphasis and belief in the role that religious interventions and support can play in behaviour change in inmates.

Final Thoughts

The review of the literature clearly indicated the lack of research on the role of religion as a form of rehabilitation in correctional settings. The knowledge regarding religious rehabilitative approaches was obtained mainly through qualitative research, which is based on subjective meaning and decreases the possibility of generalization about the effectiveness of religious programs in correctional settings. However, qualitative studies can be used to initiate some basic theoretical ideas about the role of religion in rehabilitation, which can be verified and tested on a large scale through quantitative research.

In general, the qualitative research and the limited number of quantitative studies mentioned in this chapter highlight some of the positive influences of religion in the process of counselling sessions and in rehabilitative programs. The studies also show the positive influence of these programs in terms of helping inmates cope with challenges they face in prison. Religion could also promote changes to the value systems of inmates attending these sessions, which could be a probable factor in decreasing recidivism.

Despite the secular base of these programs and sessions, chaplains emphasized the religious content in their sessions, as mentioned in Sundt and colleagues (2002). In other words, chaplains believe in changing the personal value systems of inmates by emphasizing religious values and content in their sessions.

The qualitative results generated from the literature could help us develop some initial thoughts about the relationship between religion and rehabilitation. Religion could help inmates cope with the prison environment and accept their lives in prison as a way to obtain forgiveness from God or a supernatural power based on their own faith and religious background, especially for those with strong beliefs in religious values. This could also mean accepting responsibility for their criminal actions and could lead them to think seriously about changing their lives. Feeling guilty about their past criminal actions would probably make them ready to seek change by doing better in the future.

In a Canadian case study analysis about Aboriginal spirituality in corrections, an Aboriginal inmate, Jack, stated the following:

> Actually, I seriously believe I've hurt a lot of people and I have to try to make up for it. More sweat to go through. More suffering I have to give for the people that I made suffer all my life. I wish to help some other people like the Elder .... So maybe that is the way I will pay back. (Waldram, 1994, p. 207)

As mentioned earlier in this chapter, religion provides rules and ways of living that each believer is expected to follow in life. These rules teach individuals how behave and how to avoid committing a behaviour—a "sin"—that is not acceptable to society and that religion. Religion provides directions for individuals to help them repair, correct, and refrain from engaging in wrongdoings by following certain religious and spiritual practices, actions, and observances. Such religious rules, practices, and rituals can help inmates search for a future that is better than their current life. In Dammer's (2002) qualitative study, inmates identified the role that religion played in motivating them, helping them to make meaning of religion and engaging in religious practices. The participants stated, "Religion is a guide to not get out of hand, it gives you a straight path," and that "Religion helps lead someone in the right direction. You can't help but make your life better" (p. 39). Religion was regarded as a strategy and process to help them to reform their lives of crime and make sense of their imprisonment (Dammer, 2002).

Religion could also play a therapeutic role and may lead to inner peace for believers by decreasing their inner conflict and psychological strain. Some anthropologists, such as Foster and Anderson (1978), have connected religion to the healing process in non-Western societies. In reality, the effectiveness of any treatment, especially social and psychological, should be viewed in its own cultural context (as cited by Waldram, 1994). According to the research, the psychological support provided to inmates by religion or by religious and spiritual practices can be a productive factor in the rehabilitation process. The concept of religious repentance would help inmates cope with the stress of life in prison and open new avenues for a better future.

The impact of religion and its role in rehabilitation and recidivism requires more large-scale and longitudinal research to evaluate its effectiveness. In Canada, studies about religious rehabilitation are insufficient at the methodological, qualitative, and quantitative levels. Canadian community justice researchers and practitioners, criminologists, criminal justice specialists, sociologists, and scholars in the justice field need to conduct more research in order to evaluate the correlation between religious programs in Canadian prisons and rehabilitation.

Although individuals and institutions in modern societies pursue justice through secular perspectives, religion and religious observances may play a vital role in shaping social justice in society (Todd & Rufa, 2012). Religion can play a significant role in crime reduction and prevention strategies since it is considered a key factor in social control and social cohesion, as based on structural functionalism, especially if the society maintains respect to all religions, sects, and spiritual affiliations. In other words, religion helps to develop community-based justice as a set of strategies that promote public safety, quality of life, crime reduction, and effective reintegration of offenders. Community justice can also support religion and spirituality by promoting religious values such as justice, equality, tolerance, and integration since these values are essential to community justice philosophy and practice. This support may also promote the role of religion in social life.

Summary and Conclusion

Qualitative research studies and the limited number of quantitative studied discussed in this chapter indicate the positive influence of religion in rehabilitation. Some of the mentioned research studies emphasized that religious rehabilitative programs may help inmates cope with challenges they face in prison, and could also promote changes to the value systems of inmates attending the rehabilitative programs and sessions, which could be a probable factor in decreasing recidivism. Such results may encourage researchers to further investigate the role of religion in rehabilitation, and to design some evaluation measures to assess the effectiveness of religious programs.

Discussion Questions

1. In this chapter you learned how sociologists such as Durkheim, Comte, and Weber define religion. Discuss these definitions with your classmates and come up with your own definition of religion.
2. Structural functionalists emphasize a positive role for religion in social control and social cohesion. Do you think that religion can play this role in multicultural and complex societies? Discuss this with your classmates and come up with reasonable justification for your agreement or disagreement.
3. Based on the studies reviewed in this chapter, discuss and critique how involvement in religion helps prisoners adjust to life in prison and how it could reduce recidivism.

Additional Resources

About Addiction. (2016). Faith Based Addiction Treatment and Recovery Programs. *About Addiction: Substance Abuse Referral Service*: http://www.about-addiction.com/treatment/faith-based-recovery/.

Fairhurst, L. (2006). Faith-Based Prison Programs Claim to Reduce Recidivism, but There's Little Evidence, Says FSU Research. *Florida State University News*: https://www.fsu.edu/news/2006/10/04/prison.programs/.

Government of Canada. (2013). Correctional Service Canada Healing Lodges: http://www.csc-scc.gc.ca/aboriginal/002003-2000-eng.shtml.

O'Connor, T. P., & Pallone, N. J. (2002). *Religion, the Community, and the Rehabilitation of Criminal Offenders*. Binghamton, NY: The Haworth Press.

Notes

1. The social structure in complex societies is divided into different groups and categories based on some social facts such as language, religion, culture, politics, division of labour, specialization, and social class. Modern industrial societies are good examples of complex societies.
2. Social control is a mechanism that is used by the society to protect the social order. It refers to processes and procedures that hold society together based on the main cultural values, religion, law, and public opinion.
3. As based on Durkheim, collective conscience refers to the core values and norms of a society. It represents the moral unity or the moral consensus among individuals and groups.
4. Religious commitment is the level of involvement in and commitment to religion and religious practices and observances.

References

Anderson, M. L., & Taylor, H. F. (2013). *Sociology: The essentials* (7th ed). Belmont, CA: Wadsworth Cengage Learning.

Camp, S. D., Klein-Saffran, J., Kwon, O., Daggett, D. M., & Joseph, V. (2006). An exploration into participation in a faith-based prison program. *Criminology and Public Policy, 5*(3), 529–550.

Cretacci, M. (2003). Religion and social control: An application of a modified social bond on violence. *Criminal Justice Behavior, 28*(2), 254–277.

Clear, T., & Sumter, M. (2005). Prisoners, prison, and religion: Religion and adjustment to prison. *Journal of Offender Rehabilitation, 35,* 127–159.

Clear, T., Hardyman, P., Stout, B., Lucken, K., & Dammer, H. (2000). The value of religion in prison. *Journal of Contemporary Criminal Justice, 16*(1), 53–74. doi:10.1177/1043986200016001004

Correctional Service Canada (CSC). (2013). Chaplaincy services. Retrieved from http://www.csc-scc.gc.ca/chaplaincy/index-eng.shtml

Dammer, H. (2002). The reasons for religious involvement in the correctional environment. *Journal of Offender Rehabilitation, 35*(3–4), 35–58.

Durkheim, E. (1982). *The rules of sociological method.* Steven Lukes (Ed.) & W. D. Halls (Trans). New York: The Free Press. (Original work published 1895).

Elisha, E., Idisis, Y., & Ronel, N. (2012). Window of opportunity: Social acceptance and life transformation in the rehabilitation of imprisoned sex offenders. *Aggression and Violent Behavior, 17,* 323–332. doi:10.1016/j.avb.2012.03.004

Foster, G. M., & Anderson, B. G. (1978). *Medical anthropology.* New York: John Wiley & Sons.

Goodwin, G. A., & Scimecca, J. A. (2006). *Classical sociological theory: Rediscovering the promise of sociology*. Toronto: Thomson Wadsworth.

Hirschi, T. (1969). *Causes of delinquency*. Berkeley: University of California Press.

Hirschi, T., & Stark, R. (1969). Hellfire and delinquency. *Social Problems, 17,* 202–213.

Jones, R. A. (2005). Practices and presuppositions: Some questions about Durkheim and *Les Formes elementaires de la vie religieuse*. In J. C. Alexander & P. Smith (Eds), *The Cambridge companion to Durkheim* (pp. 80–100). New York: Cambridge University Press.

LaCapra, D. (1972). *Emile Durkheim: Sociologist and philosopher*. New York: Cornell University Press.

Murray, J. L., Linden, R., & Kendall, D. (2012). *Sociology in our times: The Essentials*. Toronto: Nelson Education.

Olson, J. (1990). Crime and religion: A denominational and community analysis. *Journal for the Scientific Study of Religion, 29*(3), 395–403. Retrieved from http://www.jstor.org/stable/1386471

O'Connor, T. P., & Perreyclear, M. (2002). Prison religion in action and its influence on offender rehabilitation. *Journal of Offender Rehabilitation, 35*(3–4), 11–33.

Ritzer, G. (2000). *Sociological theory* (5th ed.). New York: McGraw-Hill Higher Education.

Stark, R. L., Kent, L., & Doyle, D. P. (1982). Religion and delinquency: The ecology of a lost relationship. *Journal of Research in Crime and Delinquency, 19*(1), 4–24.

Statistics Canada. (2001). *Religious groups in Canada*. Canadian Centre for Justice Statistics Profile Series. Catalogue No. 85F0033MIE. Retrieved from http://www.statcan.gc.ca/sites/default/files/85f0033m2001007-eng.pdf

Sundt, J., Dammer, H., & Cullen, F. (2002). The role of the prison chaplain in rehabilitation. *Journal of Offender Rehabilitation, 35,* 59–86.

Thomas, J., & Zaitzow, B. H. (2006). Conning or conversion? The role of religion in prison coping. *The Prison Journal, 86*(2), 242–259. doi:10.1177/0032885506287952

Todd, N., & Rufa, A. (2012). Social justice and religious participation: A qualitative investigation of Christian perspectives. *American Journal of Community Psychology, 51*(3–4), 315–331. doi:10.1007/s10464-012-9552-4

Waldram, J. (1994). Aboriginal spirituality in corrections: A Canadian case study in religion and therapy. *American Indian Quarterly, 18*(2), 197–214. Retrieved from www.jstor.org/stable/1185246

Wernick, A. (2004). *Auguste Comte and the religion of humanity: The post-theistic program of French social theory*. Cambridge: Cambridge University Press.

Worthington, E. (1986). Religious counseling: A review of published empirical research. *Journal of Counseling & Development, 64*(7), 421–431.

Community Injustices: Experiences of Justice among Canada's Diverse Populations

CHAPTER 5

Troubling and Disrupting the "Cradle to Prison Pipeline": The Experience of Black Youth in Ontario

Beverly-Jean M. Daniel

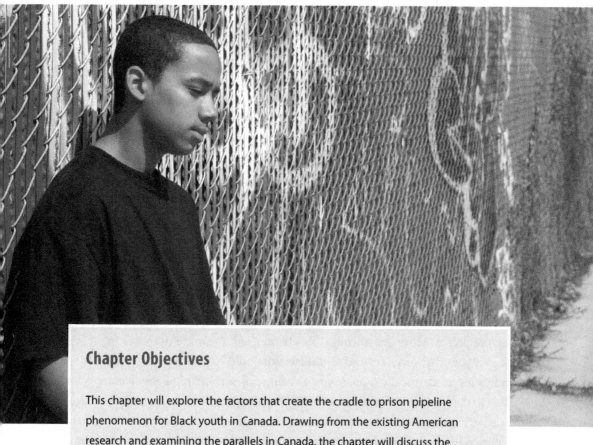

Chapter Objectives

This chapter will explore the factors that create the cradle to prison pipeline phenomenon for Black youth in Canada. Drawing from the existing American research and examining the parallels in Canada, the chapter will discuss the experiences that Black students have at various stages in their schooling journey—from birth through to early childhood education classes and into the secondary and post-secondary school systems. The chapter will use critical race theory as its primary theoretical framework.

Introduction

Education has been identified as the great equalizer in democratic liberal societies. There is an investment in the belief that if a person gets a good education, it will allow them to be successful in life. The uncritical belief in this ideology is present in every aspect of Western social, cultural, and institutional practice, to the extent that it produces an almost cult-like repetition and adherence to this idea. Western institutions of schooling operate in a manner that privileges and creates myths regarding rags-to-riches stories, while at the same time marking those who have not moved up the social, economic, or educational ladder as being weak and lazy. There continues to be a clear division between success and failure, which is regarded as a consequence of individualism or individual choice. In other words, the idea of meritocracy is based on the notion that society provides the same opportunities for all; therefore, a person will succeed or fail based on their own initiative and hard work.

Schools are central to the production and replication of the myth of meritocracy because they play a primary role in creating citizens. Schools are regarded as vehicles and tools to either take us toward success or failure depending on the way in which one engages with or is connected to the daily routines. While schools have helped, and will continue to help, some members of society experience a life of success, particularly when they have the economic resources in place, the experiences that others have in schools prepare them for a life in prison. For some students, schooling can be regarded as an unproductive march toward life or death both symbolically and literally.

This chapter will examine the processes, strategies, and practices that create the cradle to prison pipeline for Black youth within the Canadian context. It will highlight the connections between the strategies that contribute to the criminalization of students and increase their exposure to life on the street, which thereby increases the likelihood of them being watched, followed, and targeted by the police. More specifically, this chapter will examine the ways in which stereotypes that teachers and administrators hold regarding Black students as not being academically capable and as being prone to criminal involvement can lead to the "production of the criminal." The nature of these interactions between teachers and students can contribute to the criminalization of youth and their imprisonment. Further, stereotypes that teachers and principals unconsciously hold can have a negative and destructive impact on Black students' levels of academic success. Although individuals hold these stereotypes, schools and other social institutions have developed as the primary sites for the transmission of legalized practices of discrimination (racist ideologies) that are in place from the first day a student starts any form of schooling, including early child care centres. This chapter will critique the pathways from the cradle to the prison for Black youth in Canada and discuss options for disrupting this pipeline.

The Experience of Black Children from the Cradle

Edelman (2007) defines the cradle to prison pipeline phenomenon as

> a complex array of social and economic factors as well as political choices that converge to reduce the odds that poor children—especially poor Black and Latino children—will grow up to become productive adults. These factors include limited access to health care (including mental health care), underperforming schools, broken child welfare and juvenile justice systems. (p. 1)

The Cradle to Prison Pipeline campaign, which was started by the Children's Defense Fund in the United States, was aimed at reducing the number of Black and Hispanic children who are imprisoned because of ineffective schooling practices, issues of poverty, and mental health challenges. According to the research, Black boys are three times more likely to be suspended than White boys, and this pattern asserts itself from the early years of schooling (Children's Defense Fund, 2007).

Edelman (2007), citing this research, indicates that there are four main feeders into the criminal justice system: quality of health care, early childhood education, the foster care system, and schools. This chapter will focus mainly on schooling as the primary conduit from the cradle to prison for Black male youth. Although Aboriginal males in Canada also experience similar challenges, it is important not to collapse the experiences of these two groups given their differing histories and contexts.

In 2013 in Ontario, the Liberal government instituted all-day kindergarten programming, which saw a shift from half-day to full-day kindergarten classes starting at the junior kindergarten level. In its first stages, the full-day programs were implemented in schools in high-needs communities. The focus on high needs, and particularly economically deprived urban communities, was a positive step on the part of the government, which concentrated on the potential benefits of early enrichment programs. However, many teachers who work in schools in Canada continue to mistakenly believe that they are colour-blind (Lee, 1998) and are invested in multiculturalism, inclusion, equality, and liberalism (Daniel

& Solomon, 2008; Day, 2000). This means that most teachers, and most people in Canada, claim that they do not see the colour of a person's skin and that they treat all students the same. The uncritical replication of these "politically correct" sentiments by teachers limits any comprehensive analysis of the efficacy or impact of their practices on racialized students in kindergarten classes. In addition, any attempt to point out the problem with continued investment in selective tropes of colour-blindness, inclusion, liberalism (Berry, 1995), and multiculturalism is seen as reverse discrimination and an attack on "White people" (Carr & Lund, 2007; Kincheloe & Steinberg, 2000; Levine-Rasky, 2000; Lund, 2006; Sleeter, 1992), creating multiple, layered, and complex sites of resistance that can be challenging to overcome. The inclusion of these conversations about race, racism, and privilege within the field of early childhood education (ECE) has been much more limited based on the notion that children do not see race (Araujo & Strasser, 2003; Derman-Sparks, 1998; Swindler Boutte, 2008) and as such the inclusion of these ideas or practices are seen as unnecessary at that stage.

The early years are core periods of development and learning for children, and quality of schooling can have a significant impact on a child's overall life outcomes (Calman & Tarr-Whelan, 2005). In Canada, as the population becomes increasingly diverse, teachers need to be able to create differentiated learning environments that foster supportive learning for all children (Brown, Souto-Manning, & Tropp Laman, 2010; Kohli & Solorzano, 2012; Swindler Boutte, 2008). Quoting a 2001 report from the Organisation for Economic Co-operation and Development (OECD), Friendly and Prabhu (2010) state the following:

> In some kindergarten classes in Toronto, Vancouver and Montréal, more than 50% of the students were born outside Canada and most of these children came from Asia, the Middle East or Africa. Increasingly, staff in child care programs and kindergarten classes assist children who are learning English or French adapt to what may be very different norms and expectations. Neither the kindergarten nor child care workforce reflects the cultural and racial diversity of the population as a whole. Training programs for teachers and for early childhood educators are under pressure to specifically prepare their students for working in a situation of ethno cultural diversity. (p. 14)

Research on the treatment or experiences of racialized children in early childhood environments in Canada has been limited; however, anecdotal data suggests the pattern of hypervigilance of young Black male children in Canadian classrooms, including high rates of suspension and targeting for minor subjective infractions, mirrors that are evidenced in the research in the United States (Downey & Pribesh, 2004; Husband, 2011). I taught a course on race and racism in the Canadian context more than 10 years ago at an urban university in which a student recounted the differential treatment she observed of newborn babies in the pediatric unit based on their race. According to this student, the nurses appeared to cuddle and interact more frequently with the White babies and for longer periods of time than with the Black babies. In addition, the White nurses also appeared to respond much sooner to the cries of the White babies. The student asked the class to consider the messages a child receives about itself when, from the moment it is born, it is treated differently.

Another student who worked in a daycare commented on the ways in which the staff members often used negative labels and names to refer to Black and immigrant children in these settings. What these two, and many, many other, anecdotes point to is the importance of recognizing that, in a Canadian context, the differential treatment of Blacks and other racialized groups is essentially woven into the fabric of society like an invisible thread. The investment in the idea of colour-blindness, liberalism, multiculturalism, political correctness, and the cultural mosaic blinds the members of the dominant group and all too many minoritized group members to the ways in which these seemingly invisible threads bind and, at times, sever opportunities for many members of society. There is a wealth of data that speaks to the treatment of students of colour in middle and high schools (Fleming & Rose, 2007; McMurtry & Curling, 2008), and the inclusion of and research on zero-tolerance policies has served to confirm the reality that students of colour are disciplined differently than White students (Coates, 2015). As such, one would be rather naive to assume that this differential treatment only begins in the later school years given that babies and children are exposed to early childhood educators and teachers who possess many of the same dominant social stereotypes regarding Blackness. Should we assume that young Black kids are not subjected to the same modes of discipline that are deployed when they are older? Should we further assume that children who were subjected to these modes of discipline are not affected by racism and practices of racialization? These stereotypes contribute to the negative interactions between teachers and students and impact on the youth's identity development, and relationship to schooling and the larger society.

In addition, studies conducted by researchers such as Carl James and George Dei on the impact of zero-tolerance policies on the educational experiences of Canadian students (Dei, 1995; James, 2000; Puddicombe, 2011; Swain & Noblit, 2011) have reached results similar to those conducted on US school populations at the middle and secondary school levels. Research shows that children as young as three years old begin to notice and name racial differences (Araujo & Strasser, 2003; Lee, Ramsey, & Sweeney, 2008). If, for the sake of argument, it turned out to be true that children don't notice these differences, the fact of the matter is that the ECE teachers do and that they themselves have been programmed for years both at the conscious and unconscious levels with the varying discourses and practices of race and racialization. As such, in their interactions they often reify the messages to which they have been exposed. One can surmise and generalize again that these patterns do not simply emerge when students are older, but rather, by the time they have reached the middle and secondary school levels, they have been primed for failure and consequently for prison, beginning in ECE classrooms.

Teacher Discipline of Black Males and Its Impact

According to Carter, Skiba, Arredondo, and Pollock (2014), Black males are proportionally disciplined at much higher levels when subjective levels of behaviour analysis are used (Bell, 2015). However, when objective measures are employed, the ways in which teachers rated students remains relatively consistent. The unfortunate reality, however, is that the vast majority of decisions that teachers make in the context of their classrooms are often based on subjective measures, and that their varying notions and beliefs about race, class, and multiple sites of differences will inform and impact the ways in which they interact with students. After an extensive review of the literature, Caton (2012) indicates that in the majority of cases when Black males are sent to the office or removed from class, this is based on subjective behaviours such as "disrespect" or "perceived threat" (p. 1057). These are highly subjective terms, and given the social and clinical propensity for marking the Black male body as threatening, criminal, or more prone to psychological disorders (Loring & Powell, 1988; Neighbors, Trierweiler, Ford, & Muroff, 2003), the gaze of the White teacher is undoubtedly informed by these problematic social narratives of Black masculinity (Schaffer & Skinner, 2009). Caton (2012) further indicates that this pattern of suspension, which sees Black males being suspended at a rate that is four times higher than for White males, is evidenced from kindergarten to Grade 12, a phenomenon that undoubtedly contributes to the cradle to prison pipeline and can contribute to the decline in academic engagement of Black students. If students are being subjected to harsher, ongoing, and unfair penalties at school for behaviours for which other students receive less significant penalties, then as time goes by Black students will develop negative attitudes toward schooling (Codjoe, 2001; Fenning & Rose, 2015; Gillborn, 1997; Gillborn & Mirza, 2000). In addition, repeated suspensions and expulsions will create a significant delay in their learning when compared to their counterparts, thus resulting in an increased challenge in achieving academic and personal success.

In a 2004 study conducted by Downey and Pribesh, the authors examined teachers' ratings of children's behaviour in kindergarten classes. The results indicated a pattern wherein White teachers consistently rated the behaviour of Black students as representing poor citizenship and noted that they engaged in externalizing behaviour. This means that the teachers regarded Black males as behaving in ways that did not lead to the development of positive relationships in the classroom and felt that they showed anger toward others. The authors posit that this breakdown in the teacher-student relationship occurs in the early schooling years, primarily because of the often unconscious anti-Black bias of White teachers (Downey & Pribesh, 2004; McGrady & Reynolds, 2013; Sleeter, 1993) Raible and Irizarry (2010) argue that in an attempt to manage and control those children who are deemed problem children, teachers engage in a form of hypersurveillance of racially minoritized children (Schaffer & Skinner, 2009). This is not dissimilar to the hypersurveillance of Black youth by mall security, store managers, and the police. They further argue that it is this "gaze" that is constantly fixed on these children that results in them being pushed out of the classroom and into the prison. Citing Noguera (2003), the authors go on to argue that Black children are not being schooled to take on middle-class jobs. Instead, they are being made ready for the lower-end jobs in society and are provided with a lowered quality of education that disconnects them from the processes and content of schooling. This inferior quality of schooling in Canada is evidenced by the high rates of Black males who are placed in special education classes and those who are recommended for applied programs, all of which limit their ability to achieve advanced levels of schooling.

According to a report for the York Centre for Education and Community (YCEC) and the Toronto District School Board (TDSB), although Black students make up only 12 percent of TDSB students, on average they make up 29 percent of students in applied programs and 19 percent of students in Essentials programs, but only 2 percent of students in gifted education programs (James, Brown, & Parekh, 2015). The Essentials program is what used to be termed the basic education program, in which students are supported merely to attain the credits they needed for graduation. While the Applied program prepares students for college and trades and the Academic program prepares students for university, the Essentials program does little to prepare Black students for academic or career development. It is simply an exit requirement. Schools are expected to support students in exploring their future options; however, based on the current statistics, schools are sending more than one-third of graduating Black students into the world with basic or limited preparation for viable economic stability. It is not difficult therefore to make the connection between the school and the pathway to prison. Given, therefore, that racially minoritized children are exposed to teachers in their formative years, I argue that the various negative subjective judgments along with the varying sorting mechanisms (parental education, social class, school catchment area, etc.) that determine one's educational, economic, and social options, begin at first contact—in ECE. According to Hatt (2011), "the story of schooling involves low income youth of color, especially males, overwhelmingly receiving unequal educational opportunities. Simultaneously, they are often labeled from an early age as 'bad boys,' which has led to higher suspension rates" (p. 479).

Citing TDSB statistics, the work of James, Brown, and Parekh identifies the same pattern that sees Black males being suspended at twice the rate of White males (2015). The higher the rate of suspension, the less time a student spends in school, thus creating a larger academic achievement gap (Cohen, Garcia, Apfel, & Master, 2006). In her book *Are Prisons Obsolete?* (2003), Angela Davis states, "When children attend schools that place a greater emphasis on discipline and security than on knowledge and intellectual development, they are attending prep schools for prison" (p. 39). Quoting the words of Eddie Ellis from the documentary *The Last Graduation*, Davis writes, "Prisoners very early recognized the fact that they needed to be better educated, that the more education they had, the better they would be able to deal with themselves and their problems, the problems of the prisons and then problems of the communities from which most of them came" (p. 58). It is problematic and absolutely disastrous that some of the teachers of our children seem unable or unwilling to recognize the centrality of ensuring a better educated populace, rather than resorting to prison-type surveillance and disciplining in the spaces where the maximum potential of youth should be stimulated. The classrooms of our nation's schools will continue to be places where the dreams of all too many of our racialized youth die if there is no significant intervention on the part of teacher educators to ensure that teachers understand their roles and responsibilities to all students and that they are able to recognize the ways in which they replicate and reproduce deeply entrenched societal, cultural, and normative racism.

According to Swain and Noblit (2011),

> while there are many forces at play to create a punitive society, education
> is one that deserves special attention. On the one hand, there is reason to
> believe that in some real sense schools cause delinquency (Polk & Schafer,
> 1972). Schools teach students that they are failures and that they will not be
> able to use education to define a conventional life course. They structure
> peer groups by tracking and grouping students into relative winners and
> losers of the schooling enterprise. Schools use discipline and special pro-
> grams to start the exclusion process that eventually begins the school to
> prison pipeline. Moreover, education in prison is then used as part of the
> supposed rehabilitation process, which, while having benefits, fools no one
> into believing they can turn their lives around via education. Education
> then is fully embedded in, and constitutive of, the punitive society. To
> reduce the punitive nature of our society, we need to critically examine the
> roles education plays and how it interacts with other social institutions,
> including the economy, law and criminal justice. (pp. 465–466)

During the first lecture of each of my teacher education classes, I attempt to
impress upon the candidates that they essentially have the power of life and death
in their hands, both literally and figuratively. Depending on the nature of their
interactions with students with whom they are entrusted, they can provide the
foundation that builds a love of learning and opens up career and future options
for students. Alternatively, if they destroy students' desire to learn, they play a
central role in contributing to the intellectual death of those students, who may
then end up on the streets or in prison. This increases the likelihood that those
students may die on the streets, an all too common pattern for young Black
males in cities such as Toronto and Vancouver.

The Dream Killers

In 2008, McMurtry and Curling, on behalf of the Ontario Ministry of Children
and Youth Services, released the *Roots of Youth Violence* report, which specifically focused on youth violence in an urban Canadian context. The report
identified three main aspects of the educational system that have led to the

disenfranchisement of Black and Aboriginal youth in Canadian schools. These include (1) the Safe Schools Act (Bill C-12), which led to zero-tolerance policies; (2) limited cultural representation amongst staff and within curriculum; (3) and streaming.

The Safe Schools Act

The Safe Schools Act in Canada has had an extremely negative impact on the lives of racially minoritized youth and has hastened the progression from the cradle to the prison. The act and zero-tolerance policies have had an extremely disastrous impact on the lives of these youth. The act was implemented in 2001 with the primary goal of limiting or reducing the prevalence of bad behaviour in schools. It essentially gave teachers the authority to suspend or expel students, a responsibility which was previously held only by principals and school board authorities (Bhattacharjee, 2003, p. 4) and also mandated the involvement of the police for acts such as theft or simple assaults that had previously been handled by school authorities. A student could be suspended if his or her behaviour was deemed to be injurious to the school environment or persons in the school; however, such decisions are highly subjective in nature and can be influenced by the personal beliefs and biases of school officials. The Safe Schools Act was more familiarly known by respondents as the "Gang Recruitment Act" (McMurtry & Curling, 2008, vol. 3, p. 16), due to the limited educational and social options in place to deal with students who are suspended and banned from school property or expelled. It led to significant numbers of minoritized students and students with disabilities being suspended or expelled, increasing the possibility of their engagement with street life and culture. Although Bill 212, which was enacted in 2011, repealed some sections of the Safe School Act, the act essentially criminalized activities that prior to implementation could have been handled internally by school personnel. It not only removed discretionary options for discipline from the hands of staff, but also resulted in thousands of children being pushed out of school, which, as sociological and criminological research has shown, often has a direct correlation to youth becoming involved in the school to prison pipeline (Solomon & Palmer, 2006).

The common practice among teachers and school administration of removing students who are identified as problematic from school premises (Darensbourg, Perez, & Blake, 2010) resulted in shifting responsibility for controlling those bodies from the educational system to police and the justice system. Therein lies the clearest demonstration of the seamless transition from school to prison. Hatt (2011), citing Zeiderberg and Schiraldi (2002), has defined the school to prison pipeline as "the patterns of school socialization, school discipline policies, and low educational attainment by inmates that help to explain why many youth, especially low income, African American and Latino males, end up in a jail cell rather than a college classroom" (p. 477).

The gaps in their educational development as well as their unwillingness to engage with their teachers are based on the initial experiences these youth had in classrooms. As a result, the behaviours that teachers construe and construct as aggressive and disrespectful can be framed through a different analytical lens; these behaviours can be regarded as learned patterns of coping, which lead some students to compensate for and cover up their academic challenges through the stereotypical Black male and female presentation of "having attitude." A common theme that has been repeated by Black students in secondary and post-secondary settings is the impact of repeated assaults by teachers who continually challenge their academic competency and express disdain for their academic interests and pursuits. Further to this, under the Safe Schools Act principals were given the right to make arbitrary rules that determined whether the students could return to the school. These factors increased the probability that students who were removed from schools were drawn to the streets to loiter with no apparent purpose or goal, ultimately increasing their possible involvement with an existing criminal element. These students often become increasingly angry, and finally refuse to attend school altogether to avoid what can be regarded as ongoing abuse at the hands of teachers. Many students eventually start roaming the streets, some get pregnant early, and still others are arrested for drug and gun possession. The unsettling reality is that such stories are neither new nor distinct from the normative experiences that result in student disengagement. Therefore, if students are exposed to these messages at an early stage in their ECE classrooms, the cradle to prison pipeline becomes deeply entrenched and re-entrenched in Canadian classrooms. In addition, "the pipeline metaphor exists to describe the collective system of local, state, and federal policies and procedures that siphons children out of school and into prison. Ultimately under-funded, under-resourced, and stratifying schools funnel children directly and indirectly into over-crowded, dead-end prisons" (Swain & Noblit, 2011, p. 466). Unfortunately, this pipeline starts extremely early for some students.

Children who are suspended from school can be affected in several different basic ways. The time that they are out of the classroom results in a loss of instruction time and subject information. It can also lead to the development of an often conflicted relationship with the teacher and a reputation among their peers that results in stigmatization and labelling, and an ongoing sense of anomie or disengagement from schooling. Within the context of the home, the student becomes marked as a problem, given that his or her parents often have to make arrangements to meet with school officials and, at times, have to make alternative child-care arrangements based on the age of the child. Unfortunately, when students are suspended from school, there are limited options available to ensure that they are provided with the proper academic supports and access to guarantee that they are not falling behind on their studies.

In 2000, the year before Bill C-12 was fully implemented, the TDSB reported 106 expulsions. Within the first three years of enacting the bill, there were 1,901 suspensions of mostly racialized youth and youth with disabilities, resulting in the constant disruption of their learning and development. These factors coalesce in a manner that ensures the continued production of criminality in our society, a need that is central to ensure that there remains a steady stream of clients to populate the super jails being built in Canada, including Toronto. Although the zero-tolerance policies put forth in the Safe Schools Act have been repealed, there are other legal and structural developments at play that continue to produce clients for the prison-industrial complex.

A 2003 report by Bhattacharjee to the Ontario Human Rights Commission (OHRC) examined the effect of the Safe Schools Act on students in Ontario, particularly in light of the claims of disproportionate impact on students with disabilities and racially minoritized students including Aboriginal, Black, Latin American and South Asian youth. According to the OHRC report,

> there is also some suggestion that the disproportionate impact on Black students may be the result of being suspended for the more "subjective" offences, where there is greater leeway for racial stereotyping and bias to enter into the decision-making process. A high number of interviewees reported that Black students are getting suspended for being disrespectful to the teacher or questioning authority, which are more subjective offences. (Bhattacharjee, 2003, p. 11)

The OHRC report also states the following:

> Many interviewees believe that the increased suspension and expulsion of students are having a broad, negative impact on the student, his or her family, the community, and society-at-large. The most commonly identified elements are negative psychological impact, loss of education, higher drop-out rates, and increased criminalization and anti-social behaviour. (Bhattacharjee, 2003, p. 12)

The report indicates that the patterns that have been evidenced in American and British research studies are being replicated in Canada. Although Canada continues to resist the collection of race-based statistics, a 2008 TDSB report on the student demographic identified several patterns related to student enroll-ment that provide indicators that could impact on the schooling experiences of racially minoritized students. For example, 51 percent of Aboriginal and 39 percent of Black students were more likely to live with a single female parent; 64 percent of immigrant students had parents earning less than $50,000 a year, and students whose parents did not have a post-secondary education earned less than $30,000 a year; and 55 percent of Middle Eastern and 45 percent of Black students had parents who earn less than $30,000 a year. Black, Latin American, and Middle Eastern students were the three groups that experienced the great-est academic challenges, particularly in the area of math, where they scored as much as 40 percent lower on academic tests than White, middle-class students. In addition, the reading scores for children in single-parent families and families without a college education indicated a 10 to 20 percent gap in reading, writing, and math compared to their peers from two-parent, college-educated families.

Racially minoritized students also had higher rates of representation in special education classes, with, in some cases, racialized males placed in these classes at more than three times the rate of females. For example, while students with special needs represented 18.2 percent of Grade 7 students in the TDSB, males represented 64.1 percent of the students with learning disabilities, 58.1 percent of those identified as having mild intellectual disabilities (MID), and 74.2 per-cent of those with other non-gifted exceptionalities (Toronto District School Board [TDSB], 2012). Black students, who accounted for 12.4 percent of the Grade 9 cohort from 2006–2011, represented 31.5 percent of students identified with MID, 31.5 percent of those with other non-gifted exceptionalities, and 17.1 percent of those identified as learning disabled (TDSB, 2012). The data was not disaggregated for gender; however, based on the aforementioned statistics, and the overrepresentation of males within the special education designation, one can surmise that the pattern remains relatively consistent. As such, a higher percentage of Black males will be identified as having the special education designation, which can negatively impact on their options for post-secondary schooling, particularly university attendance.

When looking at post-secondary confirmation patterns, Black and Latin American students had lower confirmation rates than the overall TDSB sam-ple population. The researchers contended that those of lower socio-eco-nomic status and those in single-parent families were most affected by limited access to post-secondary education. In the 2007 TDSB census data, 70 percent of Latin American and 66 percent of Black students did not apply for post-secondary education. Among Black students, the lower rate of application was evidenced irrespective of their region of birth (TDSB, 2012). Further research at the TDSB indicates that students who feel comfortable with adults in the school environment perform better on various institutional tests such as the provincial Education Quality and Accountability Office (EQAO) assessments. However, of the students who were not comfortable with school or the overall experience of schooling, almost a third were considered highly at risk and failed reading, writing, and math assessments. In April 1968, experiential teaching done by Jane Elliot in response to the assassination of Martin Luther King, Jr., demonstrated the ease with which prejudice can be taught by exposing a group of Grade 3 students to the experience of being a minority by marginalizing students for one day based on eye colour (see PBS documentary *A Class Divided*). The students who had blue eyes were treated as "superior" and those with brown eyes were treated as "inferior." On the second day of the experiment, Elliot reversed the labels. The teacher interacted differently with the two groups, praising one group and not the other, allowing one group to go to the playground and to lunch earlier, and giving them bonus marks, while denying these privileges to the other group. By the end of the experiment, students quite easily excluded their peers based solely on a criterion that was constructed by the teacher. On the day that the students were marked as inferior, their academic performance decreased, and they experienced marginalization, anger, and frustration. Black students experience this marginalization and consequent disengagement from the day they enter the school system until they graduate. Many Black students manage to survive the ravages of the system; however, many others are forced to leave school or are pushed out of the system (Dei, 1995).

Limited Cultural Representation among Staff and within Curriculum

Another aspect of the school system identified as problematic in the *Roots of Youth Violence* report (McMurtry & Curling, 2008) is the limited cultural representation among staff and within the curriculum material. Despite significant efforts to determine the cultural representation of staff within the TDSB, no statistics are currently available. However, anyone visiting most schools within the TDSB will encounter a "sea of Whiteness" among the teaching staff and particularly among administrators and guidance personnel.

Students, in addition to feeling disconnected from staff who do not represent or understand their communities, often do not feel a sense of connectedness to the curriculum material being used in the classroom (Beyer, 1988; Codjoe, 2001; Leistyna, 2007; McKinley, 2010). Overwhelmingly, the Ontario curriculum is focused on and privileges White histories rather than being representative of the diversity of student identities. Regardless of what course is considered—whether it is reading material in English courses, research-based work in anthropology or sociology courses, homework questions in mathematics, legal systems studied in law courses, or the perspectives from which history is presented—it reflects White Western values and beliefs. In most cases, these representations and perspectives do not accurately reflect the lived experiences or histories of the students in the classroom. Additionally, curricula and examples used reinforce negative stereotypes of particular communities rather than representing the negative and positive aspects of all communities. For example, during Black History Month, the primary focus remains on the enslavement of Blacks, with limited critical analysis of the larger systems of economics, oppression, and the devastation caused by European colonization. The result is a state of simultaneous absence-presence, in that the students, though aware of their presence as members of society, are often absent from the curriculum and are not represented in the larger social and cultural domains of society in positive and complete ways.

Educators and administrators in the school system often lack the cultural sensitivity to work effectively with children from backgrounds that include multiple sites of marginalization (Blumenreich & Falk, 2006; Daniel, 2007; Hatt, 2011; Ladson-Billings, 1995; Milner, 2006). For example, a child who may be female (gender), considered to be poor (social class), and racialized (race) may have challenges connecting with the curriculum. When additional markers of identity (and often marginality) such as religion, country of origin, and sexual identity/expression are layered on, the task for teachers becomes increasingly overwhelming. Teachers often use a deficit mentality, which means that they interact with students based on what they think (personal values and beliefs) a student is missing (such as skills, economic resources, and family supports); this results in them having lowered expectations for these children. When children are exposed to these ongoing messages of deficit, minimal expectations, and higher rates and stricter forms of disciplining, as well as having to deal with the reality of their home and community environments, the end result is often a focus on survival. Schooling, then, becomes an added task or burden that they are expected to carry, thus making it more difficult to focus on achievement and find positive outlets or supports. Schools often provide limited supports or understanding, which results in students being pushed into the streets.

Educational Streaming

The final area the *Roots of Youth Violence* report identified that was specific to the education system was the practice of streaming racially minoritized children into non-academic pathways, thus limiting their opportunities to access a host of career options that require degrees. One of the respondents in the study referred to the practices of streaming as the "dream killer" (McMurtry & Curling, 2008, vol. 3, p. 16). Streaming, combined with the punitive nature of the Safe Schools Act, and along with culturally irrelevant curriculum, can lead to the alienation of significant numbers of students from our schools while preparing them for a life of limited options, one of which includes the prison system.

In addition to the previously mentioned factors, students with learning disabilities often have limited psychosocial and educational testing resources and are often labelled as disruptive or troublesome in class (Gillborn & Mirza, 2000). In such situations, teachers may use harsh disciplinary strategies such as suspensions or referral to special education classes rather than providing appropriate support services or referring the students to appropriate resources (Edelman, 2007). The combination of socio-economic struggles, learning challenges, teachers' limited cultural competency, limited resources, and the hyperdisciplinary strategies in schools creates an easy path from the cradle to the prison (Coates, 2015; Raible & Irizarry, 2010). Hatt (2011) interviewed male prisoners who indicated that their experience in schooling played a significant role in pushing them to the streets, and their eventual involvement in criminal and prison cultures. According to Michelle Alexander in her 2012 book *The New Jim Crow: Mass Incarceration in the Age of Colorblindness*, "those who had meaningful economic and social opportunities were unlikely to commit crimes … while those who went to prison were far more likely to commit crimes again in the future" (p. 8). Schools and their employees (teachers, principals, administrative staff) consciously and unconsciously target various racialized groups in our society through legalized practices of discrimination.

Within the Canadian context, it has been estimated that the dropout rate for Black students is approximately 40 percent by the time they get to high school (TDSB, 2012). It is important to remember, however, that dropping out does not start in high school. It is simply that at that juncture, school authorities and parents have less say or control over the adolescent's developmental choices; however, if we examine the experiences of children from the moment of contact with the school system and its representatives, we can plot the patterns of displacement, disengagement, and, ultimately, that eventual walk toward the prison gates. As discussed in previous sections, early teacher engagement with racially minoritized children in ECE contexts can be marred by racially stereotyped interactions and outcomes. These interactions, both negative and positive, pave the way for the students' future engagement with schooling.

According to Gillborn (2007), Black students start school functioning at a higher level than their peers, but with continued exposure to a negative school environment, their achievement levels begin to decline dramatically. His research shows that based on the information provided by local education authorities, Black students start school 20 points above their peers, but leave school 21 points behind in their general certificate of secondary education. This, he believes, is indicative of the lowered value that schools, administrators, and teachers place on Black students.

Significant patterns emerge from Gillborn's research and the potential connection to Elliot's experiential work titled "Brown Eyes/Blue Eyes" (see http://www.janeelliott.com/). The nature of Black children's schooling experiences results in a dramatic loss of academic preparedness that worsens as they spend more time in the system. Given that teachers are the primary intermediaries in the school system, the interactions or engagements that they embody result in this loss of academic achievement and possibility. And, I believe, a larger societal issue that we as Canadians must grapple with is whether or not this cradle to prison pipeline project is financially or morally sustainable. Can stemming the cradle to prison pipeline address the increasing job-skills gap that the country continues to struggle with, thus reducing the need for the importation of foreign workers? Although this discussion is out of the scope of this chapter, I believe that Canada is uniquely situated to address this scenario by adopting equitable education practices that can address the moral ineptitude evidenced within the education and social systems while simultaneously addressing larger market-level financial and economic issues.

Summary and Conclusion: Education as an Issue of Justice

This chapter has explored the ways in which the current schooling system in Canada unfairly targets, disciplines, and pushes children of certain groups from the cradle to the prison. The high percentage of racialized males and, as you will see in chapter 11, racialized and poor women who enter our prison system is evidence of this. The failure to see themselves represented in the curriculum and among the staff, and the negative experiences that students have at the hands of teachers and administrators who are ill-prepared to address the needs of the students in their classes, are issues that requires immediate attention. The preparation of teachers remains in the hands of professors whose commitment to true inclusion, social justice, and anti-oppression discourses and practices remains at best superficial and at worst completely lacking. The investment in the myths of meritocracy and liberalism remains the standpoint of most academics, teachers, and post-secondary educators, many of whom continue to feed the prison pipeline. The practices described above contribute to the disenfranchisement of communities, the destabilizing of families, and the destruction of the lives of individuals. All of these practices are the opposite of the expectations and goals of community-based justice.

A community-based justice approach to education would require that the teachers of our nation's children be prepared to address the needs of a diverse range of students. Further, teachers and school administrators have to adopt a strengths-based approach in their interactions with students and with each other. A strengths-based approach dictates that school staff identify the things that the students are good at and then build from that perspective. All too often, unfortunately, school staff adopt an attitude that starts with the areas in which students require supports, and then use that as the measure of what students are capable or not capable of doing. The problem with that approach is that it fails to provide people with an accurate baseline regarding their capacity.

A community justice approach to schooling and education would ensure that the school and its staff are connected in positive ways to local community groups, parents, and other stakeholders. The school would be a welcoming space, rather one that parents are afraid to enter. In addition, students would be provided with opportunities to engage with their wider community and school projects would be developed that allow students to examine more comprehensively the world around them. True inclusion in our society becomes the primary factor in stemming the cradle to prison pipeline.

Discussion Questions

1. What are the primary factors that contribute to the cradle to prison pipeline? Choose two of the main factors and critically discuss their relevance.
2. What role does race and class play in determining which students are streamed into lower-level academic classes?
3. What are the potential benefits of stemming the cradle to prison pipeline?
4. Based on the film *A Class Divided*, discuss ways in which you have seen students treated in your classrooms. Discuss the potential impact of such treatment on students' academic performance.

Additional Resources

Children's Defence Fund. (2016). Cradle to Prison Pipeline Campaign: http://www.childrensdefense.org/campaigns/cradle-to-prison-pipeline/.

Milligan, S. (2008). Youth Custody and Community Services in Canada, 2005/2006. *Juristat*. Statistics Canada catalogue no. 85-002-X, 28(8): http://odesi1.scholarsportal.info/documentation/PHIRN/YCCS/85-002-x2008008-eng.pdf.

Peters, W. (Producer & Director). (1985). *A Class Divided* [Film]. United States: FRONTLINE: http://www.pbs.org/wgbh/pages/frontline/shows/divided/etc/view.html.

References

Alexander, M. (2012). *The new Jim Crow: Mass incarceration in the age of colorblindness.* New York: The New Press.

Araujo, L., & Strasser, J. (2003). Confronting prejudice in the early childhood education classroom. *Kappa Delta Pi Record,* (Summer), 178–182.

Bell, C. (2015). The hidden side of zero tolerance policies: The African American perspective. *Social Compass,* 9(1), 14–22. Retrieved from http://www.ncbi.nlm.nih.gov/pmc/articles/PMC4397655/

Berry, B. J. (1995). "I just see people": Exercises in learning the effects of racism and sexism. In L. A. Bell & D. Blumenfeld (Eds.), *Overcoming racism and sexism* (pp. 45–51). Lanham, MD: Rowman & Littlefield Publishers.

Beyer, L. (1988). *The curriculum: Problems, politics and possibilities.* Albany, NY: SUNY Press.

Bhattacharjee, K. (2003). *The Ontario Safe Schools Act: School discipline and discrimination.* Toronto: Ontario Human Rights Commission.

Blumenreich, M., & Falk, B. (2006). Trying on a new pair of shoes: Urban teacher-learners conduct research and construct knowledge in their own classrooms. *Teaching and Teacher Education,* 22(7), 864–873.

Brown, S., Souto-Manning, M., & Tropp Laman, T. (2010). Seeing the strange in the familiar: Unpacking racialized practices in early childhood settings. *Race, Ethnicity and Education,* 13(4), 513–532.

Calman, L. J., & Tarr-Whelan, L. (2005). Early education for all: A wise investment. *The economic impacts of child care and early education: Financing solutions for the future.* New York: Legal Momentum.

Carr, P. R., & Lund, D. E. (2007). *Introduction: Scanning Whiteness.* Rotterdam: Sense Publishers.

Carter, P., Skiba, R., Arredondo, M., & Pollock, M. (2014). You can't fix what you don't look at: Acknowledging race in addressing racial discipline disparities. *Acknowledging Race,* 2–12. Retrieved from http://www.indiana.edu/~atlantic/wp-content/uploads/2014/12/Acknowledging-Race_121514.pdf

Caton, M. T. (2012). Black male persepctives on their educational experiences in high school. *Urban Education,* 47(6). doi:10.1177/0042085912454442

Children's Defense Fund. (2007). *America's cradle to prison pipeline: A report by the Children's Defense Fund.* Retrieved from http://www.childrensdefense.org/library/data/cradle-prison-pipeline-report-2007-full-lowres.pdf

Coates, R. D. (2015). A perfect storm. *Critical Sociology.* doi:10.1177/0896920515591449

Codjoe, H. M. (2001). Fighting a "public enemy" of Black academic achievement: The persistence of racism and the schooling experiences of Black students in Canada. *Race Ethnicity and Education,* 4(4), 343–375. doi:10.1080/13613320120096652

Cohen, G. L., Garcia, J., Apfel, N., & Master, A. (2006). Reducing the racial achievement gap: A social-psychological intervention. *Science,* 313(5791), 1307–1310.

Daniel, B. M. (2007). Developing educational collectives and networks: Moving beyond the boundaries of "community" in urban education. In R. P. Solomon & D. N. R. Sekayi (Eds.), *Urban teacher education and teaching: Innovative practices for diversity and social justice* (pp. 31–47). Mawah, NJ: Lawrence Earlbaum Associates Publishers.

Daniel, B. M., & Solomon, R. P. (2008). Tomorrow's teachers: The challenges of democratic engagement. In D. E. Lund & P. R. Carr (Eds.), *Doing democracy: Striving for political literacy and social justice* (pp. 301–317). New York: Peter Lang.

Darensbourg, A., Perez, E., & Blake, J. (2010). Overrepresentation of African American males in exclusionary discipline: The role of school-based mental health professionals in dismantling the school to prison pipeline. *Journal of African American Males in Education, 1*(3), 196–211.

Davis, A. Y. (2003). *Are prisons obsolete?* New York: Seven Stories Press.

Day, R. J. F. (2000). *Multiculturalism and the history of Canadian diversity.* Toronto: University of Toronto Press.

Dei, G. S. (1995). *Drop out or push out?: The dynamics of Black students' disengagement from school.* Toronto: Ontario Institute for Studies in Education.

Derman-Sparks, L. (1998). Educating for equality: Forging a shared vision. In E. Lee, D. Menkart, & M. Okazawa-Rey (Ed.), *Beyond heroes and holidays: A practical guide to K–12 anti-racist, multicultural education and staff development* (pp. 2–5). Upper Marlboro, MD: McArdle Printing.

Downey, D. B., & Pribesh, S. (2004). When race matters: Teachers' evaluations of students' classroom behavior. *Sociology of Education, 77*(4), 267–282.

Edelman, M. W. (2007). The cradle to prison pipeline: An American health crisis. *Preventing Chronic Disease: Public Health Research, Practice and Policy, 4*(4), 1–3.

Fleming, P., & Rose, J. (2007). Overrepresentation of African American students in exclusionary discipline: The role of school policy. *Urban Education, 42*(6), 536–559.

Friendly, M., & Prabhu, N. (2010). Can early childhood education and care help keep Canada's promise of respect for diversity? Occasional paper no. 23. Toronto: Childcare Resource and Research Unit.

Gillborn, D. (1997). Ethnicity and educational performance in the United Kingdom: Racism, ethnicity, and variability in achievement. *Anthropology and Education Quarterly, 28*(3), 375–393.

Gillborn, D. (2007). Combating racism in schooling: A critical perspective on contemporary policy and practice. In W. T. Pink & G. W. Noblit (Eds.), *International Handbook of Urban Education* (pp. 979–1006). Dordrecht: Springer.

Gillborn, D., & Mirza, H. S. (2000). *Educational inequality: Mapping race, class and gender; A synthesis of research evidence.* London: Institute of Education, Middlesex University.

Hatt, B. (2011). Still I rise: Youth caught between the worlds of school and prison. *Urban Review, 43*(4), 476–490.

Husband, T. (2011). "I don't see color": Challenging assumptions about discussing race with young children. *Early Childhood Education Journal, 39*(6), 365–371. doi:10.1007/s10643-011-0458-9

James, C. E. (2000). Rethinking access: The challenge of living with difficult knowledge. In G. J. S. Dei & A. Calliste (Eds.), *Power, knowledge and anti-racism education.* Halifax: Fernwood.

James, C., Brown, R., & Parekh, J. (2015). An educational profile of African Caribbean Canadian students: 2003–2006 cohort. Toronto: York Centre for Education and Community (YCEC) & the Toronto District School Board (TDSB).

Kincheloe, J. L., & Steinberg, S. R. (2000). Constructing a pedagogy of Whiteness for angry White students. In N. M. Rodriguez & L. E. Villaverde (Eds.), *Dismantling White privilege: Pedagogy, politics and Whiteness* (pp. 178–197). New York: Peter Lang.

Kohli, R., & Solorzano, D. G. (2012). Teachers, please learn our names!: Racial microaggressions and the K–12 classroom. *Race, Ethnicity and Education, 15*(4), 441–462.

Ladson-Billings, G. (1995). Toward a theory of culturally relevant pedagogy. *American Educational Research Journal, 32*(3), 465–491.

Lee, E. (1998). Anti-racist education: Pulling together to close the gaps. In E. Lee & D. Menkart (Eds.) *Multicultural education and staff development* (pp. 26–34). Washington, DC: Network of Educators on the Americas.

Lee, R., Ramsey, P. G., & Sweeney, B. (2008). Engaging young children in activities and conversations about race and social class. *Beyond the Journal: Young Children on the Web, 63*(6), 68–76. Retrieved from https://www.naeyc.org/files/yc/file/200811/BTJRaceClassConversations.pdf

Leistyna, P. (2007). How multicultural curriculum development often misses the mark. In J. L. Kincheloe (Ed.), *Teaching city kids: Understanding and appreciating them* (pp. 57–70). New York: Peter Lang.

Levine-Rasky, C. (2000). Framing Whiteness: Working through the tensions in introducing Whiteness to educators. *Race, and Ethnicity in Education, 3*(3), 272–292.

Loring, M., & Powell, B. (1988). Gender, race and the *DSM-III*: A study of the objectivity of psychiatric diagnostic behavior. *Journal of Health and Social Behavior, 29*(1), 1–22.

Lund, D. E. (2006). Rocking the racism boat: School-based activists speak out about denial and avoidance. *Race, Ethnicity and Education, 9*(2), 203–221.

McGrady, P. B., & Reynolds, J. R. (2013). Racial mismatch in the classroom: Beyond Black-White differences. *Sociology of Education, 86*(1), 3–17.

McKinley, J. (2010). *Raising Black students' achievement through culturally responsive teaching.* Alexandria, VA: ASCD.

McMurtry, R., & Curling, A. (2008). *The review of the roots of youth violence.* Toronto: Service Ontario Publications.

Milner, H. R. (2006). Preservice teachers' learning about cultural and racial diversity: Implications for urban education. *Urban Education, 41*(4), 343–375.

Neighbors, H. W., Trierweiler, S. J., Ford, B. C., & Muroff, J. R. (2003). Racial difference in DSM diagnosis using a semi-structured instrument: The importance of clinical judgment in the diagnosis of African Americans. *Journal of Health and Social Behavior, 43*(September), 237–256.

Noguera, P. (2003). The trouble with Black boys: The role and influence of environmental and cultural factors on the academic performance of African American males. *Urban Education, 38*(4), 431–459.

Peters, W. (Director). (1985). *A class divided* [Film]. Frontline, PBS.

Polk, K., & Schafer, W. E. (1972). *Schools and delinquency.* Minnesota: Prentice Hall.

Puddicombe, B. (2011). *Racialized terror and the colour line: Racial profiling and policing headwear in schools.* Master of Education thesis, University of Toronto. Retrieved from http://hdl.handle.net/1807/27366

Raible, J., & Irizarry, J. G. (2010). Redirecting the teacher's gaze: Teacher education, youth surveillance and the school to prison pipeline. *Teaching and Teacher Education, 26*(5), 1196–1203.

Schaffer, R., & Skinner, D. (2009). Performing race in four culturally diverse fourth grade classrooms: Silence, race talk, and the negotiation of social boundaries. *Anthropology and Education Quarterly, 40*(3), 277–296.

Sleeter, C. E. (1992). Resisting racial awareness: How teachers understand the social order from their racial, gender and social locations. *Educational Foundations, 6*(2), 7–31.

Sleeter, C. E. (1993). How White teachers construct race. In C. McCarthy & W. Crichlow (Eds.), *Race, identity and representation in education* (pp. 157–171). New York: Routledge.

Solomon, R. P., & Palmer, H. (2006). Black boys through the school-prison pipeline: When "racial profiling" and "zero tolerance" collide. In D. E. Armstrong & B. J. McMahon (Eds.), *Inclusion in urban educational environments*. Charlotte: University of North Carolina.

Swain, A., & Noblit, G. W. (2011). Education in a punitive society: An introduction. *Urban Review, 43*, 465–475.

Swindler Boutte, G. (2008). Beyond the illusion of diveristy: How early childhood teachers can promote social justice. *Social Studies, 99*(4), 165–173.

Toronto District School Board (TDSB). (2012). The TDSB Grade 9 cohort 2006–2011. Retrieved from http://www.tdsb.on.ca/Portals/0/Community/Community%20Advisory%20 committees/ICAC/research/September%202012%20Cohort%20dataAcrobat%20Document. pdf

Zeiderberg, J., & Schiraldi, V. (2002). *Cellblocks or classrooms? The funding of higher education and corrections and its impact on African American men*. Washington, DC: Justice Policy Institute.

CHAPTER 6

Decolonizing the Response to Violence against Indigenous Women and Girls through Community Justice

Jennifer Fraser

Chapter Objectives

This chapter will discuss the issue of violence against Indigenous women and girls in Canada and will provide a historical look at colonization and its impact on Indigenous women. It will explore the governmental and justice-based response or lack of response to this issue and will explore alternative options for accessing justice.

Introduction

Violence against Indigenous women and girls in Canada is an endemic, socio-historical problem that has been well-documented by researchers, governments, international humanitarian organizations, and the United Nations (e.g., Amnesty International [AI], 2004; Anaya, 2014; Brennan, 2011; Brownridge, 2008; Burns & Taylor-Butts, 2009). Indigenous women are disproportionately victims of interpersonal violence, including intimate partner abuse and sexual violence, as well as of abduction and femicide (Brennan, 2011; Royal Canadian Mounted Police [RCMP], 2014). Reports from the RCMP have estimated that nearly 1,100 Indigenous women have been murdered in Canada since 1980 and an additional 174 Indigenous women remain missing across the country (RCMP, 2014, 2015); these numbers are much higher than the working estimate of 500–600 missing and murdered used previously by Indigenous and women's organizations (AI, 2004; Native Women's Association of Canada [NWAC], 2010). However, the work of grassroots activists like Gladys Radek, who has collected the names of over 4,200 missing and murdered women and children across Canada, suggests the number might be much higher than even the RCMP reports estimate (Chartrand, 2014). Despite their overwhelming vulnerability to victimization, Indigenous women are rarely able to seek justice through the Canadian criminal justice system. Based on the Western idea of adversarial justice, Canada's criminal justice system does not "speak" for many women's needs and, for the few cases of interpersonal violence that do see a criminal trial, they often produce discourse and judicial decisions permeated with racism and sexism (McGillivray & Comaskey, 1999; Nancarrow, 2007). These tragic circumstances have sparked an outcry across many sectors, from the grassroots to the ivory tower, for the Canadian government to finally do something substantive to address this problem.

The federal political climate has not been conducive to addressing the needs of Indigenous women and girls. Stephen Harper, Canada's prime minister from 2006 to 2015, repeatedly denied the severity of violence against Indigenous women and girls by removing funding from Indigenous women's organizations, blocking attempts to study the problem at a national level, and even stating that Canada has "no history of colonization" at a news conference during the G-20 Summit in 2009 (Ljunggren, 2009). His sentiments were not necessarily supported by politicians at other levels of government, but his denial of colonization is problematic. By extension, the former prime minister's dismissal of the systemic nature of violence against Indigenous women demonstrates the continuation of centuries of racism and sexism that has permeated White settler–Indigenous relations and both illustrates and constitutes the insidious nature of institutional violence that Indigenous women face. Many Indigenous scholars and activists have turned away from the state as a site of recompense for centuries of discrimination and ongoing violence against women and girls. Indeed, community-based solutions that harness the resources of communities and the strength of individuals and that address violence from a holistic, harm reduction and healing-based approach are preferred to the institutional, incident-based criminal justice system of the state.

This chapter takes the position that violence against Indigenous women and girls is a product of the ongoing project to colonize the land that is now known as Canada and control its Native peoples. The next section will highlight some of the history of Indigenous-settler relations, focusing on some of the more significant examples of how Euro-Canadian settlers attempted to solve the "Indian problem" through assimilation and eradication. The second section will look at the particular effects this colonization project has had on Indigenous women and girls and what that means for their vulnerability to violent victimization and their access to justice. The final section will make the case for community-based responses to violence against Indigenous women and girls as a decolonial alternative to state-based interventions.

The Ongoing Colonization of Canada

The starting point for the colonization of the New World is typically designated as Christopher Columbus's landing in what is now known as the Bahamas after his voyage in search of India in 1492. While historians have no conclusive evidence of when human beings first set foot onto the territory that is now known as North and South America, most concede that peoples from Siberia first crossed the Bering Strait up to tens of thousands of years ago (Farb, 1968). Europeans exploring the New World in the 15th century were neither discovering new territory, nor were they bringing "civilization" to a supposedly savage population of "Indians." Indeed, Europeans stumbled upon a continent already occupied by hundreds of different cultural groups speaking hundreds of different languages, living in complex social groupings (Farb, 1968; Hill, 2009). Communities had systems of organization and decision-making, they sustained themselves by "living off the land" and respecting Mother Nature, and many were egalitarian with important social roles given to men, women, and two-spirit peoples throughout the life course (Anderson, 2016; Farb, 1968).[1]

European explorers to North America operated under the "Doctrine of Discovery," a set of theological principles and legal rulings that allowed Europeans to declare sovereignty over unclaimed land and subjugate peoples who posed a threat to European civilization and Christian values (Reid, 2010; Venne, 1998). Indigenous peoples' connection to the land for spiritual and physical sustenance did not extend to an assumption of ownership; indeed, as described by Leroy Little Bear, "[Indigenous peoples] are not the sole owners under the original grant from the Creator; the land belongs to past generations, to the yet-to-be-born, and to the plants and animals" (1986, p. 247). Land is conceived of by most Indigenous peoples as a resource to be respected, shared, and utilized by all, not as a "thing" to be possessed by any one group of people. Since, from a European perspective, Indigenous peoples did not own the land, explorers were able to take advantage of a welcoming Indigenous population who had no expectation that visitors would assume control over the abundant natural resources of the continent that had been shared, through oral agreements, by Indigenous communities for centuries.

In what is now North America, British and French explorers discovered the potential for financial gain through the fur trade with the abundance of beaver and other wildlife on the continent; as a result, settlement in the New World expanded rapidly. The fur trade, and the creation and expansion of the Hudson's Bay Company, are foundational to the development of Canada as a country. White fur traders' intermarriages with Indigenous women, particularly in Western Canada, was integral to solidifying strategic trading relationships, and, in this regard, some Indigenous women enjoyed the position of cultural liaison in the emerging settler society, particularly in the early years when White settlers relied on Indigenous communities for survival (Van Kirk, 1980). Of course, White fur traders' perceptions of "saving" Indigenous women from a "savage" lifestyle through marriage denied many Indigenous women's reality of having to leave their communities and adopt the patriarchal norms and values of the emerging settler society (Anderson, 2016; Barker, 2006). However, many Indigenous women, particularly those outside of Western Canada, felt the consequences of racial and class disparity, and this was certainly the case when White European women began to immigrate to the continent (Van Kirk, 1980).

Strategic alliances with Indigenous communities were integral to French and British settlers as they attempted to solidify their claims to sovereignty over the territory and expand their settlements. In the early years, the European settlers relied on Indigenous communities for survival, using their knowledges to trap and hunt animals and mine gold and silver, to acquire lands for expanded farming and agriculture, and enlisting them as allies in conflicts with other Indigenous and settler communities. But over time, Indigenous communities also began to rely on the Europeans for resources such as metal pots, knives, horses, and even guns, leading to a somewhat interdependent relationship between Indigenous communities and settlers, at least for a time. However, European expansion also meant land-clearing, deforestation, and the destruction of wildlife that had been integral to Indigenous survival; epidemics of smallpox and measles that were introduced unknowingly to the Indigenous population, and then spread knowingly by Europeans through contaminated blankets and other textiles; and ongoing struggles between different Indigenous and settler communities that resulted in massacres of Indigenous peoples by the thousands (Daschuk, 2013; Hill, 2009; King, 2012).

One of the main ways that Europeans were able to expand their settlements was by appropriating lands traditionally used and shared by Indigenous communities. Europeans saw treaty-making with Indigenous communities as a way to not only encourage peaceful relations between settlers and Indigenous peoples, but also to claim ownership over much-desired lands (Hill, 2009). Many treaties were signed without the Indigenous parties' full comprehension of what the treaties entailed, some were signed by individuals who did not have the authority of their communities to make such decisions, and others were simply broken by settlers who had no intention of co-operating with the Indigenous peoples. Treaties typically gave White settlers ownership over large parcels of land and allowed Indigenous peoples to occupy specific portions called reserves that, in many cases, were insufficient to allow the Indigenous communities to survive using their traditional skills.[2] Of course, Indigenous communities resisted this occupation and organization of land, but as Europeans settled in the Americas en masse, and Indigenous peoples continued to die from diseases, warfare, and starvation, it was increasingly difficult to maintain any control over the territory. Disputes over land culminated, for the Europeans, in the Seven Years' War and were resolved in 1763 when France ceded its colonies to the British. The Royal Proclamation of 1763 entrenched the Doctrine of Discovery and created the Indian Department, positioning Britain as the sovereign state in control of the new dominions and the Native peoples of its lands (Reid, 2010).

After the War of 1812, when Canada required the military co-operation of Indigenous communities to resist the invasion of Americans, alliances between settlers and Indigenous communities became less necessary. Settlers pursued their project of "civilizing" the Indigenous population through a series of treaty agreements and legislative changes, including the 1857 Act to Encourage the Gradual Civilization of Indian Tribes in the Province and to Amend the Laws Respecting Indians, and most notably the Indian Act of 1876. The Indian Act gave the federal government complete control over the economic, political, and social life of Indigenous peoples in Canada and, despite numerous amendments, remains in force today. The act created the "Status Indian" and imposed the governing structure of band councils on Indigenous communities, whose land base is determined by the government in the form of reserves. Historically, the act had banned spiritual and cultural ceremonies and celebrations, restricted the movements and activities of Indigenous peoples, and created criteria for the loss and acquirement of Indian status.

The Indian Act also paved the way for the entrenchment of forced attendance at residential schools for Indigenous children beginning in the late 1800s. Canada's first prime minister, Sir John A. Macdonald, saw residential schools as a way to civilize the "savage Indian":

> Indian children should be withdrawn as much as possible from the parental influence, and the only way to do that would be to put them in central training industrial schools where they will acquire the habits and modes of thought of white men. (House of Commons Debate, 1883, as cited in Truth and Reconciliation Commission of Canada [TRC], 2015, p. 6)

Industrial and boarding schools had existed for Indigenous children since the early 19th century, but they did not reach their peak of attendance until the early 20th century when, in 1920, it became mandatory for all Indigenous children to attend residential school. Of this policy, deputy superintendent of the Department of Indian Affairs at the time, Duncan Campbell Scott, remarked,

> I want to get rid of the Indian problem. I do not think as a matter of fact, that this country ought to continuously protect a class of people who are able to stand alone. That is my whole point. Our objective is to continue until there is no Indian question, and no Indian department and that is the whole object of this Bill. (Treaties and Historical Research Centre, 1978, p. 114)

It has been widely acknowledged that the residential school system was implemented to isolate Indigenous children from their families and communities in an effort to erase their cultures and replace them with a White, Euro-Canadian, Christian value system. Most schools were originally run by Roman Catholic, Anglican, United, Methodist, and Presbyterian churches, and when the federal government got involved they provided some funding to the churches to continue their work, but also opened large, federally administered residential schools across the country.

Once at the schools, children were prohibited from speaking their language, were given an English or French name to replace their Indigenous name, and were prevented from interacting with their families. Children were religiously indoctrinated and received an education that would prepare them for life in the working class: girls were taught domestic chores like sewing, laundry, and cooking, while boys learned industrial skills and performed manual labour. The abuse of Indigenous children while at residential school was common, with children physically punished for behaviours perceived as Indigenous, sexually abused by predatory school officials, and emotionally and psychologically abused by school officials who perceived them as "dirty," "uncivilized," and "evil" (Dickason, 2002; Kirmayer, Brass, Holton, Paul, Simpson, & Tait, 2007). The federal government took over the complete administration of residential schools in 1969, with most church-run schools closing in the 1980s; the last government-run school, Gordon's School near Punnichy, Saskatchewan, closed in 1996. Overall, the Canadian government estimates that 150,000 Indigenous children spent time in residential schools during their operation (Aboriginal Affairs and Northern Development, 2008).

Implemented within the residential school system, as well as a legislated public health initiative, sexual sterilization policies disproportionately targeted Indigenous women and girls throughout the country. British Columbia (1933–1973) and Alberta (1928–1972) had formal sexual sterilization policies on the books, though the practice was not uncommon in other parts of the country as well. In her dissertation and subsequent book, Karen Stote (2015) argues that the sterilization of Indigenous women and girls was a part of the Canadian government's larger colonial project involving the appropriation of Native lands, oppression of women, and denial of Indigenous sovereignty, while simultaneously reducing the number of potential dependants on the government. In this light, like residential schools, coercive sterilization was one tool of a colonial government looking to control and reduce the Indigenous population. Sterilization was useful because of the perception that Indigenous peoples were "unfit," "undesirable," or "mentally incompetent" as parents and contributed to rising rates of poverty in the 1930s. Thousands of Indigenous women and men, girls and boys were legally sterilized throughout the 20th century, many without their consent, but because the Canadian government failed to accurately maintain records of sterilizations, the actual number of Indigenous peoples affected by these policies will likely never be fully known (Stote, 2012).

As compulsory attendance at residential school was declining, other harmful colonial practices aimed at solving the "Indian problem" continued throughout the 20th century in Canada. Known as the "Sixties Scoop" because the practice peaked between the 1960s and 1980s (though it was practiced before and has been practiced since), Indigenous children were systematically removed from their homes and reserves and circulated through the child welfare system. Social workers with little knowledge of traditional Indigenous child rearing practices often interpreted the behaviour of families living in poverty or "off the land" as neglecting children, thus justifying the apprehension of thousands of children and their placement in foster homes or institutions. Removed from their families and communities, Indigenous children were typically placed in non-Indigenous homes and expected to adopt the cultural heritage of their foster family. As in residential schools, physical, psychological, and sexual abuse against children was not uncommon (Fournier & Crey, 1997). Today, Indigenous children still make up a disproportionate number of children in child welfare out-of-home care, as high as 80 to 85 percent of all children in care in the provinces of Manitoba and Saskatchewan (Sinha & Kozlowski, 2013).

Throughout the 19th and 20th centuries, residential schools, the Sixties Scoop, and discriminatory sterilization policies further erased Indigenous culture in already fragile communities and traumatized generations of individuals ripped from their families and, in many cases, subjected to various forms of abuse (Metatawabin, 2014; Stote, 2012). What was conceived of historically as solving the "Indian problem" by leaders in the European settlement of Canada, and what was implemented as a series of formal laws and policies and informal practices aimed at defining and controlling the Indigenous population, has been revised as genocide by Indigenous scholars and their allies (e.g., Daschuk, 2013; Hill, 2009; Stote, 2015). In its application, the elimination of the "Indian problem" in Canada was tackled through two primary avenues: assimilation and eradication (Hill, 2009). If Indigenous peoples could not be assimilated into Euro-Canadian society through discriminatory and violent interventions into their lives, the loss of Indigenous life due to disease, starvation, malnutrition, neglect, and abuse, reduced their numbers considerably. The pre-contact population in North America was around 10 million; today, there are around 5.2 million American Indians living in the United States and around 1.4 million Indigenous peoples living in Canada (Norris, Vines, & Hoeffiel, 2012; Statistics Canada, 2013).[3]

Today, Indigenous women and girls are living in a society with a long history of colonialist racism and violence directed toward them and in communities characterized by intergenerational trauma and gender inequality produced by that violence (Bombay, Matheson, & Anisman, 2009; Wesley-Esquimaux & Smolewski, 2004). Intergenerational trauma suggests a "historic trauma transmission" (Herman, 1997) whereby collective memories (or non-memories) of traumatic events, and the maladaptive coping mechanisms associated with those traumatic events, are passed from generation to generation (Wesley-Esquimaux & Smolewski, 2004). Individuals were, in many cases, forcibly removed from their homes, denied communication with their families, and forbidden to practice their traditional culture and spirituality. Often, these individuals were unable to maintain their native language or pass on their histories to children and grandchildren because they never learned or did not remember them (Kirmayer et al., 2007). Individuals who were also victims of physical, psychological, and sexual abuse at the residential schools not only suffered negative socio-cultural consequences, but also a range of medical, psychological, and behavioural ones. Mental health issues including post-traumatic stress disorder, addictions, and suicide are difficult to heal because of the disconnection many Indigenous peoples feel from their families, communities, and native lands (Kirmayer et al., 2007). After finishing school and returning to their communities, survivors can have difficulty maintaining healthy, functional relationships as adults, having internalized self-hatred and normalized dysfunctional behaviour (Bull, 1991; Fournier & Crey, 1997). Residential schools and other traumas that Indigenous peoples in Canada have experienced directly and indirectly through historic trauma transmission have resulted in higher rates of suicide compared to non-Indigenous peoples (Kirmayer et al., 2007), lower levels of educational attainment and income (Indian and Northern Affairs Canada, 2009), and more problems with addictions and interpersonal violence (National Collaborating Centre for Aboriginal Health, 2012).

The Canadian government has attempted to take responsibility for the horrors of residential schools with the Indian Residential School Settlement Agreement (IRSSA) announced in 2006 and a formal apology in 2008. Coming on the heels of the 1996 Royal Commission on Aboriginal Peoples, which revealed the troubling history between Canadians and Indigenous peoples, the federal government offered a $2-billion compensation package for the approximately 80,000 survivors of residential schools. The compensation package included a lump sum Common Experience Payment for former students, a settlement fund for those who had experienced the most serious abuse, healing services to be provided by the newly created Aboriginal Health Foundation, a commemoration fund for community-based and national memorial projects, and a nationwide Truth and Reconciliation Commission (TRC), which released its final report in 2015. The commission found the Canadian government guilty of committing cultural genocide against Indigenous peoples, defined as "the destruction of those structures and practices that allow the group to continue as a group" (TRC, 2015). As of writing, former prime minister Stephen Harper had not fulfilled any of the 94 recommendations of the Truth and Reconciliation

Commission's final report during his tenure; however, newly elected in October 2015, Canada's current prime minister Justin Trudeau committed to fulfilling all 94 recommendations as an election promise and launched a national inquiry into missing and murdered Indigenous women and girls on December 8, 2015.

The federal government's compensation package for survivors of residential schools illustrates the difficulty in the state attempting to "heal" an oppressed group and "reconcile" years of discrimination and violence through state-based notions of justice. In my work evaluating the health services response for the TRC National Event in Inuvik, Northwest Territories, many participants valued the opportunity to share their stories for the sake of a more accurate Canadian history, but also noted that many details of the event demonstrated disrespect, or at least ignorance, of Indigenous peoples' lives. Perhaps most troubling was that some of the event's activities took place on the site of a former residential school, potentially a very traumatic location for former students to revisit. It is in these details, or nuances, that the disconnection between Euro-Canadian settler justice and Indigenous justice becomes visible. The systemic nature of Canada's discrimination against Indigenous peoples is particularly salient when Indigenous women engage with the state and advocate for recognition of and justice for the violence they experience in their lives.

Violence against Indigenous Women and the Inaccessibility of Justice

Interpersonal and institutional violence against Indigenous women and girls, whether perpetrated by Indigenous or non-Indigenous men, has its roots in Britain and France's colonization of what is now Canada. Since the first contact between White settlers and Indigenous communities, Indigenous women have been targeted in the ongoing colonial project of assimilation and eradication precisely because of the important social, political, cultural, and spiritual roles women played in many communities. As Native American writer Paula Gunn Allen notes, "the colonizer saw … that as long as women held unquestioned power of such magnitude, attempts at total conquest of the continents were bound to fail" (1986, p. 3). Indigenous women and girls were perceived as potential targets for sexual exploitation by European explorers and settlers, as exemplified in diary records preserved from the time period; however, as these records indicate, Indigenous women actively resisted White settlers' sexual advances, refusing bribes for sexual acts and intermarriages (Barman, 2010). As stated above, some Indigenous women were able to eke out for themselves positions of influence as wives of early fur traders, but most Indigenous women were seen through the lens of rigid stereotypes. Ideas about the "Indian princess" or the worthless "squaw" (Acoose, 2016; Allen, 1986) created an enduring perception of the sexual availability of Indigenous women that has permeated Indigenous-settler relations since contact.

After Confederation, the Indian Act of 1876 embedded laws that stripped an Indigenous woman of status, access to land, and band membership if she married a non-Indigenous man. This construction of male/female relationships forced a patrilineal conceptualization of the family onto Indigenous communities, many of which were matrilineal or egalitarian before contact (Anderson, 2016; Barker, 2006; Bourassa, McKay-McNabb, & Hampton, 2004). The Indian Act also denied Indigenous women the right to hold positions in elected office on reserve, vote in band elections, or even participate in public meetings on reserve (Bourassa et al., 2004). Indigenous women were eventually granted the right to vote in band council elections in 1951 and the franchise was extended to all Indigenous people for federal elections in 1960, but the male-defined concept of "Indian status" was only amended in 1985, after the entrenchment of the Canadian Charter of Rights and Freedoms and not without considerable contest. Lawrence (1999) sees the Indian Act as producing a particular way of thinking about Indigenous peoples that has naturalized the subordinate position Indigenous women occupy in Canadian society. After more than 100 years of the Indian Act, male privilege within band governments and Indigenous organizations has come to be seen as normal and legitimate. In fact, male-dominated band councils and organizations fought against amendments to the Indian Act that would return status to women who had lost it for "marrying out." Their argument was that the Indian Act was the one mechanism through which Indigenous peoples could exercise their sacred right to self-government in Canada. Indigenous women advocating for amendments were seen to be conspiring with the racist and colonial Canadian government (Barker, 2006; Brodsky, 2014). Even though the amendments were eventually passed, and Indigenous women were given the same rights as men under the Indian Act, as Indigenous scholar Joanne Barker (2006) notes, the guise of equality rights did not "alter in any substantial way the political, economic, or social roles of Indian women within reserve and urban communities or ... (re) empower the gender-based traditions and customs of Indian governance and territorial occupation" (p. 153).

Gender inequality forced upon Indigenous communities after contact has exacerbated intergenerational trauma, translating into higher-than-average rates of interpersonal violence perpetrated against Indigenous women and girls. Most recent statistics suggest that Indigenous women are three times more likely than non-Indigenous women to suffer violent victimization, a figure that has remained constant over three cycles of Statistic Canada's General Social Survey on Victimization (Brennan, 2011). Indigenous women tend to experience more serious forms of spousal abuse than non-Indigenous women, often leading to violence and injury (Brennan, 2011). Brownridge (2003) suggests that domestic violence against Indigenous women can be explained in part by Indigenous men's adoption of White settler patriarchy, violence being one tool by which Indigenous men can exercise power and control in a society where they have very little. But Indigenous women also face violence at the hands of non-Indigenous men. Indigenous women are up to seven times more likely to die of homicide than a non-Indigenous woman in Canada (O'Donnell & Wallace, 2011). According to the RCMP, nearly 1,100 Indigenous women have been murdered between 1980 and 2010, making up about 16 percent of all female homicide victims during that period, even though Indigenous women make up only about 4 percent of the total population (RCMP, 2014). And that figure does not include all of the women and girls who have gone missing over the years, whose families and friends have contacted the police, but for whom very few resources are allocated to find. Indigenous women's groups have been organizing for decades to bring attention to missing women in Vancouver's Downtown Eastside, along British Columbia's Highway of Tears, and across Canada through organizations like Sisters in Spirit, Families of Sisters in Spirit, and, most recently, No More Silence.

Canada's pattern of missing and murdered Indigenous women and girls is particularly troubling. First identified when women, many Indigenous and involved in street-based, survival sex work and drug use, started to go missing in Vancouver's Downtown Eastside, or what has been dubbed the "urban reserve" by its Indigenous inhabitants, as far back as the 1960s (Cameron, 2010; Farley, Lynne, & Cotton, 2005). Street-based sex workers experience some of the highest rates of violent victimization. In one study of sex workers from Vancouver's Downtown Eastside, 90 percent had been physically assaulted and 78 percent raped while they were working (Farley et al., 2005). By the 1990s, the families of missing women, a few journalists, and some criminal profilers were convinced that at least one, and possibly two or three, serial killers were operating in Vancouver's Downtown Eastside, targeting poor, street-involved women, many of whom were Indigenous (Cameron, 2010). However, investigators at the Vancouver Police Department "had found no evidence to support the theory of a serial killer" (as cited in Cameron, 2010, p. 64) and persistently ignored the families of dozens of women who had disappeared. After years of bungled investigations, Robert William Pickton was finally convicted on six counts of second-degree murder in 2007, though he is believed to have killed up to 50 women. Pickton is currently serving a life sentence with no possibility of parole for 25 years.[4]

Dozens of women also continue to go missing from a 724-kilometre stretch of northern British Columbia's Highway 16 between Prince George and Prince Rupert, dubbed the Highway of Tears. Women's organizations, like the National Women's Association of Canada, estimate that up to 40 women have disappeared from this area, but the RCMP includes only 18 women in their Highway of Tears case file, as their criteria require a person to go missing within 1 mile of the highway (Human Rights Watch [HRW], 2013; RCMP, 2014). This stretch of highway is well-known because many people use it to hitchhike from one small town to another; this is a very common and normalized mode of travel, as public transportation is unavailable and the cost of having a vehicle is prohibitive. However, these missing persons cases received very little attention from the police, particularly in the beginning. In a Human Rights Watch report (2013), families of missing women note that police only began to pay attention to these cases when a 25-year-old White woman, Nicole Hoar, went missing after hitchhiking to meet her sister. Of the Highway of Tears cases, one RCMP officer was even quoted as saying, "If they're natives, nobody gives a shit" (HRW, 2013, p. 37).

Criminal justice professionals, including police officers, lawyers, and judges, have a long history of poor relations with Indigenous communities in Canada, stemming from the colonial project to solve the "Indian problem" since contact (see Comack, 2012; King, 2012; Razack, 1998). In 2010, a Commission of Inquiry was launched to look into the police investigations of missing women in Vancouver's Downtown Eastside between 1997 and 2002, right around the time that Robert Pickton was a person of interest in the case and women were continuing to disappear. Inquiry Commissioner Wally Oppal, former attorney general for the Province of British Columbia, found that a number of factors contributed to the delayed response to murdered and missing women in Vancouver's Downtown Eastside: discrimination against Indigenous peoples, including political and public indifference to their life outcomes; poor policing leadership and outdated approaches and systems; inadequate communication and information-sharing between various policing units; and internal police culture, politics, and even conspiracy and cover-up (Oppal, 2012). But the lack of a compassionate, dedicated, coordinated response to Vancouver's missing women is only part of the picture. For the Human Rights Watch report from 2013, 50 Indigenous women and girls from British Columbia, many of whom reported being physically or sexually assaulted by police officers, incarcerated inappropriately, and being stalked or verbally abused by officers, were interviewed. The RCMP responded by saying it was "impossible" to deal with accusations of police misconduct without formal allegations from the victims and asked victims to report the crimes to police for a proper investigation (see Armstrong, 2013; Commisso-Georgee, 2013).

Ongoing brutality and harsh treatment by police and other state agencies toward Indigenous communities makes many women distrustful and unlikely to contact police if they have been victimized or are unsafe (Comack, 2012; Larsen & Petersen, 2001; McGillivray & Comaskey, 1999; Nancarrow, 2007). Unfortunately for Indigenous women, gender-based violence has largely been conceptualized as a problem for the criminal justice system to solve since the early 1980s. Aggressive criminal justice interventions for violence against women were introduced in Canada in the 1980s following a decade of feminist activism to motivate the Canadian government to take violence against women seriously (see DeKeseredy & MacLeod, 1997; Dobash & Dobash, 1992). Around the same time, the Canadian Charter of Rights and Freedoms had been entrenched, a few police forces in the United States had been sued by women claiming police had failed to protect them from domestic violence, and social science research evidence was suggesting that arresting domestic abusers was the best deterrent from future violence (see Mills, 1999; Sherman & Berk, 1984).[5] In a matter of a few years, rape had been changed to "sexual assault" under the law, and mandatory arrest policies were introduced for police investigating domestic violence calls, pro-prosecution policies were introduced for Crown attorneys, and specialized domestic violence courts were created. However, few women have reaped any benefit from these policies, and they have not improved women's safety and do not speak to many women's sense of justice (Johnson & Fraser, 2011). Indigenous women in particular have borne the brunt of these policies and are more likely to be counter-charged for incidents of domestic violence when they have reacted in self-defence (Balfour, 2008). Sometimes, police do not respond or delay responding to Indigenous women who are calling because of domestic violence, and police often ignore calls from Indigenous women who experience sexual assault due to the notion that these women live a high-risk lifestyle (Fry, 2011). Thus, Indigenous women may feel forced into living with an abusive partner to avoid homelessness, involvement in sex work, or interaction with agents of the state, like police officers.

When incidents of violence reach the criminal justice system, Indigenous women are often denied "justice," as evidenced by racist and sexist language used by criminal justice professionals, delayed criminal justice processing, and lenient outcomes for offenders. Through an examination of historical records, Carter (1997) demonstrates that, at least as far back as the 19th century, White settlers have used demonizing constructions of Indigenous women to solidify the actual and symbolic boundaries between settlers and Native peoples. Consider the case of Helen Betty Osborne, a 19-year-old Cree woman studying to become a teacher, who was abducted, sexually assaulted, and murdered by four White men in the town of The Pas, Manitoba, in November 1971. It took 16 years for one of the young men to be convicted of second-degree murder in her death,[6] and he has since been released from prison after serving 10 years of a life sentence.[7] As a result of her case and another involving the death of an Indigenous man at the hands of a police officer, the Manitoba government launched the Public Inquiry into the Administration of Justice and Aboriginal People, a Commission of Inquiry that found Manitoban society at the time to be characterized by racial segregation and discrimination, and concluded that Osborne was targeted because she was Aboriginal (Chartrand & Whitecloud, 2001).

Consider the case of Pamela George, a 28-year-old mother of two who was picked up by two young White men looking for, according to testimony at their trial, an "Indian hooker" (Razack, 2000), whom they beat, sexually assaulted, and ultimately murdered in Saskatchewan in 1995. Critical race scholar Sherene Razack (2000) argues that the presumed innocence of the White men, combined with an assumed degeneracy associated with Indigeneity led Pamela George's murder to be normalized and rationalized vis-à-vis the discourse at trial and the outcome of the case. Both the Crown attorney and the judge instructed the jury to remember that Pamela George was "indeed a prostitute," presumably to undermine her status as a victim and mitigate the severity of the men's actions. Ultimately, the two men were convicted of manslaughter and each sentenced to less than seven years' imprisonment; they served about four years before they were both released on parole in 2000. Most recently, the 2015 trial for the murder of Cindy Gladue, a 36-year-old Cree woman, has sparked an outcry of injustice from Indigenous social activists and their allies across the country. Cindy Gladue bled to death in a motel bathtub in Edmonton, Alberta, from an 11-centimetre tear in her vaginal wall after participating in, as argued by the defence, consensual rough sex. Despite a blood-alcohol level that, by Canadian law, was too high to consent to sexual activity and the prosecutor's controversial decision to introduce Cindy Gladue's preserved and disembodied vagina as physical evidence at trial, the accused man was acquitted on the charge of first-degree murder.

What all of these cases of injustice, discrimination, and violence illustrate is how difficult it is for Indigenous women who experience violence to receive any type of response to their circumstances that might promote healing and ensure safety. Indigenous women are living with the burden of centuries of colonial violence upon their shoulders; they are themselves victims of violence at the hands of partners and strangers; and the Canadian state is not only unwilling in many cases to acknowledge their suffering and do something about it, but actively participates and has, at least historically, systematically organized to decimate the Indigenous population. Given this social reality, how can Indigenous women be expected to rely on the state? Rather than more government reports telling Indigenous people what they already know, myself and others (e.g., Lovelace, 2012; Monchalin & Marques, 2013) argue that what is needed is concrete preventive action to stop interpersonal violence and contextually based community justice interventions to respond to victims and offenders—alternatives to a criminal justice system so clearly rooted in Canada's ongoing colonial history.

Decolonization through Community Justice

Indigenous women living in a settler society cannot rely on the state to administer justice for institutional violence nor for interpersonal violence exacerbated by the devaluation of Indigenous life. Ongoing colonial practices have contributed to the precarious situation in which Indigenous women and girls find themselves: vulnerable to severe forms of interpersonal violence, but unlikely to receive "justice" through state-based interventions, particularly the criminal justice system. Thus, there is a strong need to identify holistic approaches and coordinate community networks and responses that will work to end the ongoing violence against Indigenous women and girls. Community-based prevention efforts and interventions for violence against Indigenous women and girls offer a decolonial alternative to state-based institutions. Indigenous activists and their allies have been vocal about decolonizing ways of knowing and being in our social world, offering alternative interpretations of, for example, socio-historically contextualized responses to gender-based violence and victimization.

Decolonization involves the dismantling of the colonial state and its many arms of government—institutions, laws, policies, practices, and discourses—as well as reimagining a way of social organization that is not predicated on the suffering and oppression of signified Others. Indigenous women's well-being and safety is intimately connected to decolonizing efforts, as women's bodies and identities have been used for centuries to progress the colonial project of solving the "Indian problem." Native American scholar and activist Andrea Smith argues,

> Rather than adopt the strategy of fighting for sovereignty first and improving Native women's status second … we must understand that attacks on Native women's status are themselves attacks on Native sovereignty. (2005, p. 138)

Thus, decolonizing responses to violence against Indigenous women and girls are imperative to break out of the cycle of violence and injustice with which

Indigenous women are faced. The historical and ongoing colonization of the territory that is now known as Canada, the rates and severity of violence committed against Indigenous women and girls, and the discrimination they face in interactions with state-based institutions, like the criminal justice system, are all indicators that the state will not be useful in solving a problem it has effectively created.

This is why the call for the federal government to launch a national public inquiry into Canada's missing and murdered Indigenous women is so puzzling.[8] Many Indigenous organizations and political leaders, including the Native Women's Association of Canada, federal opposition leaders, and leaders of the provinces and territories, are calling for a national public inquiry into the violence perpetrated against Indigenous women in Canada, based on recommendations from the United Nations Special Rapporteur on the rights of Indigenous peoples (Anaya, 2014). This recommendation is based on Anaya's (2014) assessment that Indigenous peoples' human rights are being violated in Canada, evidenced by poor living conditions on reserves, the well-being gap between Indigenous and non-Indigenous peoples in Canada, the overrepresentation of Indigenous peoples in the nation's prisons, and of course, the high rates of violence against Indigenous women and girls (Anaya, 2014). Again, the lived reality for many Indigenous people in Canada is one created by the Canadian state to either assimilate or eradicate the Indigenous population. According to Smith (2014), even the concept of "human rights" is a colonial construction; Indigenous activists and their allies must truly think outside the box of the state and, to improve the well-being and safety of Indigenous women and girls, think outside the box of the criminal justice system.

Thinking outside the box of the criminal justice system, and the state as a whole, perhaps requires an imagination for some Western thinkers. But as Smith explains, using domestic violence as an example, it is as simple as asking different questions:

> What if we do not make any assumptions about what a domestic violence program should look like, but instead ask: What would it take to end violence against women of color? What would this movement look like? What if we do not presume that this movement would necessarily have anything we take for granted in the current domestic violence movement? (2005, p. 153)

Much Indigenous activism around violence against women and girls focuses on holistic interventions that target physical, mental, emotional, and spiritual well-being. Typically, community-based, holistic interventions engage all individuals affected by violence to embark on a healing journey. After histories and personal experiences of colonization, violence, and discrimination, healing for Indigenous peoples is intimately connected with decolonization, and decolonization involves a return to traditional ways of conceptualizing and interacting with the social world. This is much broader than simply funding victim services or incarcerating a violent offender for a short period of time; Indigenous healing through decolonization means focusing on the overall, lifelong well-being of individuals and communities. Former assistant Crown attorney Rupert Ross (2014) writes of how, through his work in remote Northern Ontario Indigenous communities, he came to understand a "traditional indigenous worldview" (see also Monchalin, 2016) that involves seeing life events relationally and seeing the embeddedness and interconnectedness of oneself within the physical and spiritual worlds. Ross (2014) identifies 12 unique components of Indigenous healing that are different from Western practices:

1.   Special focus on the spirit.
2.   A "healthy person" understands their embeddedness in an interconnected physical and spiritual world.
3.   Reliance on group healing.
4.   Individual healing is connected to community healing.
5.   Importance of emotions.
6.   Importance of catharsis through ceremony.
7.   Empathetic, compassionate elders as healers.
8.   Respect for the worth of every living being.
9.   The belief that it is not always necessary to "talk" your way back to health.
10. Connection to land.
11. Adoption of complementary practices from other sources (e.g., Western therapies).
12. Healing as a lifelong journey. (Ross, 2014)

While the Canadian criminal justice system is concerned operationally with resolving individual instances of crime, Indigenous healing stemming from the endemic violence against Indigenous women is concerned with healing our whole selves as inhabitants of an interconnected world.

A reconceptualization of our existence within the physical and social world can still translate into practical programs to prevent violence against women, help victims, and work with offenders. Indigenous women report a need for outreach and prevention programs for youth and young mothers, for children who have witnessed violence, for men who are violent, and for elders who have suffered abuse as well (Lamontagne, 2011). Partnerships with band councils have been identified as integral to the survival of community-based programs, as they can help with cost-sharing, information exchange, and other resources (Lamontagne, 2011). Smith (2005) emphasizes the importance of community members, not just clients, acting as organizers in community justice interventions. When street-involved women from Vancouver's Downtown Eastside began to go missing at an alarming rate, Indigenous women were among the first people to demand attention to the issue. In 1991, Indigenous women were integral to the inaugural Valentine's Day Women's Memorial March, which marks a day of remembrance to honour the lives of women from the area who have gone missing or been murdered, an annual event that continues today (Culhane, 2003). The tenacity of the organizers of this event demonstrate the commitment family and community members have to the well-being and the safety of their women and girls, a resource that must be harnessed for implementing other community-based interventions.

There are many current initiatives that exist outside the state and also outside what has been called the "non-profit industrial complex" (INCITE!, 2009, p. 101).[9] The Native Youth Sexual Health Network is a great example of a grassroots advocacy organization that does preventive work in communities across Canada and the United States. Their Sexy Health Carnival brings information about sexual health, harm reduction, violence prevention, suicide, and other issues to youth and other community members at powwows, schools, and other community events in a fun and interactive way. At the 2015 conference Sovereignties and Colonialisms: Resisting Racism, Extraction, and Dispossession at York University in Toronto, members of the network demonstrated their carnival by setting up information booths in a classroom that conference participants were free to browse and engage with, just as children and youth would at a powwow or community event. The Native Youth Sexual Health Network is also working with Families of Sisters in Spirit and No More Silence to create a community-led database of the names of Indigenous women, girls, and two-spirit people who have gone missing or been killed across Canada. This is in response to the federal government's cancellation of the Native Women's Association of Canada's Sisters in Spirit Initiative in 2010, which collected about 600 names of missing or murdered Indigenous women while the program operated from 2005 to 2010. Families of Sisters in Spirit is an entirely volunteer-based grassroots organization that supports the families of Indigenous women who have been murdered or have gone missing and maintains an active Facebook page to track new Indigenous missing persons cases. No More Silence has garnered the research support of Dr. Janet Smylie, a Métis scholar and family physician, to help create methodologies for this project. As of mid-2015, the website had created community lists for Alberta, Ontario, and Newfoundland and Labrador, as well as one for Indigenous two-spirit and trans people who had disappeared or were murdered.

Indigenous holistic healing interventions for violence against women also tend to focus on men's behaviour much more than mainstream feminist or community services (e.g., Baskin, 2003). Community-based healing circles, though in many cases supported by at least one level of government or a government agency, have been successful in engaging men and women to heal histories of domestic violence and sexual abuse. Probably the best-known example is the Community Holistic Circle Healing Program developed in Hollow Water First Nation, about 200 kilometres north of Winnipeg, Manitoba (see Aboriginal Peoples Collection, 1997; Ross, 1996). In response to the perceived ineffectiveness of incarceration, the community in Hollow Water came together to develop its own training protocols and healing programs based on traditional teachings to address the cycle of intergenerational abuse recurring in so many of the community's families. The program consists of 13 steps, each of which involves victims, offenders, and community members working together to heal from the trauma of colonization, as well as the contemporary violence in their lives. An evaluation of the program's operation from 1986 to 2000 found that only 2 out of 107 participants had reoffended and that the program had increased community awareness of sexual abuse and family violence, increased disclosure rates, reduced rates of alcoholism, improved education standards, and increased services for at-risk children and youth (Couture, 2001). Of course, this program required significant coordination with government bureaucracies and a firm commitment from community members to hold offenders accountable for their behaviour through the circle process. Ross (2014) describes the Hollow Water organizational process as "revolutionary," so there is no reason why communities could not adapt a similar process for their own needs, this time without government input.

Conclusion

I have written about the history of colonization in Canada from a perspective that sees it as both a centuries-old political agenda and an ongoing problem out of which Canadians and Indigenous peoples have difficulty envisioning themselves. I have written about how colonization, and, in particular, the laws and policies created to solve the "Indian problem" through assimilation and eradication have shaped social constructions of Indigenous women, placing them in a vulnerable social category in which they are at grossly disproportionate odds of being victims of intimate partner abuse, sexual violence, or murder and are unlikely to receive "justice" through the adversarial Canadian criminal justice system. Criminal justice interventions in Canada individualize acts of violence against women, decontextualizing violence from patterns within relationships and socio-historical processes that place Indigenous women at a structural disadvantage in our society. Western scholars have a long way to go in terms of understanding how different understandings of violence can lead to conceptualizing entirely new non-state-based (or, in this case, old and traditional) ways to prevent and respond to that violence.

If Western scholars are willing to think outside the box, I argue that community-based justice prevention efforts and interventions are a viable, decolonial alternative to state-based responses to violence against Indigenous women and girls. As concerned students and scholars within the Western academic system, I think it is incumbent upon us to open our minds and allow for the possibility of entirely different conceptualizations of violence and responses to that violence—to decolonize ways of thinking that have been engrained since elementary school. Practically, we can support grassroots community-based efforts that already exist to prevent and respond to violence against Indigenous women and girls. Academic allies should offer their research skills to community groups that want to implement programs and evaluate their effects over the long term. Academic networks should be harnessed to uncover what communities are doing across Canada and to share ideas about what resonates with victims, offenders, and other community members. Using our positions as academics to highlight the many programs, initiatives, and events that are implemented and organized outside of the state would demonstrate a commitment to decolonial academic praxis and to promoting the well-being of Indigenous women and girls.

Discussion Questions

1. Think about what reconciliation means to you. How do you think a country like Canada can reconcile its relationship with Indigenous peoples after centuries of discrimination, abuse, and violence?
2. Indigenous interventions for violence against women often involve bringing the victim and offender together. Canada's criminal justice system typically keeps the victim and offender separate throughout criminal justice proceedings. What do you think is the appropriate role for victim and offender in "justice" proceedings?
3. Community-based interventions often suffer from lack of resources, member burnout, and high turnover, as well as larger structural obstacles. How might a community group sustain its program or services over the long term without funding from governments or government agencies?

Additional Resources

April, S., & Magrinelli Orsi, M. (2013). Gladue *Practices in the Provinces and Territories*. Ottawa: Department of Justice Canada: http://www.justice.gc.ca/eng/rp-pr/csj-sjc/ccs-ajc/rr12_11/rr12_11.pdf.

Jibwe, Y. (Director). (2014). *Missing—The Documentary* [Film]. Canada: Animiki Films: https://www.youtube.com/watch?v=3gK4S2e1HAE.

Justice Education Society of BC. (2016). *Gladue* and Aboriginal Sentencing: http://justiceeducation.ca/about-us/research/gladue-and-aboriginal-sentencing.

Notes

1. Two-spirit is an umbrella term used to describe individuals who identify with both masculine and feminine traits, and is often considered to be a third gender or on the lesbian, gay, bisexual, transgender, and queer (LGBTQ) continuum.

2. Under the Indian Act, s.18(1), "reserves are held by Her Majesty for the use and benefit of the respective bands for which they were set apart, and subject to this Act and to the terms of any treaty or surrender, the Governor in Council may determine whether any purpose for which lands in a reserve are used or are to be used is for the use and benefit of the band."

3. The estimate of the population of North and South America pre-European contact ranges from 10 to 100 million people. Today, there are approximately 40 million Indigenous people in the Americas (Haines & Steckel, 2000; Hill, 2009; Taylor, 2002).

4. Life with no possibility of parole for 25 years has traditionally been Canada's toughest sentence; however, some judges have been moving in the direction of harsher sentences. Travis Baumgartner was sentenced to 40 years without parole in 2013 for murdering three colleagues during a robbery of their armoured vehicle, and Justin Bourque was sentenced to 75 years without parole in 2014 for the deaths of three RCMP officers in the Moncton shootings. These sentences are two of the harshest handed down in Canada since the last executions were performed in 1962.

5. This research evidence would later be criticized by Faubert & Hinch, 1996; Lerman, 1992; Sheptycki, 1991; and Sherman, 1992.

6. In Canada, second-degree murder refers to murders that were not planned in advance of their commission (see section 231 of the Criminal Code of Canada).

7. A life sentence in Canada typically translates into 25 years in a federal penitentiary, though individuals may be eligible for parole before they have served the full sentence (see section 745.6 of the Criminal Code of Canada).

8. Former Prime Minister Stephen Harper flatly quashed hopes for a national public inquiry by discontinuing funding for a national database of missing and murdered Indigenous women in 2010 and stating that this violence is not part of a "sociological phenomenon" and should be "viewed as a crime" to be solved by the police (Boutilier, 2014).

9. INCITE!, a US-based activist organization of women, gender non-conforming, and trans people of colour, defines the *non-profit industrial complex* as a system of relationships between the state, the ruling classes, charitable foundations, and non-profit or non-governmental organizations that "results in the surveillance, control, derailment, and everyday management of political movements" (INCITE!, 2014).

References

Aboriginal Affairs and Northern Development. (2008). *Statement of apology to former students of Indian Residential Schools.* Retrieved from http://www.aadnc-aandc.gc.ca/eng/1100100015644/1100100015649

Aboriginal Peoples Collection. (1997). *The four circles of Hollow Water.* Ottawa: Public Safety Canada.

Acoose, J. (2016). *Iskwewak Kah'Ki Yaw Ni Wahkomakanak: Neither Indian princesses nor easy squaws* (2nd ed.). Toronto: Women's Press.

Allen, P. G. (1986). *The sacred hoop: Recovering the feminine in American Indian tradition.* Boston: Beacon.

Amnesty International (AI). (2004). *Stolen sisters: A human rights response to discrimination and violence against Indigenous women in Canada.* New York: Amnesty International.

Anaya, J. (2014). *Report of the Special Rapporteur on the rights of Indigenous peoples: The situation of Indigenous peoples in Canada.* Geneva: UN Human Rights Council. Retrieved from http://unsr.jamesanaya.org/country-reports/the-situation-of-indigenous-peoples-in-canada

Anderson, K. (2016). *A recognition of being: Reconstructing Native womanhood* (2nd ed.). Toronto: Women's Press.

Armstrong, J. (2013, February 13). RCMP responds to Human Rights Watch report. *Royal Canadian Mounted Police.* Retrieved from http://www.rcmp-grc.gc.ca/en/news/2013/13/rcmp-responds-human-rights-watch-report

Balfour, G. (2008). Falling between the cracks of retributive and restorative justice: The victimization and punishment of Aboriginal women. *Feminist Criminology, 3*(2), 101–120.

Barker, J. (2006). Gender, sovereignty, and the discourse of rights in Native women's activism. *Meridians: Feminism, Race, Transnationalism, 7*(1), 127–161.

Barman, J. (2010). Indigenous women and feminism on the cusp of contact. In C. Suzack,
    S. M. Huhndorf, J. Perreault, & J. Barman (Eds.), *Indigenous women and feminism: Politics,
    activism, culture* (pp. 92–108). Vancouver: UBC Press.

Baskin, C. (2003). From victims to leaders: Activism against violence towards women. In
    B. Lawrence & K. Anderson (Eds.), *Strong women stories: Native vision and community
    survival* (pp. 213–227). Toronto: Sumach Press.

Bombay, A., Matheson, K., & Anisman, H. (2009). Intergenerational trauma: Convergence of
    multiple processes among First Nations peoples in Canada. *Journal of Aboriginal Health*,
    5(3), 6–47.

Bourassa, C., McKay-McNabb, K., & Hampton, M. (2004). Racism, sexism, and colonialism: The
    impact on the health of Aboriginal women in Canada. *Canadian Woman Studies*, 24(1),
    23–29.

Boutilier, A. (2014, August 21). Native teen's slaying a "crime," not a "sociological phenomenon,"
    Stephen Harper says. *Toronto Star*. Retrieved from http://www.thestar.com/news/
    canada/2014/08/21/native_teens_slaying_a_crime_not_a_sociological_phenomenon_
    stephen_harper_says.html

Brennan, S. (2011). Violent victimization of Aboriginal women in the Canadian provinces, 2009.
    Juristat. Statistics Canada Catalogue no. 85-002-X. Retrieved from http://www.statcan.gc.ca/
    pub/85-002-x/2011001/article/11439-eng.htm

Brodsky, G. (2014). *McIvor v. Canada*: Legislated patriarchy meets Aboriginal women's equality
    rights. In J. Green (Ed.), *Indivisible: Indigenous human rights* (pp. 100–125). Winnipeg:
    Fernwood Publishing.

Brownridge, D. (2003). Male partner violence against Aboriginal women in Canada: An empirical
    analysis. *Journal of Interpersonal Violence*, 18(1), 65–83.

Brownridge, D. A. (2008). Understanding the elevated risk of partner violence against Aboriginal
    women: A comparison of two nationally representative surveys of Canada. *Journal of Family
    Violence*, 23(5), 353–367.

Bull, L. (1991). Native residential schooling: The Native perspective. *Canadian Journal of Native
    Education*, 18, 3–63.

Burns, M., & Taylor-Butts, A. (2009). A profile of Canada's shelters for abused women. *Family
    violence in Canada: A statistical profile 2009*. Catalogue no: 85-224-X. Ottawa: Statistics
    Canada.

Cameron, S. (2010). *On the farm: Robert William Pickton and the tragic story of Vancouver's
    missing women*. Toronto: Vintage Canada.

Carter, S. (1997). *Capturing women: The manipulation of cultural imagery in Canada's prairie west*.
    Montreal: McGill-Queen's University Press.

Chartrand, P. L. A. H., & Whitecloud, W. (2001). *Aboriginal Justice Implementation Commission:
    Final report*. Winnipeg: Government of Manitoba. Retrieved from http://www.ajic.mb.ca/
    reports/final_toc.html

Chartrand, V. (2014). Tears 4 Justice and the missing and murdered women and children across
    Canada: An interview with Gladys Radek. *Radical Criminology*, 3, 113–126.

Comack, E. (2012). *Racialized policing: Aboriginal people's encounters with the police*. Winnipeg:
    Fernwood Publishing.

Commisso-Georgee, C. (2013, February 13). RCMP calls for more info about abuse claims
    in communities. *CTVNews.ca*. Retrieved from http://www.ctvnews.ca/canada/
    rcmp-calls-for-more-info-about-abuse-claims-in-b-c-s-aboriginal-communities-1.1154727

Couture, J. (2001). *A cost-benefit analysis of Hollow Water's Community Holistic Circle Healing process*. Ottawa: Aboriginal Corrections Policy Unit.

Culhane, D. (2003). Their spirits live within us: Aboriginal women in Downtown Eastside Vancouver emerging into visibility. *American Indian Quarterly, 27*(3/4), 593–606.

Daschuk, J. (2013). *Clearing the plains: Disease, politics of starvation, and the loss of Aboriginal life*. Regina: University of Regina Press.

DeKeseredy, W. S., & MacLeod, L. (1997). *Woman abuse: A sociological story*. Toronto: Harcourt Brace & Company.

Dickason, O. (2002). *Canada's First Nations: A history of founding peoples from earliest times*. Toronto: Oxford University Press.

Dobash, R. E., & Dobash, R.P. (1992). *Women, violence and social change*. London: Routledge.

Farb, P. (1968). *Man's rise to civilization as shown by the Indians of North America from primeval times to the coming of the industrial state*. New York: E. P. Dutton & Co.

Farley, M., Lynne, J., & Cotton, A. (2005). Prostitution in Vancouver: Violence and colonization of First Nations women. *Trans Cultural Psychiatry, 42*(2), 242–271.

Faubert, J., & Hinch, R. (1996). The dialectics of mandatory arrest policies. In T. O'Reilly-Fleming, (Ed.), *Post-critical criminology* (pp. 230–251). Scarborough, ON: Prentice-Hall.

Forbes, J. D. (2008). *Columbus and other cannibals*. New York: Seven Stories Press.

Fournier, S., & Crey, E. (1997). *Stolen from our embrace: The abduction of First Nations children and the restoration of Aboriginal communities*. Vancouver: Douglas & McIntyre.

Fry, H. (2011). *Call into the night: An overview of violence against Aboriginal women*. Ottawa: House of Commons Canada.

Haines, M. R., & Steckel, R. H. (2000). *A population history of North America*. Cambridge: Cambridge University Press.

Herman, J. (1997). *Trauma and recovery: The aftermath of violence—from domestic abuse to political terror*. New York: Basic Books.

Hill, G. (2009). *500 years of Indigenous resistance*. Oakland, CA: PM Press.

Human Rights Watch. (2013, February). *Those who take us away: Abusive policing and failures in protection of Indigenous women and girls in northern British Columbia, Canada*. Retrieved from http://www.hrw.org/sites/default/files/reports/canada0213webwcover_0.pdf

INCITE!. (2009). *The revolution will not be funded: Beyond the non-profit industrial complex*. New York: South End Press.

INCITE!. (2014). Beyond the non-profit industrial complex. *INCITE!*. Retrieved from http://www.incite-national.org/page/beyond-non-profit-industrial-complex

Indian and Northern Affairs Canada. (2009). *A demographic and socio-economic portrait of Aboriginal populations in Canada*. Ottawa: INAC.

Johnson, H., & Fraser. J. (2011). *Specialized domestic violence courts: Do they make women safer? Community report: Phase 1*. Ottawa: Department of Criminology.

King, T. (2012). *The inconvenient Indian: A curious account of Native people in North America*. Toronto: Anchor Canada.

Kirmayer, L. J., Brass, G. M., Holton, T., Paul, K., Simpson, C., & Tait, C. (2007). *Suicide among Aboriginal people in Canada*. Ottawa: The Aboriginal Healing Foundation.

Lamontagne, M. (2011). *Violence against Aboriginal women: Scan and report*. Toronto: Canadian Women's Foundation.

Larsen, A., & Petersen, A. (2001). Rethinking responses to "domestic violence" in Australian Indigenous communities. *Journal of Social Welfare and Family Law*, 23(2), 121–134.

Lawrence, B. (1999). *"Real" Indians and others: Mixed-race urban Native people, the Indian Act, and the rebuilding of Indigenous nations.* Unpublished PhD dissertation, University of Toronto.

Lerman, L. G. (1992). The decontextualization of domestic violence. *The Journal of Criminal Law and Criminology*, 83(1), 217–240.

Little Bear, L. (1986). Aboriginal rights and the Canadian "grundnorm." In J. R. Ponting (Ed.), *Arduous journey: Canadian Indians and decolonization* (pp. 112–136). Toronto: McClelland and Stewart.

Ljunggren, D. (2009, September 25). Every G20 nation wants to be Canada, insists PM. *Reuters*. Retrieved from http://www.reuters.com/article/columns-us-g20-canada-advantages-idUST RE58P05Z20090926#qA9C7FBe6EoldhuO.97

Lovelace, R. (2012, December 21). Violence against Aboriginal women and the right to self-defence. *Rabble.ca*. Retrieved from http://rabble.ca/news/2012/12/right-self-defense

McGillivray, A., & Comaskey, B. (1999). *Black eyes all of the time: Intimate violence, Aboriginal women, and the justice system.* Toronto: University of Toronto Press.

Metatawabin, E. (2014). *Up Ghost River: A Chief's journey through the turbulent waters of Native history.* Toronto: Alfred A. Knopf Canada.

Mills, L. G. (1999). Killing her softly: Intimate abuse and the violence of state intervention. *Harvard Law Review*, 113, 550–613.

Monchalin, L. (2016). *The colonial problem: An Indigenous perspective on injustice and crime in Canada.* Toronto: University of Toronto Press.

Monchalin, L., & Marques, O. (2013). Preventing crime and poor health among Aboriginal people: The potential for preventative programming. *First Peoples Child and Family Review*, 7(2), 112–129.

Nancarrow, H. (2007). In search of justice for domestic and family violence: Indigenous and non-Indigenous Australian women's perspectives. *Theoretical Criminology*, 10(1), 87–106.

National Collaborating Centre for Aboriginal Health. (2012). *The state of knowledge of Aboriginal health: A review of Aboriginal public health in Canada.* Prince George, BC: NCCAH.

Native Women's Association of Canada (NWAC). (2010). *What their stories tell us: Research findings from the Sisters in Spirit Initiative.* Ottawa: NWAC.

Norris, T., Vines, P. L., & Hoeffiel, E. M. (2012). The American Indian and Alaska Native population: 2010. *2010 Census Briefs*. Washington, DC: US Census Bureau.

O'Donnell, V., & Wallace, S. (2011). First Nations, Métis, and Inuit women. In *Women in Canada: A gender-based statistical report, 2010–2011*. Ottawa: Statistics Canada.

Oppal, W. T. (2012). *Forsaken: The report of the Missing Women Commission of Inquiry.* Vancouver: Government of British Columbia. Retrieved from http://www.ag.gov.bc.ca/public_inquiries/docs/Forsaken-ES.pdf

Razack, S. H. (1998). *Looking White people in the eye: Gender, race, and culture in courtrooms and classrooms.* Toronto: University of Toronto Press.

Razack, S. H. (2000). Gendered racial violence and spatialized justice: The murder of Pamela George. *Canadian Journal of Law and Society*, 15(2), 91–130.

Reid, J. (2010). The Doctrine of Discovery and Canadian law. *Canadian Journal of Native Studies*, 2, 335–359.

Royal Canadian Mounted Police (RCMP). (2014). *Missing and murdered Aboriginal women: A national operational overview.* Retrieved from http://www.rcmp-grc.gc.ca/pubs/mmaw-faapd-eng.html

RCMP. (2015). *Missing and murdered Aboriginal women: 2015 Update to the national operational overview.* Retrieved from http://www.rcmp-grc.gc.ca/pubs/abo-aut/mmaw-fada-eng.pdf

Ross, R. (1996). *Returning to the teachings: Exploring Aboriginal justice.* Toronto: Penguin.

Ross, R. (2014). *Indigenous healing: Exploring traditional paths.* Toronto: Penguin.

Sheptycki, L. W. G. (1991). Using the state to change society: The example of domestic violence. *Journal of Human Justice, 3*(1), 47–66.

Sherman, L. W. (1992). The influence of criminology on criminal law: Evaluating arrests for misdemeanor domestic violence. *The Journal of Criminal Law and Criminology, 83*(1), 1–45.

Sherman, L. W., & Berk, R. A. (1984). *The Minneapolis domestic violence experiment.* Washington, DC: Police Foundation.

Sinha, V., & Kozlowski, A. (2013). The structure of Aboriginal child welfare in Canada. *International Indigenous Policy Journal, 4*(2). Retrieved from http://ir.lib.uwo.ca/cgi/viewcontent.cgi?article=1127&context=iipj

Smith, A. (2005). *Conquest: Sexual violence and the American Indian genocide.* Cambridge: South End Press.

Smith, A. (2014). Human rights and decolonization. In J. Green (Ed.), *Indivisible: Indigenous human rights* (pp. 83–97). Winnipeg: Fernwood Publishing.

Statistics Canada. (2013). *Aboriginal peoples in Canada: First Nations people, Métis, and Inuit.* Catalogue no. 99-011-X2011001. Ottawa: Statistics Canada.

Stote, K. (2012). The coercive sterilization of Aboriginal women in Canada. *American Indian Culture and Research Journal, 36*(3), 117–150.

Stote, K. (2015). *An act of genocide: Colonialism and the sterilization of Aboriginal women.* Winnipeg: Fernwood Publishing.

Taylor, A. (2002). *American colonies: The settling of North America.* New York: Penguin Books.

Treaties and Historical Research Centre. (1978). *The historical development of the Indian Act* (2nd ed.). Ottawa: Indian and Northern Affairs. Retrieved from http://www.kitselas.com/images/uploads/docs/The_Historical_Development_of_the_Indian_Act_Aug_1978.pdf

Truth and Reconciliation Commission of Canada. (2015). What we have learned: Principles of truth and reconciliation. Winnipeg: TRC. Retrieved from http://www.trc.ca/websites/trcinstitution/File/2015/Findings/Principles_2015_05_31_web_0.pdf

Van Kirk, S. (1980). *Many tender ties: Women in fur-trade society, 1670–1870.* Norman: University of Oklahoma Press.

Venne, S. H. (1998). *Our elders understand our rights: Evolving international law regarding Indigenous peoples.* Penticton, BC: Theytus Books.

Wesley-Esquimaux, C. C., & Smolewski, M. (2004). *Historic trauma and Aboriginal healing.* Ottawa: Aboriginal Healing Foundation.

CHAPTER 7

Dead and Gone: The Crisis of the Justice System's Non-response to the Deaths of Canadian Youth of Somali Descent

Ahmed Ilmi

Chapter Objectives

This chapter will help the reader develop an understanding of the ways in which law enforcement officials have failed to solve more than 60 murder cases in Alberta and Ontario of young Canadian males, who were born and or/raised in Ontario, Canada, of Somali descent. There is a need for society as a whole to look at unequal outcomes when it comes to issues of policing and justice.

Introduction

To critically examine the unequal outcomes of justice in an age in which debates about public safety are at the centre of our national conversations, it is essential to highlight some of the systemic challenges that contribute to miscarriages in the justice system. While there are many theories explaining how and/or why so many young Canadian men of Somali descent get killed, the lack of law enforcement response raises an alarm with regard to the value that we place on some lives and not others. In this chapter, I raise questions of identity, race, ethnicity, and citizenship to interrogate which lives are worthy of police commitment and which communities are underserved. I also look at the ways in which the Canadian Somali community is often scapegoated to account for the justice system's lack of response.

On June 2, 2012, a young man opened fire at a packed food court in Toronto's world-renowned Eaton Centre. A total of five people were shot. Twenty-four-year-old Ahmed Hassan died as a result of his injuries on the scene, while Nixon Nirmalendran died in hospital nine days later. This horrific incident received media attention from both local and international news agencies, including CNN, NBC, BBC, Al-Jazeera, CityTV, and CBC. Toronto police chief Bill Blair told a sea of reporters that "this shooting was not only wanton and incredibly dangerous, but also reckless as to the safety of others" (Taylor, 2012). He also went on to state that Hassan may have had some gang affiliation, and that this might have been a targeted killing. In response to public outrage over questions of public safety, many government officials took the stage and promised a swift response.

Given that this was not the first time that a young Black male had been shot in Toronto, why was this particular case different? Why did it get so much attention? Shouldn't all shootings of Black/African males be a question of public safety? Judging from the infamous Summer of the Gun in Toronto in 2005, when a total of 52 mostly Black male victims succumbed to their untimely deaths, giving equal treatment and relevance to their lives does not appear to be the case (Siciliano, 2010). What makes the Eaton Centre shooting different? The primary issue or question then becomes: Does the justice system place different value on the lives of Black bodies who are victims of crime? And if so, what are the factors that determine which lives are more worthy of police investigation and which murders get the necessary police support to solve the crimes?

Law Enforcement and Community Relationships

Racialized communities in Canada have historically been subjected to racial discrimination at the hands of law enforcement agencies. Discriminatory prejudice
stems from the unjust connection made by law enforcement between Blackness
and crime that dates back to the days of colonial settlement in the Americas,
and the history of slavery. Racialized communities have always been policed
differently, with an overrepresentation of Blacks in the justice system and an
underrepresentation of Black victims who experience fair treatment through
legal means. In the name of law and order, racialized communities are criminalized and subject to unequal, dehumanizing treatment. Numerous studies have
shown that Blacks/Africans are racially profiled and are subject to apprehension
and questioning without probable cause (see Chan & Chunn, 2014; Tanovich,
2006; Tator & Henry, 2006; Wortley & Owusu-Bempah, 2011). In recent years
there has been the emergence of the unconstitutional police practice of carding, in which police officers target Blacks/Africans and other ethnic minorities,
in particular young males; collect their personal information; and put it into a
database (see Meng, Giwa & Anucha, 2015; Owusu-Bempah & Wortley, 2014;
Rankin & Winsa, 2013). The logic behind this discriminatory police practice
is that young Black/African males are more likely to commit crimes, therefore
they ought to stopped and questioned. The labelling of Black males as prone to
criminality marks their deaths as being less deserving of police investigation
and resources than other members of the society because Black males represent
"the usual suspects."

On October 31, 2008, the body of 21-year-old Abas Abukar, a former Humber
College student, was found in Northmount Park in Edmonton, where he had
moved from Toronto four months earlier. About a month later, Abdulkadir
Mohamoud, 23, was also found shot to death in a park. He had also also moved
from Toronto, about two years prior to being killed (Aulakh, 2010). Violent
accounts of this nature signify the realities to which so many young Canadians
of Somali descent have fallen victim. One might raise the argument that policing and the justice system are distinctly different. But to truly understand the
historically rooted systemic inequalities that have resulted in the deaths of over
60 young Canadian males of Somali descent, one has to look at the ways in which
racism operates and manifests itself in Canadian society.

Historical Background

Members of the Somali community began arriving in Canada in the early 1990s to escape political upheaval in Somalia. The Somali community primarily settled in southern Ontario, in cities such as Ottawa and Toronto. Over the past two decades, Somalis have built communities and integrated into Canadian society like the immigrant communities that came before them. Canada has a reputation for being a tolerant society; however, racism and racial oppression have been experienced by all racialized immigrant communities, and members of the Somali community, as an African/Muslim population, continue to face systemic discrimination in employment, education, housing, and the justice system.

This discrimination in the justice system is especially visible when looking at the number of unresolved murder cases of young Canadian males of Somali descent from 2008 to 2015, which exceeds 60 cases. The majority of victims were born and/or raised in Ontario, but migrated to Alberta in search of employment opportunities shortly after the oil boom began in 2005. The concentration of these murders took place in the cities of Calgary, Edmonton, and Fort McMurray. The majority of these cases were reported in the media as senseless, violent crimes connected to gangs and drugs (Howlett, 2015; Spencer & Austin, 2011), and the victims were painted as foreign nationals with no roots in Canada. As such, these youth are always identified as Somalis (i.e., foreigners) in the media and not as Canadians of Somali heritage (see Dykstra, 2013; Hanon, 2011; Roth, 2011). The categorization of these youth as Somali in the media is problematic because it identifies who is marked as a citizen, thus indicating which crimes are regarded as worthy of attention by the authorities. This line of thinking allows for differential, unequal treatment in policing matters by creating a binary of deserving versus undeserving category/community vis-à-vis the Somali immigrant. It also permits one to connect questions of law and order in Canada to political instability in Somalia. The civil war and human devastation in that country has been well documented in Western media and movies for several years. Therefore, the assumption made about these youth by the media, law enforcement, and greater society is that they come from a violent society and that they have brought their violent culture with them to Canada, thus underscoring what has been referred to as the importation model of crime (Hall, Critcher, Jefferson, Clarke, & Roberts, 2013).

The construction of the deaths of Canadians of Somali descent as resulting from political disorder that is occurring in a foreign space enables authorities and the general public to treat these homicides as a Somali problem, rather than a Canadian issue. Given that the deaths are regarded as a foreign issue, there is limited public pressure on police agencies in both Ontario and Alberta to force them to allocate personnel resources and mandate policy changes and programs to respond to these unresolved homicides. When trying to make sense of the number of unresolved murders, one has to look at issues of identity, policing, and the broader justice system to make sense of how they are understood in society. While theoretically crime and punishment is straightforward in our democratic society, the reality is quite different when looking at racial minority communities and law enforcement. As such, Canadian youth of Somali descent have been constructed as hyperviolent criminals unworthy of justice.

The Undeserving Menace to Society

As peoples of African heritage, Somalis might not have traditionally categorized themselves as Black, as markers like ethnicity, nationality, and religion have historically had greater significance within the North American context. However, once the community arrived in North America, it was read as Black and was faced with the social reality of becoming Black. The concept of Black male youth hypercriminality is connected to the ways in which Canadian youth of Somali descent are further marginalized in our society. In fact, one of the biggest obstacles to full social participation and inclusion is the overcriminalization and social exclusion of this group as an undeserving underclass in our society. The majority of these youth have been raised in Toronto's low-income neighbourhoods (Anderson, 2010) and are therefore seen as troubled youth. These youth occupy multiple sites of intersecting oppressions, including identities as Somali, Black, Muslim, African, immigrant, and poor; therefore, often when these young men find themselves outside of their local Toronto neighbourhoods, they are immediately marked as outsiders to the space, thus increasing the level of scrutiny to which they are exposed. The general societal and mainstream institutions impose a criminal Black youth identity on these individuals. This new social reality has deep implications for how the community is seen in society, where the community fits into the Canadian landscape, and how the justice system interacts with its members.

The upsurge in the number of deaths of young Somali men between 2005 and 2014 in Alberta has been attributed to three factors. The first factor is that these young men were lured to the booming Alberta drug trade by the prospect of making up to $5,000 a day (see Wingrove & Mackrael, 2012). The second is that they were in the wrong place at the wrong time (Aulakh, 2010). The third is that many of these young men have difficulty finding viable employment because of the racial oppression that they face in the job market and in society at large (Feagin, Vera, & Batur, 2001). With Alberta's booming illegal drug trade, estimated at $5 billion a year (Aulakh, 2010), the lure of making quick money becomes too good to resist, and consequently these youth become trapped in an unforgiving underworld. The drug trade creates a get-rich-quick mindset in these youth and leads them to a very risky lifestyle, despite coming from strong families and having strong community ties. These young men may also regard their involvement in the drug trade as an opportunity to escape the inevitability of poverty, provide options for caring for their families, and afford them the opportunity of performing a role as the male breadwinner.

The Question of Urban Youth Identity: The Increasing Body Count

When looking at the unresolved murders of Canadian men of Somali descent, their cultural location within both Canadian society and their diaspora communities should not be overlooked. The reality is that in the North American context, African identities are marked by histories of racialization (see hooks, 1992; Ibrahim, 2008; Omi & Winant, 1998; West, 2000). As such, these youth occupy multiple worlds that they are expected to fit into and navigate. What is unique about this generation is that they often find themselves in a peculiar space where there is a tension between the values and expectations of their parents and the broader Canadian values that they have been exposed to through their experiences of living in Canada (see Anderson, 2010). This tension largely arises from Somali parents expecting their children to be responsible members of their community and to become productive members of society. Consequently, most of these youths left their home province of Ontario in search of employment and a better life for themselves and their families. Racism, social exclusion, and joblessness in Ontario, where youth jobless rates in 2014 were approximately 15.8 percent (Labour Market Information Division, 2014), are factors that push youth toward the booming economy of Alberta; however, the markers of social exclusion are also evident in Alberta, and the limited options for viable employment for Somali youth may drive these youth to make reckless decisions such as getting involved in the drug trade. Their involvement in the drug trade would not be condoned by their family or community and, as such, these youth find themselves out of place in their family homes and communities, as well as in mainstream Canadian society (see Ibrahim, 2008). In an attempt to remain connected to their family and community, however, these young men perform two distinct identities: one for their family homes and community, and one to deal with the tough realities they are faced with in the drug game and the outside world. This duality of identity performances, which are at times conflicting, makes it extremely difficult for family members and the greater Somali community to intervene when their sons start getting pulled into dangerous situations, and family members and loved ones often find out about the situation when it is too late. This dual identity performance has powerful implications for these youths self-perceptions in relation to how they interact in their multiple worlds. They have a difficult time exposing their drug-involved lifestyle to their family, while at the same time they are not fully accepted in mainstream society or into the drug underworld (see chapter 8 of this text) (Ngo, Calhoun, Worthington, Pyrch, & Este, 2010). The rationale for these youth is that if they are facing discrimination and racism in all spheres of society, why should they try to fit in at all. This causes a fragmentation of the self, which can be psychologically demoralizing (see Du Bois, 1989; Fanon, 1967; Ilmi, 2012; Wa Thiong'o, 1993); therefore grasping this predicament is fundamental to understanding the logic behind some of the choices made by these young men, and the potential supports or programming that can be put in place for them at the societal and community levels.

One of the most detrimental misconceptions held by some members of the Somali community, and the larger society as well, about the deaths of so many young Canadian Somalis is that these men were all drug traffickers, and as such their lives do not matter. This group of males has often been referred to as the "lost generation" (Wingrove & Mackrael, 2012). The labelling of these males as criminals, which also marks them as undeserving of societal investment, produces a logic that is articulated outside of questions of law, order, and justice in Canadian society. In other words, the construction of undeservingness is accompanied by the idea that these deaths do not require the involvement of the justice system, and that they can be regarded as an efficient form of street justice—"they got what the deserved!" This perspective reflects who is seen as fit to possess a Canadian identity, and the resulting impact of not being seen as a part of the Canadian social fabric. Without understanding how identities are rooted in specific and intersecting contexts, we risk being caught in a dehumanizing predicament in which communities gripped by violence, which are most often subjected to injustices, are asked to accept ongoing systemic injustices. How can we placidly accept the injustices faced by some communities in our society? How can we make sense of the ways in which some bodies are seen as undeserving of justice in our democratic society? And further, should we learn to accept the unfair and imbalanced ways in which the various strands of the justice system respond to different communities?

The lack of prosecutions and convictions with respect to these homicides inadvertently highlights that these African/Black bodies do not matter to law enforcement officials (Hall et al., 2013), and it is precisely because their lives are deemed unworthy that Canadians of Somali descent can be killed without prosecution of their killers. The implication is that Canadian youth of Somali descent are seen as a social threat within mainstream society and, as such, when they are being killed in local communities, their identities are rendered invisible and they become nothing more than a body count. Nothing stresses this predicament more than the number of homicides of Canadian Somali males that took place in Alberta from 2005 to 2009. The deaths of youths born and/or raised in Canada can occur and be reported in the news, and yet there have been virtually no arrests. We must question why the justice system has failed these victims and their loved ones and critically examine policing culture and the discourses that determine which deaths are worthy of being investigated.

"No Snitching": No One Is Co-operating with Our Investigation

"No snitching" refers to a street code that prevents offenders from co-operating with police, which would often result in material rewards, to implicate perpetrators of crimes (Whitehill, Webster, Frattaroli, & Parker, 2014). To solve crimes, police officers rely heavily on eyewitness accounts and the co-operation of the general public. In the event that there are no witnesses, witnesses do not come forward, or members of the general public choose not to assist with the investigation, the police use forensic evidence to solve crimes. Law enforcement agencies have always worked with and gathered intelligence on criminals and criminal organizations to penetrate this underworld (Marx, 1988). Limited co-operation on the part of witnesses and the general public to provide information to the police has been highlighted as an obstacle to solving the homicides of Canadian Somali males in Alberta vis-à-vis the "no snitching" street code (see Anderson, 2010; Wingrove & Mackrael, 2012; Paikin, 2012). The rationale put forward is that these are hardened criminals and as long as no one co-operates the police cannot solve these murders, but the reality is that it is hard to determine what the facts are when it comes to "no snitching." The police have a duty to keep the general public safe and to continue to investigate cases, regardless of the level of assistance from the public or those involved in the cases; however, the failure on the part of police to solve these multiple murders leaves one to question whether the policing organizations still have a duty to solve those crimes or if they do not have the capacity or skill to do so. The lack of public involvement or "no snitching" cannot be put forward as the reason these cases have remained unsolved. In the cycle of violent crime, "no snitching" becomes an excuse for not solving murder cases; however, a larger issue that needs to be highlighted is the lack of faith in the competency of our police forces and the increasing number of murderers who are left to wander our streets, thus contributing to the moral decay of our society. The "no snitching" street code and the failure to solve these violent crimes creates the social conditions in which these violent crimes can continue with impunity in our society. Another clear message that is sent to these youth is that their lives or deaths are insignificant, thus providing less incentive to positively invest or engage in Canadian society.

Scapegoating the Canadian Somali Community

Members of the Somali community, like most members of any community, are hardworking and law-abiding citizens. One of the most detrimental outcomes of these unresolved murders is the way in which the Canadian Somali community has been marked as deficient and irresponsible in terms of parenting practices, which suggests that they are responsible for these deaths. The failure on the part of the authorities react to these crimes contains the concealed massage that these deaths largely stem from the ungovernability of the Canadian Somali communities of Ontario and Alberta. This message is intimated in three ways. First, there are always historical links made between the crimes and deaths of these young men and the political instability in Somalia. This usually begins with a narrative that suggests that these young men and the community are affected by and connected to the violence in Somalia because their roots are in Mogadishu, the country's capital, which has been regarded as ungovernable because of the prolonged civil war that began in 1991 (see Anderson, 2010; Paikin, 2012). The links between these scenarios are quite difficult if not impossible to prove, particularly given that the young men who were killed were either born in Canada or migrated here during their formative years. Although their parents may have some relation to and been affected by the war, these youth have no direct connections to Somalia's political struggles. Those political conflicts are anchored in a power struggle with major national and international actors with competing interests, who have little to no connection to local Canadian youth violence. The challenges in Somalia are related to a different set of circumstances, which are engrained in ethnic and historical realities of a distant land. The one link that one may be able to establish between the deaths of these young men and the homeland of their parents is whether the young men have been able to form connections that have enabled them to develop drug courier links to Somalia's drug trade. Establishing this link would require further investigation and research. Any comprehensive analysis of the occurrences of violence and murder of these young men requires that we examine how their experiences of schooling, and living and fitting—or not fitting—into Canadian society have pushed them to the margins of society (Ngo et al., 2010).

Second, an argument that has been made and/or implied is that the absence of nurturing father figures (which is often a trope that is advanced to explain the involvement of Black males in criminal activities) has negatively affected these young men (see Ezeonu, 2010). This argument has been driven home by using the voices of Canadian Somali women in the media to convey the message that the homicides of so many young men are unbearable for Somali Canadian mothers, who are inadvertently a representation of the lack of legitimate father figures in the community. The conversations then become focused on the feelings of the grieving mothers, while the need to seek justice is misplaced. Moreover, the young men who are at the centre of this crisis remain voiceless—they are seldom asked or consulted about any matters related to their own issues. By putting forward the concept of fatherlessness and a lack of positive role models as problematic in the Canadian Somali community overshadows and limits the examination of the failures of the justice system and larger society.

Third, the concept of cultural difference is one of the most salient and often unquestioned factors alluded to by law enforcement agencies to explain this problem as a Somali youth problem, rather than a societal issue. In a community struggling to come to terms with these homicides, the issue is not only localized but sensationalized. Principally, the issue is then portrayed as a Somali youth problem with few repercussions for the rest of society; therefore, it is irrelevant to both law enforcement and the greater general public whether the crisis is contained or intensified (Pacentrilli, 2012). This enables law enforcement and the greater society to treat these incidents as exceptions, rather than examining the social, systemic, and structural inequities in the justice system that continue fuelling this social problem. It is, after all, policing organizations and the justice system that are principally responsible for maintaining law and order in our society. Would it ever have been acceptable for over 60 murders to take place in any other community in Canada, with no repercussions? How do we, as a society, collectively account for this gross miscarriage of justice? More importantly, what does that say about our society?

Implications

The issue of community justice is vitally important to the essence of our democracy. It is in this spirit that we question some of the structural and systemic challenges present in our justice system that contribute to unequal outcomes in our society. As a society, we need to engage in questions of community justice for all to strengthen our democracy, and we have to critically examine the ways in which racialized bodies are often unaccounted for in our legal system. Some may argue that because the issues raised in this chapter face the Canadian Somali diaspora and impact that community's youth, the community should collectively search for solutions and provide some answers. There also will be those who will push for the "tough-on-crime" approach and call for more police officers in our communities. But if we are concerned about the realities on the ground, I think that it is time that we move away from playing the blame game and toward a community justice law enforcement approach.

One the of main principles of community justice is that it is a community-oriented approach to crime prevention and is set to improve the quality of life in any given community (Karp & Clear, 2000). Its central focus is community-level outcomes, which shifts the emphasis from individual incidents to systemic patterns and larger structural issues of criminal justice within a community. Moreover, it is built on the need to collaborate with and engage communities in constructive dialogue about local justice and empowering the community (Karp & Clear, 2000). Therefore, we must creatively think of ways to develop a community justice model that could address issues of crime and punishment in the Canadian Somali community. This is not going to be an easy task. Nevertheless, we as a society must provide answers as to why there have been so many homicides of Canadian youth of Somali descent.

Conclusion

This chapter examines the failure of law enforcement agencies to solve more than 60 murder cases of young Canadian males of Somali descent in Alberta and Ontario. In this chapter, I critically examined notions of race, ethnicity, citizenship, and belonging to highlight the ways in which they impact how policing is conducted in the Canadian Somali community. I also looked at the ways in which the Canadian Somali community is often scapegoated for the violence that grips the community.

It is with a profound sense of urgency that we as a society need to rethink questions of policing and justice for all. In highlighting some of the systemic challenges imposed on Canadian youth of Somali descent that are largely responsible, in my view, for the unresolved homicides, in addition to trying to identify the causes of these deaths, we also need to ensure that our analysis can collectively account for the unequal outcomes that are entrenched in our legal system. When considering how public accountability informs how community policing is conducted, we need to challenge the ways in which some social ills in our society are ascribed to racialized bodies, in this case Canadian Somalis, and demand results from our law enforcement agencies. Questions of public safety are at the centre of national interest; however, global influence must be considered. We must examine the deep-seated values that make us Canadian and reflect on the realities faced by racial and ethnic minorities in our society. This chapter is timely in an age where violence against, and murders of, Black men are being sensationalized in American media and audiences around the world are consuming this violence, while the acquittals of those who commit the murders are being witnessed by millions. It is not acceptable for us in Canada to say that we are not the United States. It is time that we as a society start thinking about what justice looks like for young Canadian Somalis and all members of society. How many more young men have to be killed before we start paying attention? How do we socialize young African/Black boys in our society? How do we criminalize them? How does their unequal treatment in schools and the classroom socially exclude them from becoming full members of our society? Without hesitation, we should hold all violent criminals accountable for their actions—but we are also all ultimately responsible for the miscarriages of justice that occur in our democratic society.

Discussion Questions

1. How can we account for the disparities in the delivery of justice in our society?
2. Does the justice system place different value on the lives of racialized bodies who are victims of crime?
3. How can we address some of the injustices faced by some communities in our society?
4. What is our collective responsibility for building a more equitable justice system?

Additional Resources

Bader, V. (1995). Citizenship and Exclusion: Radical Democracy, Community, and Justice. Or, What Is Wrong with Communitarianism? *Political Theory, 23*(2), 211–246.

Daly, K., & Stubbs, J. (2006). Feminist Engagement with Restorative Justice. *Theoretical Criminology, 10*(1), 9–28.

Miller, D., & Walzer, M. (1995). *Pluralism, Justice, and Equality*. New York: Oxford University Press.

Spergel, I. A. (1995). *The Youth Gang Problem: A Community Approach*. New York: Oxford University Press.

Tan, K. C. (2004). *Justice without Borders: Cosmopolitanism, Nationalism, and Patriotism*. Cambridge: Cambridge University Press.

Young, I. M. (2011). *Justice and the Politics of Difference*. Princeton, NJ: Princeton University Press.

References

Anderson, S. (2010). The life and death of Abdinasir Dirie. [Television broadcast]. *The Fifth Estate*. CBC.

Aulakh, R. (2010, March 22). Somali-Canadians caught in Alberta's deadly drug trade. *Toronto Star*, A22.

Chan, W., & Chunn, D. (2014). *Racialization, crime, and criminal justice in Canada*. Toronto: University of Toronto Press.

Du Bois, W. E. B. (1989). *The souls of Black folks*. New York: Penguin Books.

Dykstra, M. (2013, March 21). Police continue to offer $40,000 cash rewards for help in solving slayings from Edmonton's Somali community. *Edmonton Sun*. Retrieved from http://www.edmontonsun.com/2013/03/21/police-continue-to-offer-40000-cash-rewards-for-help-in-solving-slayings-from-edmontons-somali-community

Ezeonu, I. (2010). Gun violence in Toronto: Perspectives from the police. *Howard Journal of Criminal Justice, 49*(2), 147–165.

Fanon, F. (1967). *The wretched of the earth*. New York: Grove Weidenfeld.

Feagin, J. R., Vera, H., & Batur, P. (2001). *White racism: The basics*. New York: Routledge.

Hall, S., Critcher, C., Jefferson, T., Clarke, J., & Roberts, B. (2013). *Policing the crisis: Mugging, the state, and law and order* (2nd ed.) New York: Palgrave Macmillan.

Hanon, A. (2011, January 30). Killings of young Somali men a complex story. *Edmonton Sun*. Retrieved from http://www.hiiraan.com/news2/2011/jan/killings_of_young_somali_men_a_complex_story.aspx

Howlett, K. (2015, January 2). Man killed in Calgary mass shooting had record for assault, drugs. *Globe and Mail*, A5.

hooks, b. (1992). *Black looks*. Boston: South End Press.

Ibrahim, A. (2008). The new *flâneur*: Subaltern cultural studies, African youth in Canada, and the semiology of in-betweenness. *Cultural Studies, 22*(2), 234–253.

Ilmi, A. (2012). Living the Indigenous ways of knowing: The African self and a holistic way of life. *Journal of Pan African Studies, 11*(9), 148–160.

Karp, D. R., & Clear, T. R. (2000). Community justice: A conceptual framework. *Boundary Changes in Criminal Justice Organizations, 2*, 323–368.

Labour Market Information Division. (2014). Labour Market Bulletin—Ontario: March 2014. Ottawa: Employment and Social Development Canada. Retrieved from http://www.esdc.gc.ca/eng/jobs/lmi/publications/bulletins/on/mar2014.shtml

Marx, G. T. (1988). *Undercover: Police surveillance in America*. Berkeley: University of California Press.

Meng, Y., Giwa, S., & Anucha, U. (2015). Is there racial discrimination in police stop-and-searches of Black youth? A Toronto case study. *Canadian Journal of Family and Youth/Le Journal Canadien de Famille et de la Jeunesse, 7*(1), 115–148.

Ngo, H. V., Calhoun, A., Worthington, C., Pyrch, T., & Este, D. (2010). The unravelling of identities and belonging: Criminal gang involvement of youth from immigrant families. *Journal of International Migration and Integration*, 1–22.

Omi, M., & Winant, H. (1998). Racial formations. In P. Rothenberg (Ed.), *Race, class, and gender in the United States* (pp. 13–49). New York: St. Martin's Press.

Owusu-Bempah, A., & Wortley, S. (2014). Race, crime, and criminal justice in Canada. In S. Bucerius & M. Tonry (Eds.), *The Oxford handbook of ethnicity, crime, and immigration* (pp. 281–320). New York: Oxford University Press.

Pacentrilli, F. (2012, April 26). Talking to the dead [Video file]. Retrieved from https://www.youtube.com/watch?v=82Bm4g949S4.

Paikin, S. (2012). Somali-Canadian killings [Television broadcast]. *The agenda with Steve Paikin.* TVO. Retrieved from https://www.youtube.com/watch?v=3ktILEAVtQs

Rankin, J., & Winsa, P. (2013, August 21). Known to police: Toronto police stop and document Black and Brown people far more than Whites. *Toronto Star*, A9.

Roth, B. (2011, June 6). The latest homicide victim was Somali. [Video]. *Edmonton Sun*. Retrieved from http://www.edmontonsun.com/videos/979651344001.

Siciliano, A. M. (2010). *Policing poverty: Race, space and the fear of crime after the year of the gun (2005) in suburban Toronto.* Doctoral thesis, University of Toronto.

Spencer, K., & Austin, I. (2011, November 10). Gangs a threat to refugee kids. *The Province*, A3.

Tanovich, D. M. (2006). The colour of justice: Policing race in Canada. *Windsor Review of Legal and Social Issues, 22,* 105–117.

Tator, C., & Henry, F. (2006). *Racial profiling in Canada: Challenging the myth of "a few bad apples."* Toronto: University of Toronto Press.

Taylor, L. (2012, June 3). Eaton Centre shooting: One dead, seven injured. *Toronto Star*. Retrieved from https://www.thestar.com/news/gta/2012/06/03/eaton_centre_shooting_one_dead_seven_injured.html

Wa Thiong'o, N. (1993). *Moving the center: The struggle for cultural freedoms.* London: James Curry.

West, C. (2000). *Race matters.* Boston: Beacon.

Whitehill, J. M., Webster, D. W., Frattaroli, S., & Parker, E. M. (2014). Interrupting violence: How the CeaseFire Program prevents imminent gun violence through conflict mediation. *Journal of Urban Health, 91*(1), 84–95.

Wingrove, J., & Mackrael, K. (2012, June 22). Why so many Somali-Canadians who go west end up dead. *Globe and Mail.*

Wortley, S., & Owusu-Bempah, A. (2011). The usual suspects: Police stop-and-search practices in Canada. *Policing and Society, 21*(4), 395–407.

CHAPTER 8

South Asian Youth and the Justice System

Beverly-Jean M. Daniel and *Sabra Desai*

Chapter Objectives

Some youth find themselves caught up in a socio-economic, educational, political, and cultural vortex, often not of their own making, that might lead to criminal behaviour. This article explores why it is necessary to examine the involvement of South Asian youth in activities that might be deemed criminal for the purposes of informing prevention, intervention, strategies, support, advocacy, and reintegration services. This chapter provides a context for the need for research and examination of issues of crime and criminal activities among South Asian youth in Canada. Through this work, we are seeking to open up spaces for dialogue and make it possible to challenge the silences and identify the issues and options for collective community-based approaches to intervention.

Introduction: Why We Need to Address This Issue

Community justice and applied social justice require developing an understanding of the existing communities and groups that will come into contact with the justice system. Knowledge and understanding of communities can help inform prevention and intervention strategies that can limit youth involvement in crime. Moreover, this work can inform support services when youth come into contact with the justice system and ensure that effective advocacy and reintegration services are available.

There is limited research on the involvement of South Asians in crime. The term *South Asian*, for the purposes of this chapter, refers to very diverse peoples whose ancestry or origins can be traced to the Indian subcontinent, including the countries of Bangladesh, India, Nepal, Pakistan, and Sri Lanka. Knowledge of the patterns of and responses to crime and criminality within South Asian communities can ensure that community justice workers have a more comprehensive understanding of the patterns that moves beyond stereotypes to ensure better service provision to these communities. According to Ngo (2010), conducting research on these issues within ethnoracial communities "encourages informed dialogues on the intersections of crime, immigration, and intergroup relations, and invites critical examination of Canada's immigration and multiculturalism policies, and responsiveness of the existing policies and services for youth from immigrant families" (p. 2). This chapter aims to explore the growing challenge of South Asian youth involved in criminal activities and the factors that promote that involvement. It also seeks to open up discussion about the importance of developing culturally based services to address the needs of the community.

As Canadian society becomes increasingly diverse and the number of second-generation immigrant youth continues to grow, it is necessary to move beyond the stereotype of the "model minority" (Yonemura Wing, 2007) when referring to South Asians (Indians, Pakistanis, etc.). This shift is important in order to examine the needs, barriers, and challenges of youth from these communities. Failing to do so can limit effective social interventions on a systemic level. This chapter is aimed at examining the emerging patterns of crime in South Asian communities, which collectively form the largest group of visible racialized people in Canada. According to the 2009 Census, there were 1.26 million people of South Asian descent in Canada, with approximately 684,000 in the Greater Toronto Area (GTA).

Despite the sizable population of South Asians in Canada, there is limited research on South Asian communities in relation to crime and justice that examines issues other than those related to spousal abuse. The authors recognize that there are multiple social, cultural, religious, and geographic diversities that exist within what has, in Canada, been termed the "South Asian community" (Ashutosh, 2008; Desai & Subramanian, 2003); however, the lack of comprehensive research on this group makes it difficult to separate the information into distinct categories that would allow for a clear analysis based on these diversities. It is not the intention of the authors to assume that the patterns and discussions that emerge within this chapter should be taken as representative of the entire community when referring to South Asians.

Thandi (2013) uses the term *communities* in his work and makes the argument that as much as we must recognize the many differences within the South Asian community, "it is equally important to recognize the commonalities found within South Asian communities in order to best serve their needs" (p. 212). This chapter aims to open up a conversation that will foster dialogue regarding the way in which the justice system addresses or fails to address the needs of South Asian communities in general and, more specifically, youth. Moreover, this chapter calls for more comprehensive exploration of and further research into the area of crime and criminality within the community, with the aim of developing effective proactive and preventive measures to address these issues.

History and Social Construction of South Asians

It is important to state that persons who have been identified as South Asian, specifically of Sikh heritage, have been in Vancouver, British Columbia, Canada, since the early 1900s (Asia/Canada, n.d.). After decades of anti-Indian legal and social racist practices (Henry & Tator, 2006), the loosening of immigration restrictions in the 1970s and the change to a point-based immigration system, which focused on increasing the number of skilled immigrants, led to a significant increase in the number of South Asian immigrants. The point system considered factors such as capacity to speak English or French, educational levels, work experience or skill levels, and a person's ability to adapt to a Canadian context, which included level of familial supports available to the applicant (Government of Canada, 2015). Many South Asian immigrants settled in the GTA in Ontario, as well as within larger urban centres in the other provinces, a pattern that many immigrants adopt (Li, 2000). In their early years in Vancouver, South Asians were regarded as dangerous, dirty, and a blight to society (Indra, 1979).

In more recent times, South Asians have often been referred to as a "model minority" group. They are seen as hardworking and industrious and as easily able to join the existing system with little or no challenge to the established power base. On the surface, this can be regarded as a positive label. In reality, this term essentially silences the group and is used in a way that limits opportunities for South Asians to challenge the system and engage in any sustained critique of systemic inequities. Moreover, this notion of model minority plays into the silencing that goes on within the South Asian communities due to cultural concepts of *sharam*, or shame, and *izhat*, or respect or honour, which are used as internal mechanisms of control and silencing all in the name of not bringing attention to the communities. However, as Ralston (1999) argues, it is important to recognize that although immigrants are active participants in the construction of their own identities, race, class, and power also play a critical role given that the dominant group of a society plays a primary part in construction of the "immigrant" identity. Further to this, it could be argued that this construction as the model minority and the resulting silencing limits dialogue across ethnoracialized minorities who are affected in similar ways by systemic oppression.

Another aspect of the model minority stereotype is the assumption that the group is academically strong (Yonemura Wing, 2007); the drawback of this is that those students who struggle often do not have a voice or a platform to identify their concerns (Navaratnam, 2011). This can result in the ongoing marginalization of South Asian students who may have learning disabilities or simply different learning styles that make it difficult for them to excel within the regular education system. If these students are not provided with the supports and tools they need to succeed, the resulting impact will be growing numbers of South Asian students who are increasingly frustrated by and disconnected from the school system. Although South Asian students have been regarded as overly focused on academics, they experience various forms of marginalization and exclusion (Houshmand, Spanierman, & Tafarodi, 2014). South Asian students face the ongoing challenges of effectively integrating into the existing school system, experiencing schooling as positive, and being able to build encouraging and supportive relationships with school staff (Navaratnam, 2011). Another challenge of this model minority status is that it limits the possibility of developing allies across groups that are also affected by oppression in Canada because these groups tend to be pitted against each other.

Disengagement from school can lead increasing numbers of South Asian students, particularly males, to drop out of school and end up on the streets; from there they can be drawn into crime and gangs, as reported by workers within the South Asian settlement and integration sectors. Furthermore, being seen as going against the goals and expectations of parents can result in the young person being labelled as a failure, bringing shame to the family (Navaratnam, 2011) and potentially leading to being rejected by both family and community.

Geographies of Race and Patterns of Settlement

Although Canada is known as a multicultural nation, the patterns of the areas in which people reside are marked by identifiable racialized geographies; people often settle into areas of the city where there are members of their own racial, ethnic, cultural, or religious communities. These ethnic enclaves are quite evident among some members of the South Asian community, which has led to changes in the population demographics of areas of cities that would historically have been predominantly White suburbs. For example, there was a significant increase in the number of South Asians who settled in Brampton and the Peel Region in Ontario between 2001 and 2006 (Kataure & Walton-Roberts, 2013). Markham and Vaughan, also in Ontario, have also seen increasing numbers of South Asians. This has led to the pattern of "White flight," the concept that explains the movement of Whites out of a neighbourhood as a reaction to racialized groups moving in. Brampton and Markham, which were once seen as great places to raise families, are now regarded as places for Whites to leave (Grewal, 2013). Brampton, for example, is often referred to as "Bramladesh" and "Browntown," both terms that are used in derogatory ways.

In areas where White flight occurs, there is typically a reduction in the quality of public services and the level of government funding for social services, housing, justice services, and schooling. The explanation provided for this reduction in funding is often connected to the decline in the tax base (Haines, n.d.), wherein the level of funding that is put back into the community is determined by the level of taxes that its community members pay. Therefore, if Whites have historically had better paying jobs due to colonization, systemic and institutional racism, and racial exclusion, racialized communities moving into White areas are unable to contribute to the tax base in the same way and then see a reduction in the amount of money being returned to the community. Bell and Machin (2013), in their research on immigrant enclaves, indicate that the socio-economic stability of an immigrant enclave can impact crime levels in those neighbourhoods. Higher income ethnic enclaves experience reduced levels of crime, while those that have higher levels of poverty experience higher levels of crime.

Geography and Poverty in the Greater Toronto Area (GTA)

According to statistics released in August 2014 by the City of Toronto, the rate of poverty in Toronto continues to grow and, in some areas of the city that have high numbers of visibly racialized populations, the rate of child/youth (0 to 17 years of age) poverty ranges from 30 to 50 percent (Hulchanski, 2007). In addition to this, the report indicates that approximately 24 percent of South

Asian families live at or below the poverty line. The *Three Cities within Toronto* report (Hulchanski, 2007) indicates that from 1970 to 2005, levels of poverty increased significantly in Toronto and the middle-class population declined. The report also shows a link between areas that have high immigrant populations and poverty. Peel Region, which includes the cities of Brampton, Mississauga, and Oakville, has seen a significant increase in the number of new and recent immigrants. According to the 2011 report *Portraits of Peel: A Community Left Behind*, 33 percent of the region's recent immigrants live in poverty, one-third of all violent crime involves youth, and the region has experienced a 40 percent increase in domestic disturbances since 2005. In addition to this, Peel Region receives significantly lower social service funding than other regions in the GTA.

Along with the patterns identified above, from 2009 to 2010 there were over 5,700 child abuse investigations by the Children's Aid Society in the Peel Region (*Portraits of Peel*, 2011). All of these factors create conditions that can potentially promote increased involvement of some residents with the criminal justice system and escalate challenges in this region. Although there are benefits to living in ethnic enclaves, such as shared language, cultures, and customs (Bell & Machin, 2013), crime levels within them will most likely increase since they are affected by high levels of poverty, increasing levels of violence, and challenges with an expanding youth population. However, Canada's failure to acknowledge and address issues relating to racial, ethnic, religious, and cultural differences within and amongst groups in society limits the ability or willingness to conduct research on this topic. This makes it challenging to understand the context that leads to criminal involvement and limits the opportunity to develop and implement effective options for reducing criminal activities and the impact of crime and criminality on the affected communities.

Factors That Can Lead to Criminal Involvement of Youth within South Asian Communities

In the previous sections, we discussed some of the factors that can lead to criminal involvement in general, including poverty, social exclusion, marginalization, and disengagement from schooling. In this section, we will explore the factors that, although not exclusive to South Asian communities, do play a significant role in increasing the probability that members of this community may come into contact with the justice system in Canada. These include the normalizing of violence; alcohol use as an aspect of male identity in the South Asian, including the Sikh, community (Sidhu, 2012); the challenges of intergenerational conflicts and identity conflicts of second-generation youth; drug use and gangs; and the role of patriarchal relationships.

Alcohol Use and the Normalization of Violence

Thandi (2011a), in a report to the Justice Institute of British Columbia, indicates that there is a relationship between alcohol usage and masculinity in South Asian communities that leads to increased rates of intimate partner violence. In addition to this, young males are exposed to cultural messages that mark violence as an acceptable form of engagement. Thandi states, "Within South Asian communities, men have been socialized to believe alcohol use and even misuse is socially acceptable. South Asian popular media emphasizes alcohol as a way to socialize and to resolve stress or conflicts and this pressure to continue drinking is normalized" (2011a, p. 19). Therefore, alcohol use and violence become normalized aspects of male development, leading to an increased risk of contact with the justice system. Young men are not often reprimanded by the family or the community for involvement in violent acts that bring them in contact with the justice system (Ngo, 2010; Sidhu, 2012; Thandi, 2011a).

One of the challenges that has been highlighted in the literature is the way in which crime and criminal behaviour is thought about in the South Asian community and the unwillingness on the part of parents to believe that their children are involved in criminal activities (Mall, 2015). Additionally, there is a sanctioned acceptance of violence as a marker of masculinity, particularly when the violence is a response or challenge to discrimination (Ngo, 2010; Sidhu, 2012; Sumartojo, 2012). Moreover, there is a level of communal and family support for ensuring and reinforcing the male as the head of the household in cases where the target of the violence is a female within the family.

Identity Conflicts

Another challenge facing South Asian youth is the identity conflicts that often plague children of immigrants. Youth are caught between multiple worlds and can experience stress and anxiety as they attempt to meet the expectations of their home and community, while at the same time trying to adapt to a Canadian context:

> They are also challenged with a complex process of creating and recreating multidimensional, shifting identities. Some South Asian youth, for example, actively make deliberate, strategic choices about whether to "brown it up" or "bring down the brown" in their interactions with other Canadians in order to attain specific goals or manage the challenges of living in a multicultural society. (Ngo, 2010, p. 8)

Ngo, citing the work of Reitz and Banerjee (2007), goes on to say that "second generation visible minority Canadians are less likely than those of non-visible minority backgrounds, and worse, their own first generation Canadian parents to feel a sense of belonging in Canada" (p. 8). Citing research by Wortley and Tanner (2008), Ngo indicates that racialized youth see their involvement in gangs as a way of feeling a sense of connectedness and identity attachment, particularly when faced with social injustice and discrimination:

> These young adults become involved in gang activity to achieve a sense of belonging in a friendly, supportive and intra-ethnic social network. In addition many sought to escape from, and find rewarding alternatives to, exceedingly unpleasant family lives … [and] find a replacement for the absent or rejecting families. (2010, p. 13)

This pattern is also evidenced in Sidhu's (2012) study on Sikh male involvement in gangs.

Another factor that has to be explored in the context of the South Asian male youth involvement in gangs is the role that family and intergenerational conflicts may play. The traditional family structure places the father or grandfather as the head of the family, and there is the expectation that children will follow the rules and expectations outlined by the family and cultural norms. In situations where youth feel caught between the culture of their parents and grandparents and the cultural practices evidenced in Canada, choosing not to follow the expectations of the family or community can result in youth being ostracized from the family, thus pushing them to identify other sources of support and identity connections.

Tummala-Narra, Inman, and Ettigi (2011) indicate that having a strong sense of community can help youth develop their own identity and positive self-esteem; however, their research also showed that there is an unwillingness on the part of the South Asian communities, either first or second generation, to talk about the reality or impact of racism. This reluctance to engage in discussions of racism limits their ability to effectively support each other to address experiences of discrimination, thus making it more difficult to develop a secure sense of identity.

Drugs and Gangs

Another factor of concern is the increasing use of drugs recreationally and the involvement of male youth in the drug trade. A common response from the young person using drugs and their family is to minimize the impact of drug use and/or to deny involvement in illegal activities (Ruggiero & Khan, 2006; Sidhu, 2012), which can lead to an increase in the abuse of drugs. Although the response might be similar in many non-South Asian families, there is the reluctance on the part of many of these families to access mainstream services for support as these services are deemed to have been designed by and for the dominant group (Ruggiero & Khan, 2006).

When exploring conversations around crime and criminality, it is also critical to examine differences between the older immigrant members of the community and the conceptions of their children, who are first-generation or naturalized Canadians. Members of the older generation who get involved in crime may have more established connections to criminal networks and organizations in their home country and may hold on to political, cultural, and religious-based tensions that may play out in gang conflicts. Those with links to organized and international crime networks would be senior members of the community. According to the research conducted by Ruggiero and Khan (2006), which focused on the pattern of drug trafficking involving British South Asian gangs, the contact that the gang members had with ethnic and family relations within South Asia, particularly Pakistan, facilitated the transportation of drugs into Europe, which could then be distributed across the continent.

The younger generation of Asian males who become involved in crime and get absorbed into gangs are usually members of less organized gangs that include more street-level activities and have more inter-ethnic affiliations. They may participate in gangs more for a sense of inclusion and identity development than as a primarily economic activity (Ngo, 2010). Sumartojo (2012) also argues that attempts to understand the ways in which second, third, and other generations of children of immigrant families become involved in gangs and criminal activities requires an understanding of the ways in which their lives are affected by the existing context of their lives in Canada, rather than focusing primarily on cultural or familial influences, given their increased exposure to mainstream culture.

Based on anecdotal data, conversations with local service providers, lawyers, and members of probation services, the areas in which there appear to be increasing levels of criminal involvement within the South Asian community include gang involvement, drug trafficking both within Canada and across the Canada/US border, sex-related crimes, and organized crime. This points to the increased urgency of conducting research on these patterns to ensure that the appropriate services are in place to address these issues before they become a crisis. Vancouver has seen increasing challenges related to gang killings, drug trafficking, and other criminal activities within South Asian communities; many of these crimes have been documented in the local newspapers, including the South Asian community newspapers (Mall, 2015).

According to Perry and Alvi (2011), a 2002 Canadian police survey on gangs indicated that 14 percent of youth gangs primarily involved East Indian and Pakistani youth. Based on this information, one can surmise that there is more South Asian involvement in crime which seemingly challenges the concept of the model minority group label. In addition, given the connection between crime and poverty and the racialization of poverty in Canada, one can further assume that there would be some level of representation of South Asian youth in crime stats.

Another important aspect of this discussion is understanding that the historical conflicts and practices that were present in the homelands of South Asian youth could also continue to exist here in Canada, some of which may increase potential involvement with the police. For example, the Tamil Tigers, which was regarded as a liberation organization in India, has been regarded by police as a criminal organization in Canada because of the fact that some in the community raised money to fund the civil war in Sri Lanka. Further to this, the street-level gangs, which seek to control predominantly South Asian neighbourhoods, reproduce the conflicts and challenges that were evidenced in their homelands, thus resulting in challenges for police in terms of crime control and management, and becomes as a drain on financial resources.

These ideas are based on the importation model of crime, which states that groups enter the country with previous linkages to criminal activities and simply continue these activities when they migrate. This model, although it may serve to explain the involvement of adult members of organized gangs, does little to explain the involvement of youth in gangs here in Canada. In Victoria, British Columbia, the concentration of South Asian (primarily Sikh) residents in parts of the city has led to various levels of conflict among rival groups, including the killings of increasing numbers of young males. According to Totten (2008), in British Columbia, South Asian youth have been involved in very high profile and public forms of violence resulting in an average of 10 murders of youth per year; these patterns have not been evidenced in the same way in the GTA. As a society, we have an opportunity to implement proactive strategies to limit such negative outcomes and interactions.

Patriarchy and Gendered Violence

In a report titled "Towards Healthy, Violence-Free South Asian Families," Thandi argues that there are some aspects of the South Asian culture that are different from the mainstream. These include the issue of patriarchy and sexism, the influence of the extended family, obligations to the family, the impact of immigration, and alcohol, all of which are factors that contribute to violence (2011b), a position supported by Totten's research (2008).

The current literature on the relationship between gender and crime in the South Asian community primarily focuses on the issue of violence against women (George & Rashidi, 2014; Sidhu, 2012; Thandi, 2011a; Toor, 2009; Tyyska, 2009). This is an issue that deserves significant focus because of the potential for women to be abused both by their spouses and by their in-laws, including the mother-in-law. The communal nature of South Asian families has the potential to be both a source of protection and a factor that limits women's options for safety (Abraham, 1999; Dua, 2000; Papp, 2011; Thandi, 2013).

As much as it may be argued that the South Asian family structure is highly patriarchal, it is important to recognize that most family patterns in Canada are also patriarchal and that there is violence within those families as well. As such, it is important not to mark the South Asian family structure as some form of unique pathology. What is unique about the South Asian context is the role that the extended family can play in reinforcing or normalizing the abuse (Bandan, 2009; Chingkhannem Tonsing, 2014; Sidhu, 2012); the role of family shame in the event that a woman does attempt to leave her husband; and the heightened use and abuse of alcohol as a coping mechanism amongst men, which is well documented in the literature. It is also important to critique the way in which media reports characterize South Asian women who are abused or who were killed by their partners.

Habitually, there is a hypersensationalism about the issue (including interviews with community leaders, discussions with religious leaders, etc.), which is not evidenced when White women are killed by their spouses (Moving beyond stereotypes, 2010). This results in marking the South Asian community and culture as more violent than other communities when, in reality, violence against women is very much a part of Canadian society, in much the same way that patriarchal practices are (Chokshi, Desai, & Adamali, 2010). It is important to note that issues that emerge as problematic in any community need to be looked at in a broader context so as to avoid marking that entire community as a problem. Domestic violence is a Canadian problem, not simply a South Asian problem; however, there are factors, as mentioned above, that can increase the probability that it may take place in South Asian families and may be long-standing if there are limited supports in place for either the perpetrator or the victim.

Lastly, there is anecdotal data that suggests that an increasing number of South Asian males are being charged and convicted for sex-related crimes, including rape, sexual assault, and incest. This pattern can be explained by the patriarchal aspects of South Asian cultures that regard women and girls as being of less importance in the community (Abraham, 1999; Ralston, 1999; Singh, Hays, Chung, & Watson, 2010). Ironically, while females are seen as being in need of protection, in particular to protect their virginity, they can be considered to be at most risk within the confines of the South Asian community given the extent to which they are subjected to sexual violence (Toor, 2009). It is these inconsistent messages, the extremely restrictive family and cultural boundaries, and lowered status of women that are potentially leading to the extremely high rates of suicide among South Asian women and girls. It is estimated that South Asian females have a higher rate of suicide and attempted suicide than any other group in Canada (Papp, 2011). However, the focus on the victim after the crime has happened does little to address the root cause of the issue. Canada continues to adopt a reactive stance to issues and social problems after these problems have occurred, although there are many signs that point to the emergence of proactive strategies that could be put in place to potentially stop the problem or at least limit its impact.

Summary

This chapter provided a discussion of some factors that can lead to the increased involvement of South Asian youth in the justice system. Increased sense of alienation from the larger society; cultural values and practices that can be challenging; historically embedded patriarchal structures; and increasing intergenerational conflicts all come into play. In addition, there are the ongoing challenges related to systemic and institutionalized injustices that inform interactions with the broader society. This chapter also speaks to the importance of recognizing the benefits of developing early intervention strategies and working alongside organizations that provide culturally relevant services and supports.

We must recognize the importance of having data and information related to specific communities in terms of risk and resiliency, opportunities and supports, to ensure that those working in the field have access to comprehensive information to make proper recommendations and case management plans. Basing his analysis on existing recommendations for supporting youth involved in gangs, Ngo (2010) suggests the importance of involving the community, social interventions, and culturally responsive justice-based supports, along with changes in organizations (such as schools and businesses), that would support the effective integration of immigrant youth into the broader society to increase their sense of social connectedness.

Discussion Questions

1. How does the marking of South Asians as a "model minority" reinforce or challenge existing power structures in Canada? And how do the markers of race, class, and power construct particular identities?
2. Gang violence among youth is a growing problem within South Asian communities. What factors should be considered in developing effective programming options for these youth?
3. What are the academic drawbacks and limitations of the model minority stereotype for South Asian students and their families? Identify and discuss.

Additional Resources

Province of British Columbia. (n.d.). Preventing Youth Involvement in Gangs: http://www2.gov.bc.ca/gov/content/safety/ crime-prevention/community-crime-prevention/gangs.

Slinger, H. (Director). (2011). *The Gangster Next Door* [Video]. Canada: CBC: https://www.youtube.com/watch?v=P4lMHZBSt2E.

Royal Canadian Mounted Police (RCMP). (2006). Youth Gangs and Guns: http://www.rcmp-grc.gc.ca/pubs/yg-ja/gangs-bandes-eng.pdf.

References

Abraham, M. (1999). Sexual abuse in South Asian immigrant marriages. *Violence against women*, 5(6), 591–618.

Ashutosh, I. (2008). From census to the city: Representing South Asians in Canada and Toronto. *Diaspora: A Journal of Transnational Studies*, 17(2), 130–148.

Asia/Canada. (n.d.). Asians in Canada. Retrieved from http://asia-canada.ca/ changing-perspectives/indians

Bandan, P. (2009). *The obstacles South Asian victims of spousal violence endure in Vancouver, Canada: Culture vs. the extended family vs. the law*. Master of Arts thesis, Simon Fraser University.

Bell, B., & Machin, S. (2013). Immigrant enclaves and crime. *Journal of Regional Science, 53*(1), 118–141.

Chingkhannem Tonsing, J. (2014). Conceptualizing partner abuse among South Asian women in Hong Kong. *Journal of Transcultural Nursing, 25*(3), 281–289.

Chokshi, R., Desai, S., & Adamali, A. (2010). Overview of domestic violence in the South Asian community in Canada: Prevalence, issues and recommendations. In J. Fong (Ed.), *Out of the shadows: Woman abuse in ethnic, immigrant and Aboriginal communities* (pp. 147–170). Toronto: Women's Press.

Desai, S., & Subramanian, S. (2003). Colour, culture and dual consciousness: Issues identified by South Asian youth in the Greater Toronto Area. In P. Anisef & K. Murphy (Eds.), *Managing two worlds: The experiences and concerns of immigrant youth in Ontario* (pp. 118–161). Toronto: Canadian Scholars' Press.

Dua, E. (2000). "The Hindu woman's question:" Canadian nation building and the social construction of gender for South Asian–Canadian women. In A. Calliste & G. J. S. Dei (Eds.), *Anti-racist feminism* (pp. 55–71). Halifax: Fernwood.

George, P., & Rashidi, M. (2014). Domestic violence. *Journal of Critical Anti-oppressive Social Inquiry, 1*(1), 67–80.

Government of Canada. (2015). Six selection factors: Federal skilled workers. Retrieved from http://www.cic.gc.ca/english/immigrate/skilled/apply-factors.asp

Grewal, S. (2013, May 24). Brampton suffers identity crisis as newcomers swell the city's population. *Toronto Star*. Retrieved from http://www.thestar.com/news/gta/2013/05/24/brampton_suffers_identity_crisis_as_newcomers_swell_citys_population.html

Haines, L. (n.d.). The effects of White flight and urban decay in suburban Cook County. *Illinois Wesleyan University*. Retrieved from https://www.iwu.edu/economics/PPE18/2Haines.pdf

Henry, F., & Tator, C. (2006). *The color of democracy: Racism in Canadian society*. Toronto: Thomson-Nelson.

Houshmand, S., Spanierman, L. B., & Tafarodi, R. W. (2014). Excluded and avoided: Racial microaggressions targeting Asian international students in Canada. *Cultural Diversity and Ethnic Minority Psychology, 20*(3), 377–388.

Hulchanski, J. D. (2007). *The three cities within Toronto: Income polarization among Toronto's neighbourhoods, 1970-2005*. Toronto: University of Toronto Cities Centre.

Indra, D. M. (1979). South Asian stereotypes in the Vancouver press. *Ethnic and Racial Studies, 2*(2), 166–189.

Kataure, V., & Walton-Roberts, M. (2013). The housing preferences and location choices of second-generation South Asians living in ethnic enclaves. *South Asian Diaspora, 5*(1), 57–78.

Li, P. S. (2000). Cultural diversity in Canada: The social construction of racial differences. *Strategic Issues Series*. Saskatchewan: Department of Justice, Research and Statistics Division.

Mall, R. (2015, January 16). Warning to South Asian parents: Do you REALLY know what your sons and daughters are up to? *Indo-Canadian Voice*.

Moving beyond stereotypes of family violence in South Asian communities in Canada. (2010, April 11). [Radio broadcast]. CBC. Retrieved from http://www.cbc.ca/toronto/features/familyviolence/

Navaratnam, S. (2011). *Guilt, shame and model minorities: How South Asian youth in Toronto navigate the Canadian educational system*. Unpublished Master of Arts thesis, Ontario Institute for Studies in Education at the University of Toronto.

Ngo, H. V. (2010). Unravelling identities and belonging: Criminal gang involvement from immigrant families. Calgary: Centre for Newcomers.

Papp, A. (2011). *Suicide among young women of South Asian origin*. Winnipeg: Frontier Centre for Public Policy.

Perry, B., & Alvi, S. (2011). South Asians and justice in Canada. In B. Perry (Ed.), *Diversity, crime and justice in Canada* (pp. 149–163). Toronto: Oxford University Press.

Portraits of Peel: A community left behind. (2011). Region of Peel: Peel Fair Share Task Force, Social Planning Council of Peel, United Way of Peel, & Region of Peel.

Ralston, H. (1999). *Identity and lived experience of daughters of South Asian immigrant women*. Paper presented at the International Migration and Ethnic Relations Conference, Rome. Retrieved from http://www.ualberta.ca/~pcerii/Virtual%20Library/ConferencePapers/ralston99.pdf

Reitz, J. G., & Banerjee, R. (2007). Racial inequality, social cohesion, and policy issues in Canada. In K. Banting, T. J. Courchene, & F. L. Seidle (Eds.), *Belonging? Diversity, recognition, and shared citizenship in Canada* (pp. 489–545). Montreal: Institute for Research on Public Policy.

Ruggiero, V., & Khan, K. (2006). British South Asian communities and drug supply networks in the UK: A qualitative study. *International Journal of Drug Policy, 17*, 473–483.

Sidhu, J. S. (2012). *Canadian youth criminality and identity formation: A South Asian (Sikh) perspective*. Master of Arts thesis, University of Windsor.

Singh, A., Hays, D., Chung, Y. B., & Watson, L. (2010). South Asian immigrant women who have survived child sexual abuse: Resilience and healing. *Violence against Women, 16*(4), 444–458.

Sumartojo, W. (2012). *"My kind of brown": Indo-Canadian youth identity and belonging in greater Vancouver*. Doctoral thesis, Ohio State University.

Thandi, G. S. (2011a). *"This is a man's problem": Strategies for working with South Asian male perpetrators of intimate partner violence*. British Columbia: Justice Institute of British Columbia.

Thandi, G. S. (2011b). Towards healthy, violence-free South Asian families. New Westminster: Office of Applied Research Centre for the Prevention & Reduction of Violence.

Thandi, G. S. (2013). A tale of two clients: Criminal justice system failing the needs of South Asian communities of Surrey, British Columbia, Canada. *South Asian Diaspora, 5*(2), 211–221.

Toor, S. (2009). British Asian girls, crime and youth justice. *Youth Justice, 9*(3), 239–253.

Totten, M. (2008). Promising practices for addressing youth involvement in gangs. In support of *Preventing youth gang violence in BC: A comprehensive and coordinated provincial action plan*. Vancouver: Victim Services and Crime Prevention Division.

Tummala-Narra, P., Inman, A. G., & Ettigi, S. (2011). Asian Indians' responses to discrimination: A mixed-method examination of identity, coping and self-esteem. *Asian American Journal of Psychology, 2*(3), 205–218.

Tyyska, V. (2009). Families and violence in Punjabi and Tamil communities. CERIS working paper no. 74. Toronto: CERIS—The Ontario Metropolis Centre.

Wortley, S., & Tanner, J. (2008). *Respect, friendship, and racial injustice: Justifying gang membership in a Canadian city*. In F. van Gemert, D. Peterson, & I-L. Lien (Eds.), *Gangs, migration, and ethnicity* (pp. 192–208). London: Willan Publishing.

Yonemura Wing, J. (2007). Beyond Black and White: The model minority myth and the invisibility of Asian American students. *The Urban Review, 39*(4), 455–487.

CHAPTER 9

Experiences of Familial Racism as a Precursor to Gang Involvement

Mark Totten, *Emily Stroebel,* and *Mia Hershkowitz*

Chapter Objectives

This chapter will help the reader develop an understanding of how early exposure to racism can, in the presence of other risk factors, lead to involvement in gangs. The reader will gain insight into the personal lives of some Canadian gang members through their narratives. Practice and policy implications are also discussed.

At the time, it was a high. A power high. It was a feeling of being king shit—no one could touch you. It was like "Ns" were to blame for everything and we made them pay for everything.[1] They were the reason we had no money, no jobs, no decent place to live. Being a part of the Front [Heritage Front] gave us a sense of belonging. We felt like we were accepted and someone cared for us. They told us we had an important job to do. We felt really important—because we were white—because we were guys. I mean skins don't exactly respect females either. A lot of them pounded on their girlfriends too. It wasn't just blacks. And gays as well. People think skins just hate blacks. It's not true. They hate gays, women—you name it. I think I was part of it because it made me feel good as a guy—respected. I had status. It was like I was a member of some very important club— doing really important work. Kicking the living shit out of anything that wasn't like me. It gave me an image—as a guy I mean. With the Docs, a shaved head, the bomber jacket, the white laces—people automatically know you're part of the Heritage Front. They're scared of you even though they know nothing about you. It's sad, really. Most of the guys into it were losers—stupid, no money, no place to stay, addicts. It's like we didn't want anyone to see that side of us—a guy who really has no balls pretending he's got the biggest [penis] in the world. It's all about fear and status. I was scared shitless inside—I felt like shit, a loser. But as soon as people knew I was a skin, that all changed. I had power. Respect. People were scared of me and didn't know all the shitty stuff inside of me that I was hiding. (Totten, 2000, p. 141)

Marty was a 16-year-old ex-skinhead, talked about the "power high ... a feeling of being king shit" he used to get when beating up visible minorities and males he believed to be gay. He described the dress and behavioural codes of the Heritage Front, and how his feelings of being "scared shitless ... a loser" were transformed into a "power high" when perpetrating violence.

When questioned about how he became involved in a White supremacist gang, Marty talked about growing up in a family where his father routinely talked about "those goddam 'Ns,'" "spics," "faggots," and "sluts." He also grew up in poverty, and both Marty and his father blamed ethnoracial minorities and people they perceived to be gay for this. Having left the gang, Marty was open to discussing the impact of being raised by racist parents. He was able to see that his behaviour was learned.

Introduction

This chapter draws upon the qualitative research on Canadian gang members conducted by Totten and colleagues over the past 25 years (Totten, 2000, 2014; Totten & Totten, 2012; Totten & Dunn, 2012a, 2012b; Kelly & Totten, 2002). Narratives from selected participants in these studies will be used to support the argument that some Canadian gang members engage in racist activities in part due to racist socialization in their families (families include biological families, foster families, and other kinship networks). This racist socialization is not the sole realm of White supremacist gangs. The chapter will begin by defining types of gangs and roles within gangs, the social construction of racial identity and parental transmission of racism, and will then provide examples of gang members who engage in racism. Participants included in this chapter were active members in the Hells Angels, Indian Posse, Manitoba Warriors, Native Syndicate, and Heritage Front.

Context and Content

Totten and colleagues have conducted in-depth interviews with over 500 gang members over the past 25 years, 75 percent of whom are male. The average age of these participants is about 18 years old and roughly 25 percent have been convicted of murder or manslaughter. Most have been incarcerated and about 40 percent grew up in the care of child welfare group homes and foster homes. Approximately 80 percent of these individuals grew up in poverty and were still living in poverty at the time of the studies. The ethnoracial backgrounds of participants were diverse: 25 percent were Caucasian, 15 percent African, 20 percent Aboriginal, 10 percent Latino, 20 percent mixed race, and 10 percent Asian.[2]

In most of these studies, researchers spent time socializing with gangs, getting to know the members, and building trust. Gang members were then asked if they would consent to participate in confidential, audiotaped, in-depth interviews to explore the meaning of various activities, violent crimes, and gang culture from the perspective of gang members. Another objective was to trace the lives of gang members from infancy to adulthood. The average interview time in the qualitative studies was approximately eight hours.

Methods used to analyze the in-depth interview data are based on the techniques of ethnographic data analysis (Glaser & Strauss, 1967). This is an approach that generates theory from observation. Rigorous methods for assessing truth status have been previously described and were utilized in these studies. They include triangulation of data sources (Denzin, 1989) and investigative discourse analysis (Rabon, 1994). A small number of cases were excluded from the analysis due to concerns about accuracy.

Categories of Canadian Gangs

Gang involvement in Canada exists on a continuum and there are three broad types of gangs: street gangs, mid-level gangs, and organized crime groups. *Street gangs* are visible, entrenched groups that come together for profit-driven criminal activity and often severe violence. Communication rituals and public displays of gang-like attributes are common (Totten & Totten, 2012). Street gangs are involved in serious and violent crimes and have some stability over time, yet membership is often fluid. Street gangs control an area or turf, which they protect from rival gangs. This may be a housing project or an area they claim to be their own for drug trafficking. Members identify themselves through a common name, tattoos and symbols, colours, graffiti, clothing styles, bandanas, and hats. Violence by senior gang members is typically used on new recruits entering the gang and is also employed as an exit ritual. This in part shields the gang from other individuals wanting to do harm to the gang (such as infiltration by rival gang members). Aboriginals and marginalized ethnoracial minorities are overrepresented in street gangs. While some gangs have members mainly from a single ethnic or racial group, multi-ethnic membership is also common. Many members have grown up in severe poverty, and drug and alcohol abuse is common.

Mid-level gangs have characteristics of both street gangs and organized crime groups. These gangs can be racially diverse, although some gangs in Western Canada are exclusively Aboriginal. Members may come from different socio-economic backgrounds, but the vast majority of Aboriginal and African Canadian gang members have grown up in poverty. Like street gangs, mid-level gangs are typically formed in schools, young offender group homes, and foster homes. Many members come from families where there is intergenerational gang involvement. Unlike organized crime groups, mid-level gangs are made up of disorganized smaller groups or cells. Like street gangs, relationships with other cells and groups are fluid and opportunistic—often organized around making money from crimes (such as operating drug lines). Drug, gun, and human trafficking are common, as are fraud, extortion, home invasions, and armed robberies. Violence is often initiated in response to perceived threats from other gangs, whether real or not. Members rely on violent entry and exit rituals to protect the gang from outsiders. Mid-level gangs are more sophisticated and disciplined than street gangs (Totten & Totten, 2012). For example, street gangs typically engage in very public acts of violence, often on a senseless and impulsive basis, and it is relatively easy for the police to apprehend street gang members because their crimes are so visible.

According to the Canadian Security Intelligence Service (CSIS) (2010) and Public Safety Canada (2012), *organized crime groups* share common attributes. The structure of criminal organizations is comparable to that of legitimate business enterprises, with rules, bylaws, and constitutions. Organized crime groups have been in existence for long periods of time and are widely respected and feared (a good example is the Italian Mafia). Family, race, and ethnicity determine membership. These groups engage in countrywide and international crimes, and frequently launder the proceeds of crime through legitimate businesses.

The degree of organization in most gangs is defined by the following: the gang's structure and hierarchical nature; the relationship with organized crime groups; longevity; codes of conduct and bylaws; recruitment practices; and the sophistication of interrelationships of members (Totten & Totten, 2012; Mellor, MacRae, Pauls, & Hornick, 2005).

Membership and Roles

Gang membership can be conceptualized as concentric circles: wannabees/posers, "hangers-on"[3] and "floaters" (individuals who are marginally involved but have friendships with confirmed gang members).[4] New recruits and prospects are in the outermost ring, leaders are in the innermost ring, and floaters are in between. The leadership structure is made up of the original founder and core members who started the gang. Membership commitment can be measured in a hierarchical ranking system within the gang (Totten & Totten, 2012). Although there are a number of people who direct other members, older members have more influence than young members. Leaders (also known as bosses or presidents) actively promote and participate in serious criminal activity. These members are most often males in their mid-twenties or early thirties, although emerging data in one Canadian study has documented the role of women in senior positions (Totten, forthcoming). Veterans (also known as captains, sergeants-at-arms, or higher-ups) decide which criminal activities the gang will participate in and are considered to be faithful in their loyalty to the gang.

Along with leaders, the veterans are responsible for settling internal conflicts within the gang. These conflicts typically arise from members having friendships with rival gang members, those who engage in sexual relations with girlfriends of fellow gang members without their expressed consent, or those who steal money from criminal profits or illicit drugs. Consequences range from severe beatings to death. Core members (also called associates or affiliates) have usually been with the gang since it started and are experienced, proven members. Wannabees are at particularly high risk of being victimized by violence at the hands of legitimate gang members. These youth are looking for a sense of belonging and family, and go to great lengths to mimic gang membership through tattoos, dress, display of colours, and hand signals.

Overrepresentation of Racially Minoritized Groups in Gangs

Data on the ethnoracial backgrounds of Canadian gang members is very limited. A handful of studies have been based on urban gangs in various parts of the country, there are provincial estimates by police,[5] and a few studies have focused on incarcerated gang members (Correctional Services Canada [CSC], 2008). Existing data on street and mid-level gangs suggest that most gang members are racially minoritized: Aboriginals, African Canadians, and Asians make up the highest proportion of members, followed by Caucasians, Latinos, Middle Eastern members, and members from other backgrounds. The majority of these gang members live in poverty and experienced poverty during both their childhood and teen years. About one-third of gang members in British Columbia are Asian, almost all Saskatchewan gang members are Aboriginal, just under two-thirds of both Manitoba and Alberta gang members are Aboriginal, approximately one-third of Ontario gang members are African Canadian, and roughly one-half of Nova Scotia and Quebec gang members are African Canadian (Totten & Totten, 2012). About one-third of gang members in prison are African Canadian, followed by Aboriginal, Asian, and members from other backgrounds (CSC, 2008). Aboriginal prison gangs are the fastest growing group in Canadian federal correctional facilities.

Today, about one-third of Canadian gangs are ethnically diverse, compared to 30 years ago when most gangs were ethnically homogeneous. Gangs that appear to be rigidly homogeneous today include White supremacist gangs, Aboriginal gangs, and some African gangs. Saskatchewan and Manitoba street gangs are the most homogeneous, with the vast majority of gangs in those provinces being exclusively Aboriginal. Examples include Native Syndicate, Manitoba and Alberta Warriors, Redd Alert, and Indian Posse. In central Ontario and the Maritimes, many gangs are primarily African Canadian (such as North Preston's Finest).

Current examples of multi-ethnic gangs include the Independent Soldiers and the United Nations, both of which originated in British Columbia. In addition to Aboriginal gangs, other ethnically homogeneous groups in Canada include the Chinese Big Circle Boys and Fresh off the Boat; the Vietnamese Viet Ching; the African Mad Cowz and African Mafia; and the Latino Mara Salvatrucha 13. The Hells Angels, which is an almost exclusively Caucasian outlaw motorcycle gang, is international in scope and has many Canadian chapters. Interestingly, many of its puppet clubs comprise Aboriginal, African, and Asian members (such as the Red Liners, Fallen Saints, and Zig Zag Crew). Puppet clubs do the "dirty work" for the Hells Angels. There are no published data in Canada examining the racial makeup of the leaders of ethnically diverse gangs and those who occupy the lower rungs of ethnically diverse gangs.

Why is it that minority groups dominate gang membership in Canada? Immigrant, refugee, and ethnoracial youth are vulnerable to social exclusion and negative physical and mental health outcomes. They are at increased risk for gang recruitment because of acculturation stress, poverty, and language barriers (Anisef & Kilbride, 2000; Berry, Phinney, Sam, & Vedder, 2006; Beiser, 2005; Khanlou & Crawford, 2006). They experience blocked access to good jobs and post-secondary education. Young refugees from war-torn countries are susceptible to recruitment into gangs like the Mad Cowz and African Mafia (Totten, 2014). They have experienced the violence of war and many were forced to become child soldiers. They are traumatized and accustomed to a violent lifestyle. They are seeking a place where they are not marginalized and, as such, they are easily recruited into gangs.

The Special Case of Aboriginal Gangs

Cultural genocide has contributed to the growth of Aboriginal gangs in Western Canada and Northern Ontario. Colonization, forced assimilation, the mass removal of children from their biological families (residential schools; the Sixties Scoop, during which thousands of Aboriginal children were taken from their parents and placed in the child welfare system; and today's foster homes), and intergenerational trauma are factors related to gang involvement. The practice of forced removal was put in place and enforced by the Canadian government. Aboriginal children who experience multiple child welfare placements are at particularly high risk for gang involvement. It is not unusual for a gang member to have been placed in dozens of foster and group homes and young offender centres (Totten, 2014). Other factors related to Aboriginal gang involvement are the loss of land, traditional culture, spirituality, and values; the breakdown of community kinship systems and Aboriginal law; and the destruction of traditional family units and parenting capacity (through the residential school system and placement of children in foster and group homes).

Although most Aboriginal communities are strong and resilient, many have high rates of psychosocial problems, including poverty and unstable housing, health problems and suicide, addictions, crime, family violence and homicide, sex trade involvement, school dropout and unemployment, and institutionalization into child welfare, correctional, and mental health facilities (Totten & the Native Women's Association of Canada, 2010).

Gangs can provide a sense of family and belonging, friendship, an identity, and income for marginalized Aboriginal young people facing these psychosocial challenges. Gangs offer a job, protection, and shelter from racism and trauma. Some members report that the gang is a space to combat social injustice. For example, Kim, a Cree 21-year-old, stated the following about her experience as a gang member: "I was beating up White girls who were being mean to me. They called me squaw—they were racist." She talked about how being the only Aboriginal girl in her all-White school led her to "act out." Because she was the only student with dark skin, other students and teachers assumed she was black and called her derogatory names. "I was the only Indian in an all-White school…. It kind of made me feel embarrassed. I knew that they were thinking: 'What's wrong with your family, and why are you in there?'" (Totten, 2014, p. 33). Quickly, she came to the conclusion that the only way to cope was to fight, then run away. She was convicted of a string of assaults on Caucasian females.

Pathways into Street and Mid-Level Gang Involvement

Research out of Canada has identified a number of pathways into gang life: victimization by chronic and severe violence at a young age, particularly in families; multiple placements in child welfare and youth justice facilities; and being born into "super-gang families," where there is intergenerational gang involvement. In addition, experiencing brain injuries and serious mental health and behavioural disorders, addictions, the formation of hypermasculine and sexualized feminine gender identities, and social exclusion and racial marginalization can all be potential pathways. In this chapter, we will focus on this last pathway. Gang involvement is typically the result of a multitude of risk factors across many domains, including, for example, family, peers, school, community, and psychological (Totten & Totten, 2012). Some gang members are located on one primary pathway; others become gang-involved through a number of different pathways. Aboriginal and minority youth are more vulnerable to these conditions compared to other youth, and are therefore at greater risk of going down these paths. Evidence supporting the existence of these pathways comes from the work of Totten and colleagues and a small number of Canadian studies on this issue (for example, Dickson-Gilmore & Laprairie, 2005; Weatherburn, Fitzgerald, & Hua, 2003).

The Construction of Racial Identity

How do gang members develop, express, and construct their racial identity? How do they "do" race? The family is an important site of socialization, and reinforcement of racist ideologies by caregivers can lead to gang involvement. Social interactions in the family impact the development of racial identity (Burton, Bonilla-Silva, Ray, Buckelew, & Freeman, 2010; Shorter-Gooden & Yi, 1999). Negative interactions that are racialized may contribute to the development of a negative racial identity (Golash-Bonza & Darity, 2008), which can lead to experiences of marginalization and exclusion. Racial identity is influenced by early childhood experiences with parents, guardians, and other family members. School and peer groups are also areas of influence. In addition, the media plays a significant role in constructing identities for racially marginalized groups, particularly in adolescence, when youth spend more time in peer groups and begin separating from their families. Most parents are extremely upset about their children being involved in gangs (Totten, 2012), but once youth enter the teenage years, the level of control parents have to fight the images that the media portrays is significantly reduced. For vulnerable youth, media popularization of gang culture makes this lifestyle seem appealing. The representation of gang culture in movies, hip-hop music, and clothing has resulted in the integration of gang culture into general youth subculture (Office of Juvenile Justice and Delinquency Prevention, 2010).

The practice of colourism is one way social interactions in the family are influenced by race (Neegan, 2008). Colourism is defined by Burton and colleagues (2010) as "the allocation of privilege and disadvantage according to the lightness or darkness of one's skin" (p. 440). Dark-skinned minorities are more likely to experience negative social outcomes, including poverty and substance abuse (Hochschild & Weaver, 2007). Parents may even place higher value on their own minority children who appear to be or can pass as White. White gang members adopt racist ideas and beliefs about non-White groups, while racialized groups internalize the negative ideas about their group.

The following quote from Brian, a 14-year-old skinhead gang member, is illustrative of the role played by experiences of racist socialization at a young age. Brian had recently returned home after living on the streets for a couple of years. Growing up, Brian remembered his father frequently beating his mother, and calling her "N" often (both of his parents were White). Brian reported that his father routinely sat him down and told him to never be friends with Blacks, explaining that they were racially inferior. In turn, Brian engaged in racial violence with his gang:

> If I can't work it'll be hard to get people to respect me. It's like a kind of status. But I know as long as people know not to "f" with me—well, I'll always have that. As long as I've got my balls, I'll be all right (laughing). A guy's nothing without that. No, let's say I wasn't a fighter or I was a [gay man] or I was a "N." Now that would be bad. They ain't got nothing—no respect, no power. It's all about power really. I mean, I get what I want because people know if I don't get it, I'll kick the shit outta them. (Totten, 2000, p. 92–93)

Like gender, race is not a fixed characteristic—it is fluid, and constructed with resources at hand. It is both a social construction and a social reality: "Race, as other social categories such as class and gender, is socially constructed ... but it has a social reality. This means after race—or class or gender—is created, it produces real effects on the actors racialized as 'black' or 'white'" (Bonilla-Silva, 2006). Racism is structured and systemic. It has both an ideology that legitimizes White dominance—and leads gang members to believe that the system is just—and a set of social structures where those racialized groups that have been marked as non-dominant actually have less access to power. Gangs reproduce racial privilege. There is an unequal distribution of power in gangs for members with White skin. The Hells Angels, for example, have the power to negotiate business deals with racially minoritized street gangs and puppet clubs. They can develop a code of conduct within and between gangs, which results in the dominance of White gang members over other groups that have been oppressed.

Racism in gangs is not just a matter of the openly White supremacist gangs, like the White Boy Posse, Heritage Front, and Aryan Nations. Many other gangs engage in racially coded activities and behaviour at both an individual and a social level. Their members are racially oppressed and also engage in discrimination (for example, see Feagin, 2000). Racism requires systemic and institutional power. Racialized groups do not have the access to power that Whites have; therefore, racialized groups engage in discrimination, not racism. Whites are the only group in society that has the power to control and dominate racially minoritized groups, and to produce racialized categories that limit the options of those groups.

Race is a central component of identity (Burton et al., 2010), and is developed in the context of social interactions, "which are the medium for the construction of the self" (Lindgren, 2005, p. 6). One's racial identity is fluid and is constantly being developed, expressed, and acted out within broader structures of inequality such as class, gender, and ability. Our participants "do" race within the context of their families, peers, neighbourhoods, and gangs. Poverty and gender are important points of intersection. This means that racial identities are not static, but instead are created and recreated daily, within the limits of other forms of oppression. Unequal relations of social class and gender overlap with racism and contribute to a unique social space where racial identity is developed and expressed.

Racialization is the "assignment of racial meaning to real, perceived, or ascribed differences among individuals or groups, which produces hierarchies of power and privilege among races" (Burton et al., 2010, p. 445). Racialized groups such as Aboriginals and Blacks are labelled as different and, as a result, experience unequal access to power and privilege. Our participants, during childhood, experienced unequal treatment because of their race. They were the only or one of the only dark-skinned students in their class. Because of physical characteristics like skin colour and hair texture, and other characteristics, such as their names, they were subjected to differential and discriminatory treatment. This inequality continued into adulthood.

Transmission and Internalization of Racism

The seeds of racism are planted at home. Through their socialization practices, family members "overtly and covertly support or diminish the proliferation of racial stratification systems within their children" (Massey, 2007, p. 445). In general, children are likely to adopt the values and beliefs of caregivers. Research shows that children internalize their parents' racial attitudes and prejudices, which results in implicit (Sinclair, Dunn, & Lowery, 2004) and explicit racial attitudes and prejudices within the child (Carlson & Iovini, 1985; Fishbein, 2000). The transmission and internalization of racism is dependent on the degree of identification between the parent and child (Sinclair et al., 2004). Jones (2000) defines the internalization of racism as the acceptance by members of the stigmatized races of negative messages about their own abilities and intrinsic worth. It is characterized by their not believing in others who look like them, and not believing in themselves. It involves accepting limitations to one's own full humanity including one's spectrum of dreams, one's right to self-determination, and one's range of allowable self-expression. (p. 1213)

Frank's case highlights how racism can be internalized in gang members. A 41-year-old Aboriginal inmate in a medium security correctional facility, he talked about how he experienced racist parenting at home.

My mom took us out [of the reserve to a different province and city] …. And then we were abandoned …. The man that my mom stayed with was Native in ethnic origin, he was a racist, and he was abusive to our mother, and he didn't look after us kids. He used to beat my mother when they were drinking. He used to beat my youngest brother because he had blue eyes and that's when I decided that me and my younger brothers, we weren't going to stay at this place. (Kelly & Totten, 2002, p. 67)

Frank took his brothers from home to live on the streets for a couple of weeks. The police apprehended them and placed them with racist foster parents.

Um, and when the foster home father came home that day [the first day they were in the foster home] and the foster mother—they got together and they laid down the rules. And the rules that they laid down I didn't like at all and that was the basis of my rebellion. First of all they said, "you're no longer an Indian. Your hair is coming off." Things along those lines that were just … blatant, but they cut right through you. … We couldn't have our friends, we couldn't associate with Indian people, we couldn't talk if you knew any Indian words. (Kelly & Totten, 2002, p. 67–68)

Frank's internalization of this racism led him to develop an intense dislike for Aboriginals in general and for himself in particular. He has been an addict for most of his life and has attempted suicide many times. Frank has also been in prison most of his life following a homicide he committed against a rival Aboriginal gang member.

The case of Susan, a 24-year-old member of a Black street gang, provides another example of how racism is transmitted to a gang member. In her case, it was students at her elementary and high schools. Susan was the only visible minority in all-White, middle-class school. She was biracial, and remembers being called an Oreo cookie by other students: "They said I was White on the inside, Black on the outside" (Kelly & Totten, 2002). Throughout her childhood and early adolescence, other kids told her to make up her mind: was she Black or White? She was teased because she came from an affluent home, where her adoptive parents both had professional careers. Susan killed a White youth who had a drug debt with her gang. She claimed that the victim's racist comments triggered the homicide.

For our participants, the internalization of racism is the acceptance of racial stratification that places their racial groups at the bottom. It is the acceptance of negative stereotypes about their race, and it is the embracing of Whiteness while devaluing the Black or Aboriginal self. It is characterized by shame of racial identity and culture. Considering the history of colonization is important when contextualizing the experiences of Blacks and Aboriginals. According to Speight, "the effects of racism are cumulative, spanning generations" (2007, p. 127). This can contribute to how racism is transmitted through the family.

The internalization of racism has caused Indigenous peoples to view themselves, their people, their family members, and their communities as "racially and culturally subhuman, deficient and vile" (Poupart, 2003, p. 87). First Nations people have been "traumatized by racism and attacks on their culture" (McCaslin & Boyer, 2009, p. 63). Parental attendance at residential schools has resulted in the transmission of their racialized experiences to their children. This has created an intergenerational effect of racism (Bombay, Matheson, & Anisman, 2014). Beyond those effects, the internalization of racism leads one to "internalize racism psychologically" and to externalize it physically (Stone, 2007); the externalizing quality can lead to involvement in gangs, participation in violence, and an intense dislike for others like the self. The internalization of racism has negative psychological consequences (Nyborg & Curry, 2003), which can contribute to the expression of violence (Poupart, 2003), mental health challenges including depression, eating disorders, and substance abuse (Carr, Szymanski, Taha, West, & Kaslow, 2013).

Theresa's case is representative. She is a 44-year-old biracial woman. Her mother is White and her biological father is Black. Her mother was given up at birth to a White woman (who Theresa calls "grandmother") who was a friend of the family. Theresa's grandmother could be mean. Theresa said: "It wasn't nice for my mom, you know, to be told every day of her childhood, 'you're not my daughter I just raised you, you came from the gutter.'" Theresa's mother was 15 when she started to date Theresa's biological father, who was a much older Black man. Her mother married him at age 16, and her grandmother immediately disowned her: "She said, no, I don't want nothin' to do with you because of the mixed marriage." When Theresa's mother started having children (who were biracial), her grandmother "didn't want no part of us." This was devastating for Theresa, who adored her grandmother. This was the start of a downward spiral into self-hatred for Theresa, which would last for more than 20 years.

As children, many gang members have been socialized into a world of hatred—told by parents, foster parents, guardians, and other children that they are racially inferior. These children start to believe that they are indeed second-rate, thus resulting in psychological distress. Theresa reported that she started hating the Black part of herself when she was very young. She said that these feelings were rooted in three areas: her grandmother's rejection, the absence of her father, and racist attacks at a young age. Theresa's father left her mother during the pregnancy and Theresa had no contact with him until she was in her early twenties. Theresa said: "I hated him so therefore I hated all Black people." And her mother used to call Theresa and her siblings "f'n little Ns" when she was mad at them. Theresa knew that "N" was a bad word.

At school, she never played with Black children. Frequently, she was the target of racist attacks and slurs—until she "started going crazy and beating people up." Theresa stated: "The funny thing is I'm half Black but my whole life I had a hard time accepting the fact. ... I totally hated it, I totally hated being half Black. ... I never hung out with Black people—all my friends were White." Theresa had adopted a White supremacist ideology that resulted in self-hatred and hatred of Black people. She despised her skin, hair texture, and eye colour. She used bleaching creams to whiten her skin and ironed her hair to make it look straight. She discriminated against other Blacks and refused to date them or hang out or do gang business with them. Theresa's experience is a clear example of the psychological impact of the internalization of racism and racist stereotyping on the life of a person.

Self-Hatred and Violence

Neegan (2008) states that the impact of colonization is self-hate among the colonized. A negative racial identity can lead to ethnic self-hatred (Cokley, 2002). Self-hatred has been linked to both internalized violence (suicide, drug overdoses, and self-injurious behaviour) and externalized violence, such as homicide and assaults (Lanier, 2010; Totten, 2009). It can be expressed as violence against gang members of the same race (both within a gang and against members of rival gangs). Self-hatred is rooted in White domination. Aboriginal gang members can turn on each other to destroy the Indian stereotype—in reality, themselves; Black gang members can do the same. When they attack or kill a rival, they are thus destroying themselves. African young men who live in poverty can use violence against other African young men. Bryant (2011) considers this to be a "national public health issue" (p. 691). He argues that the "lack of self-respect and/or negative attitudes" one has toward their own race is believed to "result in a greater propensity to engage in acts of violence" against them (p. 691). Racism results in Black self-hate, which consequently leads to excessive rates of Black male homicide (Hall & Pizarro, 2010). It is important to understand that poverty plays a key moderating role here—more affluent or middle-class Black men are not typically involved in homicides. Blacks who are middle and upper class possess the necessary economic resources to limit their involvement in street-level gang violence. This reality underscores the notion that gang involvement, as indicated above, is primarily about lack of economic resources rather than an issue of race.

In our research, there are many examples of Black and Aboriginal gang members who have been oppressed by racism and support the domination of Whites in broader society. In addition to the internalization of racism, the psychological trauma, and the externalization of hatred, these racially minoritized groups also engaged in extreme hatred for other racialized and oppressed groups. For example, Martha, a 35-year-old Aboriginal ex-gang member who had been involved in the sex trade since age 11, supports the superiority of White sugar daddies and tricks. She will only date or trade sex with White men. She was involved in the sex trade for many years, and she never associated with Aboriginal or Black tricks. She believed that they were violent, dirty, had diseases, and did not have enough money. She says: "I hate Black guys, I just can't stand them … I just, just these Black guys are just … I've had bad experiences with them in the past and I just don't trust them." She also did not want to have Aboriginal customers because she believed that they could be related to her—possibly a cousin or uncle. So her tricks were White: "I knew they were gonna pay it. They have more money … but a lot of Blacks are starting to date a lot of Native women. So that their children could be you know could live here and have free education you know." Jane, a 32-year-old Métis woman who has been an "old lady" for Hells Angels' boyfriends and other men who are in puppet clubs of the Hells Angels, has always worn contact lenses that make her eyes look blue. She has always dyed her hair blonde and used white hair extensions. These women although not White, adhere to attitudes and behave in ways that overtly support the presumed supremacy of White people.

The psychological impact of self-hate was evident in Theresa's teen years. When experimenting with acid as an adolescent, she tried to cut the skin on her face and arms, thinking that there would be White skin underneath her Black skin: "I just hated being Black so much that it would just drive me to the point where I actually thought if I cut so many layers off of my face I could get to the White part of me." Theresa never dated a Black man, despite the fact that she reported that many Black guys wanted to date her.

> Some Black guys used to say how come you hate on us … and I'd be, like, sorry man that's just not my cup of tea and they'd be like, why what's wrong, you don't like your own kind? … yeah so it was really hard for me, um, like I used to hate when people'd say, oh you know that Black girl, I would just fly off the handle and end up kickin' the shit outta them … and say, don't ever call me that Black girl 'cause I'm not Black.

Martha recalled going to school where there were few Aboriginal kids. She frequently got called "squaw," "dirty little Indian," "wagon burner," and "N." She stated, "I'm like a darker kind of Native you know, I was like really dark. They used to call me Black and I hated being called Black even though I'm like this just like the dark Métis you know." She was in nursery school when it first began: "Well I knew it was bad, like, I knew it was a bad thing but I was just really offended because I wasn't, you know?" At one point, she found the only African kid in her school and dragged this girl to show to other students what a Black girl looked like: "And I was, like, okay this is a Black person here so I was, like, do I look that colour and they're, well, no, and I was, like, there you go, figure it out for yourself." Her siblings and mother called her an "N" at home. Martha said: "Oh yeah, my family, my sisters and, um, everyone actually called me 'N' and I was, like, oh really so that means my dad is Black? No, well shut the 'f' up. Who you callin' me a 'N' if I'm not a 'N' then?" Martha was married to a White man, eight years her senior. He used to buy sex from her and he beat her relentlessly. The above cases highlight the impact of internalized racism and the experience of race-based oppressions.

A final case involves Jeremy, 26 years old and Aboriginal, who identified as White and belonged to a White supremacist prison gang. Jeremy hated Aboriginals. Although most of his family was involved in an Aboriginal gang, he thought they were stupid and could not negotiate a good business deal. He worked for a Vietnamese organized crime group when out on the street. Although he hated Aboriginals, he associated with his family's gang when he needed their protection—he routinely ripped off guns and drugs he was transporting for the

Vietnamese, and when fingered for these thefts, he took cover in the Aboriginal gang. His family protected him. Jeremy was a crack addict and needed access to drugs when incarcerated. His involvement with the White supremacist gang began many years ago, when he was looking for the drug and also protection in prison: "I gave this White supremacist [name of a gang] guy smokes and weed on the bus transporting us from remand to the prison. He said to me, 'I'll take care of you.' And he did" (Totten, 2014).

Jeremy also despised Blacks: "I just always have beefs with Black guys. ... Once, I had just finished off a drug deal at this restaurant. ... This Black guy ... told me to 'f' myself. I chased him and he squirrelled off. I heard 'pow, pow, pow.' My friend shot that Black guy in the head. He deserved it but he lived" (Totten, 2014). Jeremy said that his life would have "been shit" if he had remained with his family in the Aboriginal gang. According to him, Aboriginal gang members lived in poverty and never had nice clothes or cars, and the leaders never took care of their members.

Jeremy stated that his opinions on these racial groups were formed through both direct personal experiences and contact with his "crazy uncle," a retired veteran who did a couple of tours in Iraq and Afghanistan. Jeremy was sent to live with him as a child because his parents could not handle him. It is interesting that Jeremy routinely attempted suicide and talked about how much he hated himself. When not high on crack, he did have lucid moments. During these times, he reported that his self-hatred was linked to being Indian and being rejected by his family due to his association with the White supremacists.

Summary and Conclusion: Practice and Policy Implications

The pathways into gang life are complex, and have been described elsewhere.[6] There are many risk factors, which, in the absence of protective factors, can interact to put a young person on a trajectory into gang involvement. It is much more effective to prevent gang involvement in the first place than it is to intervene after individuals are already engaged in gang life. In particular, criminal justice responses are very expensive and not particularly successful in terms of rehabilitation (Totten, 2015).

What works with high-risk young people? Children who have gang-involved family members—parents, siblings, cousins, aunts, and uncles—are likely to become gang members. This is particularly true for children who experience poverty and domestic violence, and who grow up in a succession of child welfare and youth justice facilities. Ethnic and racially minoritized children who experience racism, in addition to the above risk factors, are especially vulnerable. Prevention initiatives should be embedded in the multiple sectors of a young person's life—family, school, peer group, and community—and should address racism in each sector. At home, it is widely acknowledged that quality parenting programs can be effective at reducing violence (Totten & Totten, 2012). At school, research has demonstrated that whole-school approaches that focus on improving school climate are particularly successful. Anti-racism models have been tested and are known to work (Ontario Ministry of Education, 2014). Schools are a good place for peer group programs as well. Finally, we know that children who reside in mixed income, stably housed, and racially diverse neighbourhoods typically make a successful transition into adulthood (Totten & Totten, 2012).

It is important to focus scarce resources on those children who are at elevated risk. Approaches need to include intensive supports and supervision. Two interventions, both cross-sectoral, have proven to be very effective: multi-systemic therapy (MST) and wraparound support services (Henggeler, Schoenwald, Borduin, Rowland, & Cunningham, 2009; Walker, Bruns, Rast, et al., 2004). Multi-systemic therapy focuses on working with youth and their families in their own environment, such as their home or school, and seeks to improve positive behaviours by providing supports within the multiple environments that youth frequent. Wrap-around services is a case management approach that seeks to provide youth and their families with the various forms of support services they may need. Various support teams work together to develop a comprehensive treatment plan and to ensure that necessary services are provided and all parties are working together to support the client (Henggeler, Schoenwald, Borduin, Rowland, & Cunningham, 2009; Walker, Bruns, Rast, et al., 2004). Both types of programs engage parents and guardians (such as foster parents) intensively. This is crucial, given the fact that the seeds of racism are often found at home.

Discussion Questions

1. What factors can explain the high representation of racialized youth in urban gangs?
2. Among gangs in Canada, research indicates that White gangs have the greatest amount of power and control. What is the relationship between colonialism and the dominance of White gangs?
3. What are the most important strategies that can lead to the reduction of the number of youth involved in gangs?
4. What is the relationship between the experience of racism and possible gang involvement?

Additional Resources

Homeboy Industries: www.homeboyindustries.org
> Homeboy Industries is a not-for-profit organization that started in 1988 in Los Angeles. It serves high-risk, formerly gang-involved men and women with a continuum of free social services and programs, and operates several social enterprises that serve as job-training sites.

Oshkiiwaadizag Mino Niigaaniiwad—Youth Leading in a Good Way
> Project: https://www.publicsafety.gc.ca/cnt/cntrng-crm/crm-prvntn/brf-smmrs/2013-2014-eng.aspx#mb
> This project targets approximately 100 Aboriginal youth per year, in care of the West Region Child and Family Services, a large Aboriginal child welfare agency in Manitoba. Both males and females, ages 13 to 21, living on and off reserve, who are at high risk of gang involvement and/or are known to be gang involved, take part in the wrap-around project.

Public Safety Canada's National Crime Prevention Centre:
www.publicsafety.gc.ca/cnt/cntrng-crm/crm-prvntn/ntnl-crm-
prvntn-cntr-en.aspx
The National Crime Prevention Centre (Public Safety Canada) is
an excellent source of information on evidence-based approaches
for crime prevention and gangs.

Safer Schools Together: www.saferschoolstogether.com
Vancouver-based Safer Schools Together trains schools throughout North America in bullying and violence prevention and
intervention strategies. The goal is to promote safe, caring schools
through the development of effective practice, policy, protocols,
and programs.

REACH Edmonton: www.reachedmonton.ca
The WrapEd youth gang prevention project was created by
REACH Edmonton and is a collaboration with the Africa Centre,
Edmonton John Howard Society, Edmonton Police Services,
Native Counselling Services of Alberta, and YOUCAN. The goal
of this five-year project, funded by the National Crime Prevention
Centre, is to prevent at-risk youth from falling into a life of drugs,
violence, and gangs.

Notes

1. "N" is used to replace a derogatory racial slur directed at Blacks.
    "Ns" is the plural form.
2. Readers seeking an in-depth discussion of sample characteristics
    can review publications by Totten and colleagues.
3. A term commonly used for those on the outside of outlaw
    motorcycle gangs.
4. This term was first used by Spergel (1995).
5. Including the Astwood survey which asked police officers to esti-
    mate the number of youth gangs in their jurisdiction (2004).
6. For example, see Totten and Totten (2012).

References

Anisef, P., & Kilbride, K. (2000). *The needs of newcomer youth and emerging "best practices" to meet those needs.* Toronto: Joint Centre of Excellence for Research on Immigration and Settlement.

Astwood Strategy Corporation. (2004). *2002 Canadian police survey on youth gangs.* Ottawa: Public Safety and Emergency Preparedness Canada.

Beiser, M. (2005). The health of immigrants and refugees in Canada. *Canadian Journal of Public Health, 96*(2), 30–44.

Berry, J., Phinney, J., Sam, D., & Vedder, P. (2006). Immigrant youth: Acculturation, identity and adaptation. *Applied Psychology, 55*(3), 303–332.

Bombay, A., Matheson, K., & Anisman, H. (2014). The intergenerational effects of Indian residential schools: Implications for the concept of historical trauma. *Transcultural Psychiatry, 51*(3), 320–338.

Bonilla-Silva, E. (2006). *Racism without racists: Color-blind racism and the persistence of racial inequality in the United States.* New York: Rowman & Littlefield.

Bryant, W. W. (2011). Internalized racism's association with African American male youth's propensity for violence. *Journal of Black Studies, 42*(4), 690–707.

Burton, L., Bonilla-Silva, E., Ray, V., Buckelew, R., & Freeman, E. (2010). Critical race theories, colorism, and the decade's research on families of color. *Journal of Marriage and Family, 72*(3), 440–459.

Canadian Security Intelligence Service. (2010). *2010 annual report on organized crime.* Ottawa: CSIS.

Carlson, J. M., & Iovini, J. (1985). The transmission of racial attitudes from fathers to sons: A study of Blacks and Whites. *Adolescence, 20*(77), 233–237.

Carr, R. E., Szymanski, M. D., Taha, F., West, M. L., & Kaslow, J. N. (2013). Understanding the link between multiple oppressions and depression among African American women: The role of internalization. *Psychology of Women Quarterly, 38*(2), 233–245.

Cokley, O. K. (2002). Testing Cross's revised racial identity model: An examination of the relationship between racial identity and internalized racialism. *Journal of Counseling Psychology, 49*(4), 476–483.

Correctional Services Canada (CSC). (2008). *Managing the inter-connectivity of gangs and drugs in federal penitentiaries.* Ottawa: CSC.

Denzin, N. (1989). *Interpretive biography.* Newbury Park, CA: Sage.

Dickson-Gilmore, J., & Laprairie, C. (2005). *Will the circle be unbroken? Aboriginal communities, restorative justice, and the challenges of conflict and change.* Toronto: University of Toronto Press.

Feagin, J. (2000). *Racist America: Roots, realities and reparations.* New York: Routledge.

Fishbein, H. (2000). *Peer prejudice and discrimination: The origins of prejudice.* Mahwah, NJ: Lawrence Erlbaum.

Glaser, B., & Straus, A. (1967). *The discovery of grounded theory.* Chicago: Aldine.

Golash-Boza, T., & Darity, J. W. (2008). Latino racial choices: The effect of skin colour and discrimination on Latinos' and Latinas' racial self-identifications. *Ethnic and Racial Studies, 31*(5), 899–934.

Hall, E., & Pizarro, M. (2010). Unemployment as conduit of Black self-hate: Pathogenic rates of black male homicide via legacy of the antebellum. *Journal of Black Studies, 40*(4), 653–665.

Henggeler, S., Schoenwald, S., Borduin, C., Rowland, M., & Cunningham, P. (2009). *Multisystemic Therapy for antisocial behaviour in children and adolescents*. New York: Guilford Press.

Hochschild, L. J., & Weaver, V. (2007). The skin color paradox and the American racial order. *Social Forces, 86*(2), 643–670.

Jones, C. P. (2000). Levels of racism: A theoretical framework and a gardener's tale. *American Journal of Public Health, 90*(8), 1212–1215.

Kelly, K., & Totten, M. (2002). *When children kill: A social-psychological study of youth homicide*. Toronto: University of Toronto Press.

Khanlou, N., & Crawford, C. (2006). Post-migratory experiences of newcomer female youth: Self-esteem and identity development. *Journal of Immigrant and Minority Health, 8*(1), 45–56.

Lanier, C. (2010). Structure, culture, and lethality: An integrated model approach to American Indian suicide and homicide. *Homicide Studies, 14*(1), 72–89.

Lewin, K. (1948). *Resolving social conflicts*. New York: Harper and Row Publishers.

Lindgren, S. A. (2005). Social construction and criminology: Traditions, problems and possibilities. *Journal of Scandinavian Studies in Criminology and Crime Prevention, 6*(1), 4–22.

Massey, D. S. (2007). *Categorically unequal: The American stratification system*. New York: Russell Sage Foundation.

McCaslin, D. W., & Boyer, Y. (2009). First Nations communities at risk and in crisis: Justice and security. *Journal of Aboriginal Health, 5*(2), 61–87.

Mellor, B., MacRae, L., Pauls, M., & Hornick, J. (2005). *Youth gangs in Canada: A preliminary review of programs and services*. Prepared for Public Safety and Emergency Preparedness Canada. Calgary: Canadian Research Institute for Law and the Family.

Neegan, E. (2008). Constructing my cultural identity: A reflection on the contradictions, dilemmas, and reality. *Alberta Journal of Educational Research, 54*(3), 272–282.

Nyborg, V. M., & Curry, J. F. (2003). The impact of perceived racism: Psychological symptoms among African American boys. *Journal of Clinical and Child and Adolescent Psychology, 32*(2), 258–266.

Office of Juvenile Justice and Delinquency Prevention. (2010). *Gang prevention: An overview of research and programs*. Washington, DC: US Department of Justice.

Poupart, L. M. (2003). The familiar face of genocide: Internalized oppression among American Indians. *Hypatia, 18*(2), 86–100.

Public Safety Canada. (2012). *Organized crime research brief 28: Data mining for possible organized crime*. Ottawa: Public Safety Canada.

Rabon, D. (1994). *Investigative discourse analysis*. Durham, NC: Carolina Academic Press.

Shorter-Gooden, K., & Yi, K. (1999). Ethnic identity formation: From stage theory to a constructivist narrative model. *Psychotherapy, 36*(1), 16–26.

Sinclair, S., Dunn, E., & Lowery, B. S. (2004). The relationship between parental racial attitudes and children's implicit prejudice. *Journal of Experimental Social Psychology, 41*(3), 283–289.

Speight, L. S. (2007). Internalized racism: One more piece of the puzzle. *The Counseling Psychologist, 35*(1), 126–134.

Spergel, I. A. (1995). *The youth gang problem: A community approach*. New York: Oxford University Press.

Stone, A. (2007). Internalized racism: Physiology and abjection in Kerri Sakamoto's *The Electrical Field*. *Canadian Literature, 193*(193), 36–52.

Totten, M. (2000). *Guys, gangs and girlfriend abuse*. Toronto: University of Toronto Press.

Totten, M. (2009). Aboriginal youth and violent gang involvement in Canada: Quality prevention strategies. *Institute for the Prevention of Crime Review, 3*, 135–156.

Totten, M. (2012). Gays in the gang. *Journal of Gang Research, 19*(2), 1–24.

Totten, M. (2014). *Gang life: Ten of the toughest tell their stories*. Toronto: James Lorimer.

Totten, M. (2015). An overview of gang-involved youth in Canada. In J. Winterdyk & R. Smandych (Eds.), *Youth at risk and youth justice*. Toronto: Oxford University Press.

Totten, M. (forthcoming). *The construction of female gangs in Canada*. Toronto: University of Toronto Press.

Totten, M., & Dunn, S. (2012a). *Final evaluation report for the Prince Albert Outreach Program Inc. Warrior Walking Gang Project*. Gatineau, QC: Mark Totten & Associates Inc.

Totten, M., & Dunn, S. (2012b). *Final evaluation report for the North Central Community Association RAGS Project*. Gatineau, QC: Mark Totten & Associates Inc.

Totten, M., & the Native Women's Association of Canada. (2010). Investigating the linkages between FASD, gangs, sexual exploitation, and woman abuse in the Canadian Aboriginal population: A preliminary study. *First Peoples Child and Family Review, 5*(2).

Totten, M., & Totten, D. (2012). *Nasty, brutish and short: The lives of gang members in Canada*. Toronto: James Lorimer.

Walker J., Bruns, E., Rast, J., et al. (2004). Phases and activities of the wraparound process. Portland, OR: National Wraparound Initiative, Regional Research Institute, Portland State University.

Weatherburn, D., Fitzgerald, J., & Hua, J. (2003). Reducing Aboriginal over-representation in prison. *Australian Journal of Public Administration, 62*(3), 65–73.

CHAPTER 10

LGBTQ Issues in Policing and Prisons: Understanding Gender/Sexuality as It Intersects with the Justice System[1]

Marty Fink

Chapter Objectives

This chapter will help the reader develop an understanding of how the criminal justice system affects queer and trans inmates. Issues relating to the criminalization of gender and sexual difference will be defined and discussed through historical and contemporary contexts. Students will learn to think through issues of sexual and gender-based oppression using an intersectional framework.

Introduction

This chapter will first look to Canadian history to understand current queer and trans prison issues. Next, it will explain how this concept of intersectionality works within the Canadian criminal justice system. Understanding how queer and trans issues are intersectional will point to possibilities for changing the ways that prisons and policing target queer and trans populations. This chapter will also look at ways of supporting queer and trans prisoners and will suggest alternatives to the criminalization of gender and sexual difference.

Context and Content: Defining Queer/Trans Issues within the Criminal Justice System

Understanding the Canadian justice system requires an understanding of how policing and prisons affect queer and trans populations. In the following sections, I will provide a definition of some of the common terms associated with the LGBTQQ communities.

Queer is an umbrella term that includes a broad spectrum of identities. Some of these identities are included in the acronym LGBTQ2IAA+ (lesbian, gay, bisexual, transgender, questioning, two-spirit, intersex, asexual, and allies). The "+" at the end of the acronym signifies that this long amalgam of letters is not extensive and can also include a wide range of other identities. Anyone can be queer if they self-identify as queer. Queer can even include straight people who are allies to those who face discrimination on the basis of gender and sexual difference.

Trans is a word that refers to people whose gender identities are different from the gender they were assigned at birth. When we are born, doctors assign each of us a sex (male or female) based on the appearance our genitals. Many people feel that their gender is at odds with the sex/gender they were assigned at birth. When a person's experience of gender is different from the gender they were assigned by doctors when they were born, that person is trans. Some trans people take hormones and/or have surgeries to make their bodies reflect their chosen gender identities. Some trans people choose not to make any medical or physical modifications to their bodies. Anyone can be trans if they self-identify as trans. Accessing hormones or surgeries is not necessary for all trans people; however, some trans people need to access these medical procedures in order to feel like themselves. This is called *gender self-determination*. The idea behind gender self-determination is that we should all be given the power to choose our own genders, rather than having that decision made for us on the basis of what our genitals look like. Trans women are women who were assigned the gender of male at birth. Trans men are men who were assigned the gender of female at birth.

Gender non-conforming people may have gender identities or gender presentations that conform to neither male nor female gender norms. It is useful to consider gender as a spectrum, where male and female are two possibilities, but are not the only two options that people can choose from. Many people have genders that do not conform to male or female conceptions of gender.

Intersex is a medical classification of people who are born with genitals that are neither male nor female. Intersex people face different medical and political challenges than trans people because they are often given surgeries and hormones while they are still infants rather than having the opportunity to self-determine their bodies and their gender identities.

Queer and trans people face oppression on the basis of gender- and sexuality-based discrimination. This experience of discrimination is compounded by a range of intersecting oppressions. Gender and sexual discrimination are intersectional because they interface with discrimination connected to other factors, including race, class, age, citizenship status, and disability, as well as other forms of oppression.

Gender-based oppression is also connected to ongoing Canadian histories of colonization. Prior to contact with Western colonizers, racist legislation including the Indian Act, and other forms of institutionalized colonial violence, Indigenous communities supported and honoured the lives of people who did not conform to Western understandings of gender and sexual identity (Yee, 2011). In Indigenous communities before contact, individuals were valued for their differences when they did not fit into existing male/female categories of gender or into straight categories of sexual orientation (Rifkin, 2011). *Two-spirit* is a term that is used to represent the identities of Indigenous people whose genders and sexualities do not fit into colonial, binary systems of gender and sexuality. Because colonization and institutional violence against Indigenous peoples continues to create an overrepresentation of Indigenous populations within the criminal justice system, the framework for eliminating sexual and gender-based violence in Canada today must include the struggle for Indigenous sovereignty and decolonization.

Criminalization in Context: A History of Criminalizing Queer/Trans People

To understand the current context of queer and trans justice issues, it is necessary to understand the history of policing and incarceration of queer and trans people. The Stonewall Riots of 1969 was a critical event in queer and trans history. Though this event took place in New York City, it marked a significant political shift in Canada as well (Kinsman, 1996, p. 290). These riots took place against the police to make a statement that queer and trans people would no longer tolerate police brutality and criminalization simply for being queer and trans. These riots mark the birth of the modern gay rights movement (Carter, 2010). Each year on the anniversary of the riots, cities across North America celebrate by hosting an annual pride parade.

During the 1950s and 1960s (and in periods predating the historical moment of the riots), people were arrested, imprisoned, and subjected to police brutality simply because they were queer or trans (Silverman & Stryker, 2005). The very act of having queer sex (often referred to as "sodomy") was considered a criminal act (Kinsman, 1996, p. 64). Those reported for having engaged in queer sex lost their homes, their children, and their jobs. There was no legal protection for people who were sexual minorities (Kinsman, 1996, p. 64). Queer bars were raided frequently by the police and those in attendance were put into custody where they often experienced physical and sexual violence (Silverman & Stryker, 2005).

During this period, people were also arrested and charged for failing to conform to the gender they were assigned at birth (Silverman & Stryker, 2005). If a person's birth certificate said they were male, they needed to be wearing at least three pieces of men's clothing. If their birth certificate said they were female, they needed to be wearing at least three pieces of women's clothing (such as a bra, women's underpants, and a skirt) (Silverman & Stryker, 2005). Trans people, drag queens, and gender non-conforming people were all subject to police harassment, violence, and criminalization simply for dressing in accordance with their chosen gender identities. Trans people were also denied access to housing, social services, and employment, and had no legal protection from violence and harassment (Silverman & Stryker, 2005).

These laws that established gender and sexual difference as criminal were also supported by medical experts and by the field of psychology. The DSM (*Diagnostic and Statistical Manual of Mental Disorders*) contains the guidelines by which doctors diagnose mental illnesses and recommend treatment. Because both gender identity disorder (GID) and homosexuality were listed in the DSM, those who displayed "symptoms" of these "disorders" could be institutionalized and required to undergo corrective treatments (Spurlin, 2009, p. 92). Treatments ranged from electroshock therapy, lobotomies, and institutionalization, to therapies mandating adhesion to gender normativity and heterosexuality (Spurlin, 2009, p. 92).

Queer activists therefore fought to have homosexuality delisted from the DSM, which was achieved in 1973 (Stryker, 2008, 74). However, they did not advocate for the rights of trans people who fought alongside them in the Stonewall Riots to put an end to police harassment faced by both communities (Stryker, 2008, p. 74). Gender dysphoria—the mental diagnosis assigned to people who feel uncomfortable living in the gender identity of the sex they were assigned by doctors at birth based on the appearance of their genitals—remains listed in the current DSM (Stryker, 2008, p. 134). Diagnoses in the DSM of gender dysphoria and gender identity disorder in children (GDIC) create an opportunity for parents to institutionalize youth within the criminal justice system for failing to conform to gender and sexual norms such as adopting gender-conforming clothing, hairstyles, ways of speaking, moving, romantic partner choice, and so forth (Spurlin, 2009, p. 79).

These issues, therefore, do not impact only adult populations. When youth do not conform to the gender they were assigned at birth, parents can still place their children in the juvenile justice system for behavioural correction. In these institutions, youth are forbidden from wearing clothes or hairstyles, or exhibiting behaviours that correspond to their chosen gender identities (Ware, 2011, p. 79). Queer and trans oppression is not limited to public institutions, and youth face discrimination within their own families. Queer and trans youth are frequently pushed out of their homes and committed through the front doors of the juvenile justice system for failing to conform to gender-based and sexual norms (Ware, 2011, p. 79). When youth are placed into this system by their own families, they often remain in the criminal justice system where they are cut off from other queer and trans youth and from community resources they could turn to for support (Ware, 2011, p. 78).

Often such children who do not conform to social norms of masculinity are placed into corrective institutions not because their parents are afraid that they will become women, but because they are afraid that they will become homosexuals (Spurlin, 2009, p. 1992). Therefore, even though homosexuality was delisted from the DSM, there remains an overlap between transmisogyny (hatred toward trans women) and heteronormativity (the idea that everyone should be straight). The criminal justice system reflects the idea of cissexism (the idea that no one should be trans and that everyone should adhere to the gender they were assigned at birth), thus understanding the problems that queer and trans adults face within prisons requires an understanding of how the system itself is set up to police and eradicate queerness and transness in youth both publicly and in the domestic sphere.

These practices are rooted in Canadian legal policy and Canadian history. The Canadian Criminal Code has historically defined queer desire as immoral and illegal. For example, Canada has adopted and adapted Britain's anti-sodomy and anti-buggery laws since Confederation (Kinsman, 1996, p. 129). These criminal codes continued to adapt themselves within Canadian law from 1890 to the 1950s in response to the newly defined medical and social concept of the "homosexual" (Kinsman, 1996, p. 129). In England in the late 19th century, the term *homosexual* was invented by doctors and implemented as a criminal type within the legal system (Foucault, 1978, p. 54; Marshall, 1990, p. 22). The courts publicized these laws by imprisoning the famous playwright Oscar Wilde for being a homosexual despite his celebrity and upper-class status to set a precedent for the legal control over homosexual sex. The Oscar Wilde trials at the turn of the 20th century also informed Canadian anti-sodomy laws that have been used to institute ongoing colonial violence, racist immigration policies, anti-feminist controls over sex work, women's autonomy within the public sphere, and patriarchal nuclear family structures (including the requirement for marriage) by rendering queer sex a crime under Canadian law (Kinsman, 1996, p. 134).

These laws thereby constructed queerness as a crime through the Canadian legal system. The ongoing implementation of this legislation is demonstrated by the Klippert case from 1965, in which a man was prosecuted under Canadian law for having queer sex in his car (Filax, 2007, p. 80). This law was intended to render homosexuality a crime, sending a message that queer desire could not be expressed in public spaces outside of the home (Filax, 2007, p. 80). Laws that specifically criminalize queer sex extend to Canada's age of consent laws that render the legal age of consent for homosexual sex 18 years old, even though heterosexual consent can be given at the age of 16. It is through Canada's laws that queer/anal sex is defined via the criminal justice system as criminal and immoral (Smith, 2015, p. 51).

As mentioned in the introduction to this chapter, understanding the nuances of how this system operates also requires an understanding of intersectionality. The following section will explain how intersectionality works in practice and within the criminal justice system.

Intersectionality: What It Means and How It Operates within Policing and Prisons

Intersectionality is a framework that understands people's complex experiences of oppression as overlapping and informing one another rather than existing in isolation. People who experience oppression relating to gender and sexuality do not experience this oppression in isolation. People's experiences of sexual and gender-based discrimination are connected to their experiences of discrimination on the basis of race, religion, age, disability, citizenship status, and socio-economic class, among other institutional factors of oppression. All of these oppressions affect how sexual and gender-based oppression takes place within the criminal justice system. The following is an example of intersectionality and the justice system.

CeCe McDonald is a young, Black trans woman from Minneapolis who was attacked by a White man on the street in June of 2011 (Malloy, 2014). When she attempted to run away from her attacker, she was followed until she defended herself with a pair of scissors from her purse, killing her attacker. She was subsequently tried for murder and imprisoned. CeCe was incarcerated in a men's prison even though she is a woman and was denied access to hormones (Malloy, 2014).

We cannot identify with certainty which part of CeCe's identity rendered her vulnerable to this violent attack on the street by a stranger. Intersectionality teaches us that we cannot separate CeCe's experience of racism from her experience of gender-based violence as a Black trans woman. Her experience of violence is therefore best understood through intersectionality. We also cannot know what part of CeCe's identity rendered her vulnerable to criminalization by the justice system. CeCe was regarded as a criminal rather than as a victim of violence. Racism—especially anti-Black racism and anti-Indigenous colonialism—is a factor that plays a part in determining who is viewed as a criminal and who is viewed as a victim of violence under the law (Spade, 2011). Trans women are frequently subjected to violations and harassment both individually and institutionally. For instance, trans women are frequently treated with hostility and violence in Canadian health care and educational settings, in housing and shelter programs, by police and jail guards, and by employers and employment services (Namaste, 2011).

We cannot know which part of CeCe's identity caused her to be charged and imprisoned rather than regarded as acting in self-defence, which was necessary to her survival. Intersectionality is again a helpful framework for understanding how CeCe's experiences of racism and gender-based violence overlapped and informed her criminal sentencing. Understanding the application of intersection-ality can also account for CeCe's lack of access to gender-appropriate housing within the justice system and for her being denied access to hormones by the prison workers (Spade, 2011).

CeCe's situation, unfortunately, is not unique and her experience was not an anomaly, but rather a reflection of how the majority of queer and trans people who are put into the criminal justice system face not only sexual/gender-based oppression, but also intersecting oppressions on the basis of race, citizenship status, disability, and class. Intersecting experiences of racism and poverty, for instance, make queer and trans people increasingly susceptible to policing and incarceration (Spade, 2011).

Another example of intersectionality is that many people who are disabled and also racialized are placed into the prison system rather than granted access to health care and other disability-related accommodations (Withers, 2012). Along such intersectional lines, disabled people without access to employment are often faced with poverty and are criminalized instead of given access to the support services they need in order to work and to live with bodily autonomy and self-determination (Withers, 2012).

CeCe's experience of violence can also be understood as a hate crime, enacted as a result of intersecting factors including racism, homophobia, and transmis-ogyny. There has been a movement in the United States and Canada to increase sentencing for perpetrators of hate crimes; however, increasing the policing and incarceration of those who commit hate crimes only increases the violence faced by queer and trans people (Stanley, 2011). Policing and incarceration tar-gets communities that face intersectional experiences of racism, disability, and poverty. The increased sentencing targets people of colour, many of whom also face gender-based and sexual oppression (Stanley, 2011). An increase in police presence creates more, rather than less violence for queer and trans people. As was demonstrated in the individual case of CeCe, queer and trans people of colour are targeted not only by civilians, but also by the police at alarmingly high rates in cities across North America (Bernstein Sycamore, 2008, p. 283; Stanley, 2011, p. 3).

Policing and incarceration also happen after a violent crime is already commit-ted. In order to prevent violence, queer and trans people need protection from the violence that occurs because of barriers to housing, education, employment, health care, social services, and citizenship status (Spade, 2011). Because of lim-ited access to social services and social supports that can lead to stable forms of employment and independence, queer and trans people remain vulnerable to criminalized forms of employment such as sex work. Increasing police presence that targets queer and trans communities therefore increases the incarceration of sex workers, many of whom are trans women and members of other vulnerable populations with precarious access to legal employment (Spade, 2011).

The decriminalization of poverty—which includes the decriminalization of sex work and other criminalized employment—and not the increase of policing and incarceration is necessary to reduce levels of violence within queer and trans communities (Spade, 2011). In order to support queer and trans people, it is necessary to reduce—rather than increase—the number of queer and trans people who are charged and imprisoned. Decarceration is the movement to reduce the number of people who are imprisoned. Decarceration requires alternatives to the prison system such as community-based rehabilitation and restorative justice (Sayers, 2015). Decarceration also relies on the decriminalization of migration and forms of employment that those living in poverty or without status in Canada rely upon for work. This concept of decarceration can also be better understood by looking to examples of policing and incarceration from Canadian history.

Canadian History: Policing and Incarceration in Queer and Trans Communities

In spite of this need for decarceration, in present-day Canada, the residents of Montreal's Gay Village are lobbying for an increase in the police presence within their neighbourhood (Burnett, 2011). As a result, arrests continue to increase as police target queer youth; racialized, Indigenous, and non-status communities; disabled people; people living in poverty; and trans women. The presence of these groups within the Gay Village is criminalized in intersectional ways that are discussed in the previous section. This trend toward calls for increased policing and incarceration is not only present in Montreal but can be traced across the country (Piché, 2012).

Gentrification is a process by which longstanding residents of a neighbourhood are forced out of their homes due to an increase in property values. Within this process, lower-income residents are often displaced and removed from Canadian cities along intersectional lines. Processes of gentrification within Canadian cities serve to remove certain bodies from public space by eliminating affordable housing and disrupting established communities. Alongside the increase in housing values comes a corresponding increase in police violence and an increase in the criminalization of queer and trans people of colour (Delany, 1999; Hanhardt, 2013).

Reflecting these processes of gentrification, the people who are calling for increased policing in their neighbourhoods are largely White, middle class, and male (Burnett, 2011); while White male queer and trans people might still experience harassment related to their sexualities, their calls for increased policing within the neighbourhood reflects their experience of privilege in equating policing with increased personal safety rather than with risk of violence and criminalization (Delany, 1999).

What is interesting about the call for more policing in Montreal's Gay Village is that it stands in opposition to the history of the neighbourhood, where queer people (many of whom were White, middle class, and male) fought to remove the police presence from their public and private lives. The request for increased policing reflects the increased housing prices in the area and the removal of queer and trans people of colour from the neighbourhood over time, as well as a shift in the relationship between queer and trans communities and the police (Fink, 2015).

The Sex Garage Riots of 1990 took place in Montreal's Gay Village, and marked a pivotal moment reminiscent of the Stonewall Riots of 1969. Although in the 1990s homosexuality was no longer an illegal act or an official psychological disorder, queer and trans communities were nevertheless still being targeted as criminal. Police continued to raid clubs and bars in the Gay Village, subjecting residents of the neighbourhood to police violence and imprisonment (Fink, 2015; Herland, 1993). Once again, a riot occurred to signal to the police that the physical and sexual harassment of queer and trans people would no longer be tolerated. The following year, another demonstration occurred in front of the neighbourhood precinct to address ongoing issues of police brutality and criminal charges leveraged against queer and trans communities. Each year in Montreal, a Pride Parade also takes place in August to mark the anniversary of the riots, when queer and trans communities protested against policing and harassment within their neighbourhood. This city-wide movement of demonstrations for queer rights remains significant in creating a culture wherein queer and trans people can occupy public space without fear of police violence and incarceration (Fink, 2015).

The HIV/AIDS crisis of the 1980s and early 1990s also contributed to the increase of police violence within queer and trans communities during this period (Gould, 2009, p. 77; Patton, 2002, p. 66). Many people were dying very suddenly from a new type of illness and the causes of this illness remained unknown. Canada's gay communities were particularly affected at the start of the pandemic. Although large numbers of gay men became ill, national and city leaders failed to provide housing, research, drug treatments, or economic supports to communities in need (Schulman, 1994). Instead, it became commonplace for institutions and individuals to respond to those living with HIV/AIDS with stigma, hatred, and fear. Hospital workers refused to enter the rooms of patients with the illness and would slip their meal trays under closed doors. People living with HIV/AIDS were evicted from their apartments and fired from their jobs (De La Cruz, 1990; Stockdill, 2003). The medical effects of this illness were severely worsened because of the negative stigma and poverty faced by those who were HIV-positive (Sontag, 1989). This included White, middle-class men who previously had access to various kinds of institutional supports. If White males who had access to power lost their social, institutional, and economic privileges when they were diagnosed with HIV/AIDS, the impact was significantly worse for racialized communities (Cohen, 1999).

The increase of queer and trans people living with disabilities and in poverty resulted in an increase in policing that was driven by HIV/AIDS stigma. There was also a corresponding increase in policing that accompanied the government's forced closing of queer and trans spaces including bathhouses, sex clubs, and areas in which criminalized activity such as sex work and drug injection took place (Kinsman, 1996). The rationale for the increased policing was based on the stereotype that HIV/AIDS was being transmitted through homosexual sex and, as such, the reduction in opportunities for gay males to engage in homosexual acts would reduce the number of people being diagnosed. The resulting moral panic also provided further rationale for the broader social discrimination against gay communities (Crimp, 2002). The government's failure to provide resources to address the crisis in these communities resulted in queer and trans people organizing to provide resources to meet the needs of their own community members who were living with severe illness, stigma, and homophobia.

During this period, the Canadian government continued to use the legal system to block access to HIV/AIDS and safer sex materials. In 1994, these practices were opposed by a lawsuit led by the Lesbian Avengers and Vancouver's Little Sister's Bookstore (Busby, 2004). This civil suit challenged the power of the Canadian customs and border control to censor queer and HIV/AIDS resources in a moment when Canadians were dying of AIDS and looking to this material to support queer cultural and physical survival (Busby, 2004). Similarly, in Surrey, British Columbia, in 1997, the government used censorship and legal measures to ban books representing queer families in schools. Books that affirmed queer family models were banned by the school board, and this decision was not overturned by the Supreme Court of Canada until 2002 (Smith, 2012, p. 133).

To counter government opposition and neglect, HIV/AIDS activists used legal means, civil disobedience, and direct action to develop a range of housing, hospice, medical, and support programs to care for people living with HIV/AIDS (Schulman, 1994). Queer and trans activists also focused on the development of safer sex and advocated for the distribution of condoms and safer sex education materials within schools and communities (Schulman, 1994). HIV/AIDS activists established underground needle exchange programs and fought in court to challenge laws prohibiting the distribution of clean needles in order to prevent HIV-transmission. Although needle exchanges and safer injection sites drastically reduce the incidence of HIV infection among intravenous drug users, this practice continues to be criminalized by Canadian laws and remains subject to underfunding and closure across Canada today (PASAN & the Canadian AIDS Legal Network, 2007).

Direct action was a tactic through which those affected by HIV/AIDS protested the needless death toll increasing rapidly due to government neglect. These protests included everything from marches, sit-ins, die-ins, poster campaigns, and political funerals to placing an enormous condom over the house of Senator Jesse Helms, who blocked safer sex education in schools (Brier, 2009, p. 107). Queer and trans activists used non-violent civil disobedience strategies adopted from the civil rights movement of the 1960s. Many queer and trans people were arrested and experienced police brutality and incarceration in response to these displays of non-violent protest (Schulman, 1994); however, these tactics succeeded in securing access to health care, drug treatments, housing, and education, and eliminating HIV/AIDS stigma.

Two Examples of Prison Activism within Queer and Trans Communities in the 1990s

ACT UP/Montreal was an HIV/AIDS organization that fought to provide HIV/AIDS treatment and education to everyone affected by the pandemic. The organization recognized that prisoners were a population whose needs were not being addressed by the government. Prisoners were denied access to condoms, clean needles, and HIV/AIDS education (ACE Program, 1998). Infection rates in prison were significantly higher than infection rates on the outside, and yet drug treatments and medical care were denied to prisoners (Herland, 1993).

Prisoners living with HIV/AIDS were often placed in solitary confinement and unsanitary living conditions; were undiagnosed, untreated, and even left dead in their cells for hours; and subjected to harassment, stigma, and violence from other inmates and guards (Slade & Sweney, 1992). HIV/AIDS activists recognized that members of queer and trans communities were being abandoned inside prisons. HIV/AIDS activists on the outside organized to join together with prison activists on the inside to decrease stigma and to increase access to education and care for everyone affected by the pandemic.

Peter Collins, a prisoner facing a life sentence in Ontario, organized from inside prison to address the crisis of HIV/AIDS. Collins's work is an example of how HIV/AIDS activists brought education programs into prisons and developed comprehensive HIV/AIDS education programs while incarcerated (Dias & Collins, 2009). Prisoner-driven HIV/AIDS education movements continued to influence the success of HIV/AIDS education programs on the outside. Prisoners built innovative prevention and support programs in collaboration with community-based organizations in cities including Toronto and Montreal. The linkages and collaborations that were formed between queer and trans prison movements in and out of prisons reduced HIV/AIDS stigma. Such alliances also raised awareness of the intersectional issues of policing and incarceration faced by marginalized populations. Prisoners, moreover, were regarded as important members of queer and trans communities who had been removed from their support networks by the criminal justice system (Fink, 2015).

In light of these histories, it is therefore troubling that many of these gains of the early 1990s have since disappeared. HIV/AIDS education and condom access in prisons remains precarious. New HIV infections occur in prisons at a rate nine times higher than those on the outside (Talvi, 2007). Prisoners are still denied access to clean needles and consistent access to the HIV medications required to sustain their lives and to prevent viral mutations that result from irregular doses of antiretroviral drugs. Prisoners in contemporary Canada are subject to ongoing stigma and harassment for being trans and for being queer, as well as for being HIV-positive (PASAN & the Canadian AIDS Legal Network, 2007).

HIV/AIDS Activism Continues Today

HIV criminalization is another issue at the forefront of HIV/AIDS activism today. Activists and artists across Canada are producing educational materials and demonstrating in public to challenge current Canadian laws that criminalize HIV transmission (Greyson, 2011). HIV criminalization laws can lead to the incarceration of HIV-positive people for failing to disclose their HIV-positive serostatus (the appearance of the antibodies for HIV within a blood test) to their sexual partners (Symington, 2009). People have been charged and imprisoned even in consensual situations wherein both partners are consenting adults and no viral transmission occurs (although one partner is seropositive, the other partner remains seronegative, continuing to test negative for HIV antibodies and remaining HIV-negative) (Symington, 2009). In blaming HIV-positive people for instances of HIV transmission (or even the perceived risk of transmission), the responsibility is removed from HIV-negative people to take joint responsibility with their partners for their sexual risks and choices. The law makes sexual situations dangerous for HIV-positive people because they face the risk of violence that comes with HIV disclosure within intimate sexual situations. This law—from the 1998 Supreme Court decision *R vs. Cuerrier*—also inhibits people from being tested for HIV and knowing their serostatus, for fear of being criminalized. HIV criminalization laws deter people from accessing HIV testing, and therefore create a barrier to accessing life-saving HIV treatment.

Finally, understanding the impact of this law again requires a framework of intersectionality: those who face the risk of violence, policing, and incarceration as a result of HIV-criminalization laws are those who also face racial, economic, and other intersecting oppressions (Symington, 2009). It is, therefore, necessary to think about what can be done to reduce the criminalization of HIV in the present, and what can be done to reduce the incarceration of queer and trans people more broadly.

Queer and Trans Prisoners: Intersecting Oppressions within the Justice System

Queer and trans prisoners face a range of issues within the prison system. For those who are questioning their gender, sexuality, or who are coming out in prison, it is difficult to gain access to a community and to essential forms of interpersonal support (Stanley, 2011). Homophobia and heteronormativity are institutionalized and normalized by the prison system; having queer sex in prison is illegal. If prisoners show affection toward one another—such as holding hands or giving one another a back rub—they can be separated or put into solitary confinement. Prisoners are therefore often segregated from their lovers and from other queer and trans prisoners they may depend on for support and acceptance within an intensely homophobic environment (Stanley, 2011). Queer and trans prisoners are also forbidden from corresponding with one another by mail, creating a grave sense of isolation.

Queer and trans prisoners are also cut off from queer and trans communities outside of prisons. Many prisons forbid materials containing sexual content from entering prisons. Some prisons have restrictions against coming out materials, queer/erotic literature, HIV/AIDS information, and hormone and transitioning information. Some Canadian prisons even have a ban on photocopies, prohibiting the entry of all resources that may provide necessary support to those who are queer and trans (Fink, 2015). Without access to these materials or to the Internet, prisoners cannot acquire information that affirms their identities and cultures.

Queer and trans inmates also endure an extremely high risk of physical and sexual violence from other inmates and from prison guards (Mogul, Ritchie, & Whitlock, 2011). This violence is often experienced without legal recourse or administrative protection. The lack of access to the queer and trans community also creates barriers to healing and receiving the support needed to deal with the coexisting traumas of violence and isolation. Queer and trans prisoners actually face such high rates of physical and sexual violence in prisons that they are often placed in solitary confinement as a way to "protect" them from these dangerous environments (Bassichis, Lee, & Spade, 2011, p. 34). Confined alone, queer and trans prisoners lose access to educational, vocational, social, and early release programs they could only access from within the general prison population. This practice of isolation therefore remains an untenable strategy for preventing sexual and gender-based violence targeted at queer and trans prisoners (Mogul et al., 2011).

Trans prisoners face an additional set of issues related to their gender and access needs. Trans prisoners who have been taking hormones for years or who have already decided to undergo surgeries before entering prison are frequently denied continuing access to these medical necessities once they are incarcerated. These barriers to hormones and surgeries create extreme bodily and psychological trauma, as well as increased susceptibility to gender-based violence (Spade, 2011). Prisoners who discover that they are trans while they are incarcerated are also often denied access to the hormones and surgeries that they need to support their transitions and to live in their current gender identities.

Trans prisoners are even prevented from choosing gender-affirming hairstyles or clothing items such as makeup and bras (Donahue, 2011). This creates extremely damaging psychological and physiological effects. Prisons are also organized according to a binary gender system, where one must fit into a male or female gender category in order to be housed. Many people do not conform to male or female gender norms, making this system hostile to their identities (Ware, 2011).

Trans people, moreover, are not housed according to their chosen genders or even according to the genders they have lived in for years outside of prison. Prisoners instead are housed according to the gender marker on their birth certificates. This results in the incorrect housing of trans prisoners. This misgendering is not only deeply traumatic for trans people but is also extremely dangerous: trans women housed in men's prisons face daily acts of sexual and physical violence by male inmates and prison guards. This creates increased susceptibility to trauma, suicide, and sexually transmitted infections including HIV (Donahue, 2011).

In confronting these issues, prison administrators have proposed the creation of separate prisons for queer and trans inmates. Lawyers and activists including Dean Spade warn against the enactment of this proposal, cautioning, "if they build it, they will fill it" (Bassichis et al., 2011, p. 34). This warning suggests that the desire to create segregated housing for queer and trans inmates would further criminalize queer and trans people and their communities in order to fill prison beds.

The violence faced by queer and trans prisoners is intersectional, as the sexual and gender-based violence prisoners face is connected to other oppressions including racism and colonial violence, which will be discussed further in the following section.

Belonging, Citizenship Policing, and Colonial Practices: The Canadian National Context

Across Canada, our prison populations reflect national ideas of who is seen as belonging within the Canadian nation, and whose lives are considered criminal by the state. Legal reforms and police presence targeting certain communities create an overrepresentation in prisons of those who are most marginalized by the Canadian nation.

Canada's legal system was founded within a history of colonization and genocide. Indigenous peoples of Canada have lost their lands, their legal sovereignty, their children, and their rights to practice their cultural beliefs and traditions. In many cases, entire populations have been murdered or have witnessed the murders and sexual violence committed against their families and communities by the state (Lenon & Dryden, 2015). This process of colonial genocide is supported by policies and laws such as the Indian Act, and those that led to the residential school system and support the medical system. Another example of genocide was when Indigenous communities were given blankets by settlers that carried the smallpox virus, resulting in the deaths of large numbers of people. These violent histories have all been supported by the Canadian criminal justice system (Dhoot, 2015).

This genocide continues today within Canadian prisons. Although Indigenous people make up only 4 percent of the Canadian population, they represent 23.2 percent of our prison population (Office of the Correctional Investigator, 2013). The incarceration rate of Indigenous women is even higher, comprising 33.6 percent of all federally sentenced women within Canada (Office of the Correctional Investigator, 2013). Again, because prisons are segregated into two categories (men and women), such statistical reporting fails to acknowledge the complex experiences of Indigenous groups that exist outside of Western gender classifications.

Before North America was colonized, patriarchal and binary gender systems (systems with only two genders, men and women, wherein men hold legal power over women) did not exist. Indigenous communities did not uphold family systems based on heterosexuality because some members of their communities were classified as neither men nor women, and could therefore be neither straight nor gay (Rifkin, 2011). As discussed earlier in this chapter, two-spirit peoples were celebrated within Indigenous cultures, and such individuals were regarded as powerful and important members of their communities. With colonialism came the legal elimination of such cultural modes of acceptance. Today, two-spirit people face extreme violence within a prison system that is hostile toward people whose genders fall outside of male and female classifications (Lenon & Dryden, 2015).

Indigenous people also experience higher rates of violence within the prison system. According to information released by the Government of Canada, Indigenous prisoners are

- routinely classified as higher risk and higher need in categories such as employment, community reintegration, and family supports;
- released later in their sentences (lower parole grant rates)—most leave prison at statutory release or warrant expiry dates;
- overrepresented in segregation and maximum security populations;
- disproportionately involved in use of force interventions and incidents of prison self-injury; and
- more likely to return to prison on revocation of parole, often for administrative reasons, not criminal violations (Office of the Correctional Investigator, 2013).

In addition, Indigenous youth are also sentenced at alarmingly high rates, as 21.3 percent of incarcerated Indigenous people are youth, compared to 13.6 percent of non-Indigenous people (Office of the Correctional Investigator, 2013).

The incarceration of Indigenous peoples is best understood intersectionally, as it reflects the complex set of factors that criminalize Indigenous communities: the lack of access to health care, education, housing, and employment; the criminalization of substance use and sex work; the violent intervention in family structures by the state, from residential schools to the Sixties Scoop, and the ongoing removal of children from Indigenous families today; and the increased policing and criminal sentencing within Indigenous communities, such as the harsh sentencing of Indigenous women for non-violent offenses (Dhoot, 2015).

Decolonization, the returning of sovereignty and land to the Indigenous populations of Canada, is a process connected directly to LGBT rights, as well as to queer and trans decriminalization. It is not until the harms of colonization are reversed that we will see a reversal in the overrepresentation of Indigenous populations in prison (Dhoot, 2015).

These disproportionately high rates of incarceration do not promote a reduction in violence, given that Indigenous communities still face alarmingly high rates of violence along intersectional and gender lines. The harm faced by these communities is not merely interpersonal but institutional; this violence reflects a long history of government oppression via Canadian laws and social systems. The overrepresentation of Indigenous peoples within Canadian prisons thus reflects their exclusion from—and oppression by—the Canadian nation. This idea that certain groups are excluded from cultural belonging within the Canadian nation also extends to other marginalized groups, including racialized and immigrant populations living in Canada (Lenon & Dryden, 2015).

Police and state violence against Indigenous and racialized populations in Canada can also be understood through the queer framework of "homonationalism." Homonationalism is a concept that addresses the issue of who is included and who is excluded by the nation (Puar, 2007). Homonationalism refers to the practice of only including queer and trans people within the Canadian nation if they are White; although there has been a vibrant movement to secure the rights of queer and trans people within Canada, these rights are frequently not extended to the Indigenous, racialized, and non-status queer and trans people within the Canadian justice system who face violence daily within Canadian institutions and prisons and at the hands of the police (Thobani, 2007). In order to address LGBT rights and justice issues in Canada, we must not overlook the struggles of Canada's most vulnerable queer and trans populations.

Queer and Trans Resistance and Resilience within the Justice System

In spite of the violence faced by queer and trans people within the criminal justice system, communities continue to demonstrate resistance and resilience in the face of sexual and gender-based oppression. Youth who are prohibited from expressing their gender identities in prison continue to risk punishment in order to style their hair, paint their nails, and sustain support-based and romantic relationships with one another. HIV/AIDS activists inside of prisons continue to distribute safer sex and harm reduction information to one another and to provide informal networks of interpersonal care and support. Examples of such programs include the activist work of Peter Collins and PASAN in Ontario (Dias & Collins, 2009). Queer and trans communities outside of prisons continue to support queer and trans communities inside of prisons by mailing in queer and trans resources, and distributing prisoners' art and writing to communities on the outside (Fink, 2015).

Activists and grassroots community organizations continue to fight against police brutality and incarceration. Organizations including the Native Youth Sexual Health Network, AIDS Action Now Toronto, Reclaim Turtle Island, and Black Lives Matter are all working to end the criminalization of racialized and Indigenous communities, including queer and trans members of those communities (Yee, 2011).

Summary and Conclusions

This chapter has focused on histories of queer and trans communities working together to address issues of criminalization and discrimination while employing an intersectional analysis. Everyone working to end police violence and incarceration, and working toward models of harm reduction, community support, and decolonization is making a difference in the lives of queer and trans people within the criminal justice system. For instance, working toward the decriminalization of poverty, migration, sex work, and substance use will create a drastic increase in sexual and gender autonomy and community resilience. Through historical and contemporary examples, this chapter investigated the need for queer and trans people to gain justice and belonging within Canada. To facilitate this, we must find alternatives to the criminalization, policing, and incarceration of all queer and trans people.

Discussion Questions

1. Discuss the connections between histories of criminalizing queer and trans people and how the criminal justice system operates today. Do policy changes decrease the violence queer and trans people face? Why or why not?
2. Discuss how oppression relating to gender and sexuality intersects with experience of oppression based on race. How do racialized and Indigenous communities become targeted within the criminal justice system? How does this relate to histories of anti-Black racism and colonialism in Canada?
3. Discuss something that can be done to decrease the experience of violence that queer and trans people face within the criminal justice system? What concrete changes could be recommended that would decrease the criminalization of all queer and trans people in Canada today?

Additional Resources

Baus, J., Hunt, D., & Williams, R. (Directors). (2006). *Cruel and Unusual* [Film]. United States: Outcast Films.

Davis, Angela. (2003). *Are Prisons Obsolete?* New York: Seven Stories.

Doroshwalther, B. (Director). (2014). *Out in the Night* [Film]. United States: ITVS: http://www.outinthenight.com/.

Native Youth Sexual Health Network (NYSHN): www.nativeyouthsexualhealth.com.

Prisoner Correspondence Project: www.prisonercorrespondenceproject.com.

Reimagining: Reigning in the New Skool. (2015). [Online magazine]: https://reimaginingthenewskool.wordpress.com/.

Silverman, V., & Stryker, S. (Directors). (2005). *Screaming Queens: The Riot at Compton's Cafeteria* [Film]. United States: Frameline.

Stanley, E., & Smith, N., Eds. (2011). *Captive Genders: Trans Embodiment and the Prison Industrial Complex*. Oakland, CA: AK Press.

Sylvia Rivera Law Project (SRLP): www.srlp.org.

Note

1. This chapter is adapted from Marty Fink's "Don't Be a Stranger Now: Queer Exclusions, Decarceration, and HIV/AIDS." Reprinted with permission of the Publisher from *Disrupting Queer Inclusions* edited by Omisoore H. Dryden and Suzanne Lenon © University of British Columbia Press 2015. All rights reserved by the Publisher.

References

ACE (AIDS Counselling and Education) Program. (1998). *Breaking the walls of silence: AIDS and women in a New York State maximum-security prison*. Woodstock, NY: Overlook.

Bassichis, M., Lee, A., & Spade, D. (2011). Building an abolitionist trans and queer movement with everything we've got. In E. Stanley & N. Smith (Eds.), *Captive genders: Trans embodiment and the prison industrial complex*. Oakland, CA: AK Press.

Bernstein Sycamore, M. (2008). Gay shame: From queer autonomous public space to direct action extravaganza. In M. Bernstein Sycamore (Ed.), *That's revolting: Queer strategies for resisting assimilation* (pp. 268–295). Brooklyn, NY: Soft Skull.

Brier, J. (2009). *Infectious ideas: US political responses to the AIDS crisis*. Chapel Hill: North Carolina University Press.

Burnett, R. (2011, December 19). Violence in Montreal's Gay Village has locals up in arms over safety and future of gay tourism. *Montreal Gazette Online Blog*. Retrieved from http://blogs.montrealgazette.com/2011/12/19/violence-in-montreals-gay-village-has-locals-up-in-arms-over-safety-and-future-of-gay-tourism/

Busby, K. (2004). The queer sensitive interveners in the Little Sister's case: A response to Dr. Kendall. In T. G. Morrison (Ed.), *Eclectic views on gay male pornography: Pornucopia*. Binghamton, NY: Harrington Park Press.

Carter, D. (2010). *Stonewall: The riots that sparked the gay revolution*. New York: St. Martin's.

Cohen, C. (1999). *The boundaries of Blackness: AIDS and the breakdown of Black politics*. Chicago: University of Chicago Press.

Crimp, D. (2002). *Melancholia and moralism: Essays on AIDS and queer politics*. Cambridge, MA: MIT Press.

De La Cruz, I. (1990). Sex, drugs, rock n' roll, and AIDS. In ACT UP/New York Women and AIDS Book Group, *Women, AIDS, and activism* (pp. 131–134). Boston: South End.

Delany, S. R. (1999). *Times Square red, Times Square blue*. New York: NYU Press.

Dhoot, S. (2015). Pink games on stolen land: Pride house and (un)queer reterritorializations. In O. H. Dryden & S. Lenon (Eds.), *Disrupting queer inclusion: Canadian homonationalisms and the politics of belonging* (pp. 49–65). Vancouver: UBC Press.

Dias, G., & Collins, P. (2009). *An intersectional strategy to address HIV/AIDS and hepatitis C in Ontario prisons*. Toronto: PASANs.

Donahue, J. (2011). Making it happen, Mama: A conversation with Miss Major. In E. Stanley & N. Smith (Eds.), *Captive genders: Trans embodiment and the prison industrial complex* (pp. 267–280). Oakland, CA: AK Press.

Filax, G. (2007). *Queer youth in the province of the "severely normal."* Vancouver: UBC Press.

Fink, M. (2015). Don't be a stranger now: Queer exclusions, decarceration, and HIV/AIDS. In O. H. Dryden and S. Lenon (Eds.), *Disrupting queer inclusion: Canadian homonationalisms and the politics of belonging* (pp. 150–168). Vancouver: UBC Press.

Foucault, M. (1978). *The history of sexuality: Vol. I*. R. Hurley (Trans.). New York: Vintage.

Gould, D. B. (2009). *Moving politics: Emotion and ACT UP's fight against AIDS*. Chicago: Chicago UP.

Greyson, J. (2011). Prick. *Poster/Virus*. Toronto: AIDS Action Now.

Hanhardt, C. (2013). *Safe space: Gay neighbourhood history and the politics of violence*. Durham, NC: Duke University Press.

Herland, K. (1993). Interviews for CityPulse News. *ACT UP Videotape Collection, 1990–1993*.

Kinsman, G. (1996). *The regulation of desire: Homo and hetero sexualities* (2nd ed.). Montreal: Black Rose Books.

Lenon, S. & Dryden, O. (2015). Introduction: Interventions, iterations, and interrogations that disturb the (homo)nation. In O. H. Dryden & S. Lenon (Eds.), *Disrupting queer inclusion: Canadian homonationalisms and the politics of belonging* (pp. 3–18). Vancouver: UBC Press.

Malloy, P. M. (2014, March 23). CeCe McDonald: Rebuilding her life after 19 months in prison. *The Advocate*. Retrieved from http://www.advocate.com/politics/transgender/2014/03/03/cece-mcdonald-rebuilding-her-life-after-19-months-prison

Marshall, S. (1990). Picturing deviancy. In T. Boffin & S. Gupta (Eds.), *Ecstatic antibodies: Resisting the AIDS mythology* (pp. 19–36). London: Rivers Oram Press.

Mogul, J. L., Ritchie, A. J. & Whitlock, K. (2011). *Queer (in)justice: The criminalization of LGBT people in the United States*. Boston: Beacon Press.

Namaste, V. (2011). Beyond image content: Examining transsexuals' access to the media. In *Sex Change, Social Change* (2nd ed.) (pp. 41–59). Toronto: Women's Press.

Office of the Correctional Investigator. (2013). Backgrounder: Aboriginal offenders—A critical situation. *Government of Canada*. Retrieved from http://www.oci-bec.gc.ca/cnt/rpt/oth-aut/oth-aut20121022info-eng.aspx

PASAN & the Canadian AIDS Legal Network. (2007). *Hard time: Promoting HIV and hepatitis C prevention programming for prisoners in Canada*. Toronto: Canadian AIDS Legal Network.

Patton, C. (2002). *Globalizing AIDS*. Minneapolis: Minnesota University Press.

Piché, J. (2012). Accessing the state of imprisonment in Canada: Information barriers and negotiation strategies. In M. Larsen & K. Walby (Eds.), *Brokering access: Politics, power, and freedom of information in Canada* (pp. 234–260). Vancouver: UBC Press.

Puar, J. (2007). *Terrorist assemblages: Homonationalism in queer times.* Durham, NC: Duke University Press.

Rifkin, M. (2011). *When did Indians become straight?: Kinship, the history of sexuality, and Native sovereignty.* New York: Oxford University Press.

Sayers, N. (2015). Restorative justice and mental health as a young Indigenous woman. *Reimagining: Reigning in the New Skool*, 58–60.

Schulman, S. (1994). *My American history.* New York: Routledge.

Silverman, V. & Stryker, S. (Directors). (2005). *Screaming queens: The riot at Compton's cafeteria* [Motion picture]. USA: Frameline.

Slade, E., & Sweney, M. (Directors). (1992). *Acting up for prisoners* [Motion picture]. USA: Frameline.

Smith, M. (2012). Identity and opportunity: The lesbian gay rights movement. In M. Fitzgerald & S. Rayter (Eds.), *Queerly Canadian: An introductory reader in sexuality studies* (pp. 121–138). Toronto: Women's Press.

Smith, M. (2015). LGBTQ activism: The pan-Canadian political space. In M. Tremblay (Ed.), *Queer mobilizations: Social movement activism and Canadian public policy* (pp. 45–63). Vancouver: University of British Columbia Press.

Sontag, S. (1989). *Illness as metaphor* and *AIDS and its metaphors.* New York: Farrar, Straus, & Giroux.

Spade, D. (2011). *Normal life: Administrative violence, critical trans politics, and the limits of law.* Boston: South End.

Spurlin, W. J. (2009). *Lost intimacies: Rethinking homosexuality under national socialism.* New York: Peter Lang.

Stanley, E. (2011). Introduction: Fugitive flesh; Gender self-determination, queer abolition, and trans resistance. In E. Stanley & N. Smith (Eds.), *Captive genders: Trans embodiment and the prison industrial complex.* Oakland, CA: AK Press.

Stockdill, B. C. (2003). *Activism against AIDS: At the intersections of sexuality, race, gender, and class.* Boulder, CO: Lynne Reinner.

Stryker, S. (2008). *Transgender history.* Berkeley, CA: Seal Press.

Symington, A. (2009). Criminalization confusion and concerns: The decade since the Cuerrier decision. *HIV/AIDS Policy and Law Review*, 14(1), 1–10.

Talvi, S. J. A. (2007). *Women behind bars: The crisis of women in the US prison system.* Emeryville, CA: Seal Press.

Thobani, S. (2007). *Exalted subjects: Studies in the making of race and nation in Canada.* Toronto: University of Toronto Press.

Ware, W. (2011). Rounding up the homosexuals: The impact of the juvenile court on queer and trans/gender-non-conforming youth. In E. Stanley & N. Smith (Eds.), *Captive genders: Trans embodiment and the prison industrial complex.* Oakland, CA: AK Press.

Withers, A. J. (2012). *Disability politics & theory.* Halifax: Fernwood.

Yee, J. (2011). *Feminism for real: Deconstructing the academic industrial complex of feminism.* Toronto: Canadian Centre for Policy Alternatives.

Building Communities of Justice: Working Toward a Solution

CHAPTER 11

Gendering Justice: Exploring Community-Based Options for Women and Girls

Rai Reece

Chapter Objectives

This chapter will explore a variety of community-based justice options for women and girls who are involved in the Canadian criminal justice system. Although the number of women who are in prison or involved in the justice system continues to be significantly lower than the number of men, the potential impact on the family when women are incarcerated tends to be higher. In addition, there continues to be an increase in the number of Aboriginal, Black, and poor White women who are entering the Canadian criminal justice system. Consequently, this results in gendered dimensions and configurations that come into play when examining pre- and post-release strategies for women and girls. This chapter will help the reader develop an understanding of the importance of exploring how effective reintegration strategies can provide support for women and girls who are leaving custody and returning to their respective communities.

ranges

ranges

Prison is being naked emotionally for the first time in your memory, with nowhere to hide. ... I build walls around my feelings and barricade my heart as best I can. I count my months, my days, until canteen, until lock-up, until release. I feel anxiety and deep depression sometimes when I look at the calendar. The world is farther away with every season. My survival here is all I have.

— Prisoner at Prison for Women, prior to its closing (Task Force on Federally
    Sentenced Women, 1990)

Introduction

Exploring community-based options for women and girls involved in the Canadian criminal justice system asks fundamental questions: First, what are key social determinants that may have affected women and girls prior to contact with the criminal justice system? Second, (how) does race, class, gender, and ability factor into effective program planning for women and girls post-release? Third, how can community-based options for women and girls exiting custodial institutions be sustained when systemic oppressions such as poverty, lack of education, lack of employment skills, and inadequate health care persist in their respective communities? We ask these questions in order to begin working toward strategies to best support short-term and long-term initiatives for women and girls in custody and post-release.

Women and girls who are involved in the Canadian criminal justice system represent a small cohort of the overall numbers of persons in pretrial custody, on bail, incarcerated, or under community supervision. According to Mahony (2011), most information regarding women and girls in custody is taken from recorded criminal incidents that are reported to police and/or are processed through the courts and correctional systems—these are referred to as administrative data sources. In April 2014, there was a total of 1,098 federally sentenced women in Canada, with 628 (57 percent) serving time in federal institutions and 470 (43 percent) under community supervision (Correctional Service Canada, 2015). In regard to the overall Canadian prison population, women prisoners comprise approximately 5 percent of that total population (CSC, 2015). In Canada the overall rate of youth (ages 12 to 17) charged has declined between 2007 and 2012 (Public Safety Canada, 2013). For example, in 2011/2012 in Ontario there were 13,958 youth admissions to correctional services, and, of these, 2,733 (19.6 percent) represented girls under some form of custodial supervision, and 415 (5.3 percent) were identified as Aboriginal (Public Safety Canada, 2013). Comparatively, in 2013/2014, for nine reporting jurisdictions (excluding Nova Scotia, New Brunswick, Quebec, and Alberta), there were 9,458 youth being supervised on an average day (Statistics Canada, 2015). Most youth admitted to correctional facilities are, on average, 15 years of age and male (Perreault, 2014). Although the youth crime rate has been decreasing over the last decade (Boyce, 2014, cited in Statistics Canada, 2015), it is important to note that similar to adult women in the federal and provincial system, there is overrepresentation of Aboriginal youth in Canadian correctional services. In addition to this, there is little information about the numbers of other racialized girls in contact with the criminal justice system.

The number of women and girls involved in the Canadian criminal justice system is relatively low compared to men. The critical needs of this population tend to be examined less through a political, bureaucratic, and socially responsive lens. Historically, programming for women and girls often relied on male-centred cognitive models as primary templates for reintegration processes. This means that issues specific to women and girls, such as sexual and domestic violence trauma, substance use, the feminization of poverty, and un/underemployment, were often ignored. According to the Correctional Service Canada (2015, March 5), incarcerated women require considerable support in terms of academic and vocational skills, and behavioural and emotional needs. Furthermore, women seeking work often have little education and/or previous employment experience (CSC, 2015, March 5). In order to examine the importance of relevant post-release community-based programming for women and girls, we can explore how gender and anti-racist feminist theory can be beneficial for practical program planning. Furthermore, any analysis of gendered incarceration has to take into account the role and status of women and girls in relation to Canada's social welfare state. According to Kim Pate (2011),

> as we see the further erosion of Canada's international reputation as human rights defenders of women, children, especially those most vulnerable because of multiple intersections of marginalization and discrimination, be it race, sexual orientation, ability—particularly disabling mental health issues—or those escaping violence, we are witnessing the exponential growth of women in prison. Women and girls are the fastest growing prison population worldwide. (para. 4)

In this chapter, we refer to Canada's social welfare system as that which includes, but is not limited to, immigration, education, and health care systems that are designed to maintain an adequate level of social well-being for members of Canadian society. Moreover, Canada's social welfare system is also very much a "raced" social welfare system whereby the creation of moral panics around immigration, terror, and all forms of violence fulfills and fuels conservative rhetoric that bolsters and supports law and order agendas. The term *moral panic* refers to the fear of some form of a threat—perceived or real—to society. The term was first popularized in Stanley Cohen's 1972 book *Folk Devils and Moral Panics: The Creation of Mods and Rockers*. In our contemporary society this term is often used sociologically in reference to perceived threats to social order (e.g., terrorism, human trafficking, crime increases). With regard to Canada's social welfare system, moral panic leads to heightened police surveillance and targeting of racialized and socio-economically deprived communities, and results in a disproportionate number of Aboriginals and Blacks in the Canadian criminal justice system, discriminatory police carding practices, anti-Muslim mosque vandalism, and the streaming of racialized children via the school to prison pipeline (see chapter 5 in this text). The Canadian state was "amongst the first countries to be impacted by the regressive, so-called law and order agenda, which [is] making prisons the default option for those most significantly impacted by the destruction of social safety nets, and the evisceration of medical, economic and education standards and services" (Pate, 2011, para. 5). Furthermore, the Canadian state has become complicit in criminalizing poverty and relying on prisons as a primary means of social control (Pate, 2011, para. 12).

Social control refers to the many institutional, systemic, and sometimes overt processes that are directly connected to the racialization of crime. Evidence of social control can be seen in practical and bureaucratic ways. One practical example is the employment of school resource officers (SROs), also known as police officers, in Canadian high schools as a way to curtail violence or other student disruptions. Although the presence of SROs in high schools may seem like a proactive measure to address violence, some have argued that this form of policing disproportionately affects racialized students who have experienced police discrimination in their neighbourhoods, and that this discrimination carries over into their educational environments. Another practical example of social control is the increase of criminalizing people in poor communities of colour. Over-policing practices such as racial profiling or racialized carding can result in an increase in the number of people of colour coming in contact with the criminal justice system and, therefore, potentially with the jail and prison systems. Bureaucratic examples of social control can be seen via immigration and refugee policies and practices of discrimination that make entry and permanent stay in Canada challenging. In Canada, immigration policy is the responsibility of the federal government. In 2012, the government placed a two-year moratorium on the sponsorship of parents and grandparents. Beiser and Bauder (2014) explain that although the moratorium was lifted in 2014, immigrants who wish to sponsor family members require a 30 percent higher minimum income than previously. In addition to this, immigrants were previously required to support sponsored family members for 10 years, but the new requirement is now 20 years (Beiser & Bauder, 2014). The reality of more stringent immigration policies is that families working to provide better life circumstances for their loved ones are placed in greater economic distress while trying to meet the requirements. Under the previous Conservative government, becoming a Canadian citizen was made more difficult because the application fees were tripled and the residency requirement increased from three years to four (Beiser & Bauder, 2014). These realities make it imperative to critically examine how social control practices, such as increasingly stringent immigration requirements and the racialization of crime, affect community-based justice options for women and girls.

The Relevance of Anti-Racist Feminist Theorizing for Community-Based Justice Approaches

Anti-racist feminists focus on deconstructing race and gender in an effort to focus on historic patterns of racialization in Canada (Dua, 1999) and can help us understand the experiences of women and girls in prison. One way to do this is to examine how anti-racist feminism can shed light on how the intersectional experiences of women's lives are important to understanding factors that may contribute to women and girls coming into contact with the Canadian criminal justice system. Anti-racist feminism emerged in the 1990s, and it continues to recognize the intersectionality of race, class, gender, dis/ability, and sexuality. This theory is important because it brings the experiences of racialized, differently abled, and, in some cases, poor White women and girls to the forefront of debates that traditionally negated or compartmentalized their narratives.

In this context, anti-racist feminist theorizing is connected to community-based justice approaches for women and girls because the theory investigates how the reproduction of racism cements interlocking oppressions such as those based on race, class, gender, and ability, and how these issues are connected to relevant post-release programming. In Canada, "democratic racism" (see Henry & Tator, 2009) refers to institutionalized and systemic racism that is embedded in political and social procedures and policies that disproportionately affect racialized people. Since race relations discourse has traditionally revolved around ethnicity dynamics[1] and racism is connected to power, we can use anti-racist feminism to explore the ways in which community-based justice options would be most beneficial for racialized women and girls in penal institutions.

Theoretically, anti-racist feminism centres the narratives of racialized women's experiences in the criminal justice system. For example, Black women in Canada are experiencing rising rates of incarceration due to their socio-economic status and tend to be incarcerated for poverty-related crimes such a drug muling[2] (Reece, 2010). Furthermore, Aboriginal women make up a disproportionate number of women in prison and historically have the highest rate of incarceration for women. According to the *2013–2014 Annual Report of the Office of the Correctional Investigator*, the total number of Aboriginal women prisoners has more than doubled since 2004–2005 and one in three women prisoners are Aboriginal (Sapers, 2014). Both of these groups of women experience social marginalization due to racism that manifests itself in high rates of physical, emotional, and sexual abuse; homelessness or under-housing; and mental health challenges. Both groups also experience high rates of lone parenthood and trauma due to lack of bonding and separation from their children.[3]

An anti-racist feminist lens provides a framework for addressing the specific needs of racialized women that may be overlooked in program design. It is important to take into account and understand these issues when designing and planning community-based programming. For Aboriginal women, this means taking into account their traumatic histories, which include cultural genocide, social exclusion, and marginalization. Program development and implementation should take into account cultural teachings, such as respect for traditional ways of dealing with intra- and interpersonal harm. For example, many Aboriginal communities use restorative justice healing circles as a way to begin repairing harm done to an individual and the community. Restorative justice approaches focus on perpetrator responsibility, healing, community restoration, and victim empowerment. It is necessary to consider these principles when implementing community-based programs in order to promote inclusivity and equity. Anti-racist feminist theorizing examines the fact that in Canada, women without legal status, with no political power, who are living at or below the poverty line, and who are racialized and minoritized are literally displaced within the Canadian landscape. Strategically, this renders women and girls who reside in these categories invisible and means that those who are in prison face numerous challenges in addition to having a criminal record. Having a criminal record further complicates reintegration for women and girls due to social stigma and discrimination.

Effective community-based justice programming should directly examine how women and girls in custody and upon post-release have experienced multiple oppressions, such as poverty, racism, disability, and/or sexism—all factors that may have contributed to their contact with the law. For example, programming that addresses domestic violence and women abuse ought to be contextualized based on cultural understandings of this issue, rather than through a Eurocentric lens. Additionally, community-based justice programming that addresses residual trauma, stigma, healing, and reunification for women and girls and their families would serve as beneficial for safe family reunification.[4] With these factors in mind, effective socially conscious community-based programming for women and girls must underscore and practice applied social justice.

Gendered Community-Based Responses for Women and Girls

The women's risk/needs assessment (WRNA) is a tool that can be used as a starting point to identify gender-specific issues that affect the "pathways to prison" pipeline for women and girls (Van Voorhis, Bauman, Wright, & Salisbury, 2009). Canadian scholars Andrews, Looman, and Gendreau (see Van Voorhis et al., 2009) have conducted extensive studies that examine the effectiveness of WRNA as a resource for community-based reintegration and rehabilitation. The risk-needs-responsivity model (RNR) was developed by Canadian scholars Andrews and Bonta (see Looman & Abracen, 2013) and emerged as the premier treatment approach for prisoners in Canada. The model is highly regarded as a reliable assessment tool for identifying which prisoners pose the greatest risk for recidivism based on criminogenic needs. Assessments based on this model are designed to address the crime a person has been convicted of, the reasons why that crime may have been committed, and the type of programming that should help address their specific situation. In particular, the RNR principles gained popularity due the fact that treatment approaches resulted in a reduction in sexual offence and violent crime recidivism (Hanson, Bourgon, Helmus, & Hodgins, 2009, as cited in Looman & Abracen, 2013). The RNR model has been popular in Canada and internationally in the United Kingdom, New Zealand, and Australia for decades (Looman & Abracen, 2013), because it was specifically designed for use in prisons and jails. Conversely, the RNR model has been criticized due to the fact that it was designed with male prisoner populations in mind, and therefore lacks a gendered perspective. As indicated earlier, the numbers of women and girls in the Canadian criminal justice system have been low; therefore the specific needs of women were not recognized as necessary to rehabilitation programming. However, feminist criminologists such as Chesney-Lind (2006) and Daly and Maher (1998) have sought to shift this theoretical paradigm by expressing the need for a gender-responsive model to address women and girls' involvement in the criminal justice system (Bloom, Owen, & Covington, 2003, as cited by Van Voorhis et al., 2009). The specific gendered challenges that women and girls face can include a range of traumas, sexual and/or physical abuse, parental stress, mental health challenges, homelessness, under-education, and addictions. Given that most women and girls are incarcerated for property-related or drug offences, gendered assessments and responses to these types of offences will help support rehabilitation that specifically addresses women's economic deprivation to include more nuanced approaches to the needs of women and girls.

Community-Based Justice Programs at a Glance

Community-based programs are not new to the terrain of correctional programming. The United States has long since implemented diversion programs for youth and in-house correctional programs that address cognitive behaviour changes. Historically, youth-based programs have employed group behavioural modification, and community intervention through employment and education (Ross & Gendreau, 1980). Hyper-sensationalized contemporary representations of community-based justice programs for youth take the form of media-glamorized Scared Straight programs that are designed to subject groups of "at-risk" youth to the threatening antics of "big bad prisoners." The undercurrent tagline for this sort of media circus is supposed to provide enough of a "real-life" scare tactic to remove negative stimuli from youth and replace it with positive stimuli, and therefore effect behavioural change. Evidence-based research has suggested that Scared Straight programs provide Band-Aid solutions and do not tackle the institutional and systemic oppressions that are mitigating factors that contribute to youth in the criminal justice system (Finckenauer, 2005).

In Canada, the colonial legacy and cultural genocide that has been and continues to be perpetuated toward Aboriginal communities via conservative agendas persists in fracturing Aboriginal families, and contributes to the socio-cultural and political destruction of their communities. This has resulted in a disproportionate number of Aboriginal women and girls in the Canadian criminal justice system. Between 2002 and 2012, the number of Aboriginal women incarcerated in federal institutions grew by 97 percent; in comparison, the number of incarcerated Aboriginal men grew by 34 percent during the same period (Rennie, 2014). The 2013 Federal Department of Justice report containing this information argues that "much of the attention to this overrepresentation has been focused on aboriginal people as a whole, without giving appropriate attention to the unique situation of aboriginal women as offenders" (Rennie, 2014). Addressing the needs of women and girls in the Canadian criminal justice system also requires a financial investment in community-based justice programs. In 2014, Canada's Economic Action Plan included a proposed $22.2 million over two years for the Aboriginal Justice Strategy (AJS) (Canada, n.d.). As part of this strategy, in March 2015, the Canadian government announced funding for Aboriginal justice programs[5] in the Northwest Territories. The funding of $631,204 over two years for the Northwest Territories Department of Justice Community Justice Division is intended to provide restorative justice services and crime reduction programs with additional community supports in 13 communities across the territory (Department of Justice Canada, 2015). A critical aspect of the program also is aimed at reintegration support for prisoners and on-the-land programs[6] for youth (Department of Justice Canada, 2015). The program's strategy utilizes two key funds: (1) the Community-Based Justice Fund, which supports community-based justice programs in partnership with Aboriginal communities and is designed to reflect Aboriginal cultural values; and (2) the Capacity-Building Fund, which focuses on professional development, vocational training, and building partnerships between the mainstream justice system and Aboriginal communities (Department of Justice Canada, 2015). The AJS may be a long overdue step in the right direction for Aboriginal women and girls under correctional jurisdiction, but for many other racialized women and minoritized women, community-based options continue to be limited.

Black women, women who are differently abled, women with mental health challenges, poor White women, and women who identify as LGBTQ+ are minoritized members of the prison populations whose specific needs also require a critical lens. The material conditions of minoritized and racialized women's lives are grounded in the realities of class, gender, and racial oppression. Anti-racist feminist theorizing can address how to best create sustainable and applicable community-based justice options for women and girls by examining the complex variables that are magnified when one is incarcerated. For example, in a recent article based on research conducted by Flora Matheson of the Centre for Research on Inner City Health of St. Michael's Hospital in Toronto, she argues that "from a Canadian perspective, it actually shows that you know the women are crying out for help with their experiences of trauma, that they want some services" (CBC News, 2015). Furthermore, according to the Canadian Association of Elizabeth Fry Societies, "about 80 per cent of women serving two years or more in federal custody had histories of physical or sexual abuse, which increased to 91 per cent among Aboriginal women" (CBC News, 2015). Applied social justice community-based programming that utilizes a gendered lens can begin to address the afore-mentioned issues by exploring and developing individually tailored best prac-tices for post-release that address addictions, reunification/reintegration, and separation anxiety and trauma.

Research has indicated that women in prison are expressly concerned with housing and employment once released and that pre-release integration pro-grams are lacking in terms of preparing women to navigate the job market, par-ticularly with a criminal record (Blanchette & Dowden, 1998; Reece, 2010). Due to the high turnover rate in the provincial system for women and the fact that most youth are sentenced to probation, the efficacy of work-release programming for women and girls in the provincial system is challenging; however, it has been noted that in the federal system community-based work-release programs for women are lacking, and could be beneficial to reintegration processes (Delveaux, Blanchette, & Wicket, 2005). Organizations cannot develop effective community-based approaches for women and girls without first addressing systemic and rampant violence against women, poverty, racism, sexism, homophobia, classism, and ableism. Given that there continue to be challenges addressing these issues in Canadian political circles, and since the criminal courts are a part of our govern-ance, it becomes increasingly difficult to address and develop gender-responsive programming that has long-term results that are beneficial to women and girls.

Gender-Responsivity: Working Toward a New Paradigm

Work and a roof over my head are my two biggest concerns.
— **39-year-old woman serving time at Grand Valley Institution for Women**
(Reece, 2010)

Developing community-based justice programming for women and girls can be a complex process due to the fact that traditional rehabilitation and reintegration tend to focus on prisoner recidivism rather than addressing the root causes of crime (Reece, 2010). Hence, one of the critiques of the RNR model mentioned earlier is that the primary premise of the model focuses on the idea that risk assessment is the most important variable to reducing recidivism; however, many of the choices that women and girls make prior to coming in contact with the law ought to be understood in conjunction with challenges they are experiencing in their lives. Evidence-based research from a 2008–2009 study found that women in provincial and federal custody are less likely to have a high school diploma and more likely to be unemployed than women in the overall Canadian population (Mahony, 2011). Among women prisoners in provincial institutions, 50 percent of did not complete secondary school, while 43 percent had a high school diploma and 12 percent had completed some post-secondary education (Mahony, 2011). The middle-class measuring rod dictates that one key to social mobility and success is education, and little or limited education reduces one's chances for personal success. Other intersecting variables, such as lack of adequate health care, violence against women, mental health challenges, poverty, racism, and sexism, only exacerbate this issue and significantly reduce a woman's chances for success.

In order for community-based justice programs to be relevant to incarcerated women and girls, they must be connected to social justice frameworks that operate within an anti-racist and anti-oppressive framework. Justice programs should be developed in consultation with women and girls regarding their needs, and work with and build coalitions with community groups interested in working with and maintaining connections with incarcerated women and girls. In addition, community-based justice programs should take into account the multiple sites of diversity among women and girls and acknowledge the effects of systemic and institutional oppression that have an indelible impact on their lives.

In general, Correctional Service Canada (CSC) is mandated to provide programming in four areas: correctional, educational, social, and vocational (CSC, 2014). At Grand Valley Institution for Women (GVIW) in Kitchener, Ontario, there are several programs aimed at preparing women for life post-release that fall under one of these categories. Programs such as the Chaplaincy Program, Alternatives to Violence, Woman Offender Substance Abuse Program (WOSAP), and the Stride program are offered at GVIW. It is important to note that women entering GVIW on drug-related charges are required to participate in WOSAP, whether or not their charge is related to using drugs or muling drugs. The Stride[7] program perhaps offers one of the most useful reintegration programs for women, since it matches women in prison with a volunteer from the community who then assists them in the process of social reintegration. The premise behind Stride is that is it a multi-stage program, meaning that it is designed to assist incarcerated women take various strides toward social development in the areas of employment, housing, and personal growth. Similarly under the social programs category, the Social Integration Program for Women is designed to target community living issues and help women plan for a healthy lifestyle, which includes teaching them how to form and maintain healthy relationships in the community, and provide information on employment and other aspects of community living (CSC, 2014); however, due to limited program spots, there is often a wait-list for women to enter these programs (Thompson, 2015).

According to METRAC,

> the needs of provincially-imprisoned women include education upgrading, vocational training, job-search skills, job skills, life skills, addictions treatment, counseling, financial planning skills, health-care, and housing advocacy. ... [and] [m]arginalized women in prison, especially Aboriginal women, are at a systemic disadvantage that can be compounded by legal issues. (2008, para. 9)

Although programming differs in the provincial and federal systems, clearly the common factors for reintegration success are the same for women exiting either system; the requirements of family and community support upon release are critical factors for societal reintegration.

An integrated approach to community-based justice programming should also examine what has and has not worked in terms of sentencing and post-custodial responses for women and girls in the Canadian criminal justice system. In an effort to work toward solutions, we turn our attention to discussions concerning recommendations and suggestions that would be beneficial to women and girls especially for community agencies that want to work with this population. This process could begin with community agencies, shelters, employment agencies, treatment centres, education institutions, and health care facilities working with women and girls on pre-release planning that is applicable to their specific needs. Similarly, community-based justice programming should also begin prior to women and girls exiting custodial settings.

At GVIW, the federal prison was originally designed to accommodate 130 women, and a 40-bed minimum-security unit was added in 2015. As of March 2015, 183 women were incarcerated at the institution (Thompson, 2015). With this increase in capacity, it is unlikely that the available programming inside the prison will be able to meet the demands of the population, and women who require specific programming as a fundamental condition of their release will be put in jeopardy for non-completion of requirements. Consequently, conditions for their release become tenuous and make the possibility for effective post-release community-based programming challenging. A solution to this problem begins during the sentencing phase of the criminal court process. Given that women and girls tend to be incarcerated for poverty-, drug use- or sex work-related offences, it is more practical to recommend women for treatment programs or community-service related programs that would be of greater benefit to them than incarceration. Furthermore, women and girl probationers tend to be a generally low-risk group compared to men, although they may struggle with completing supervision successfully (Salisbury, Van Voorhis, Wright, & Bauman, 2009). As mentioned earlier, community-based justice programs that include trauma counselling and that implement and provide "holistic, wraparound services that target past and current victimization, depression and anxiety, substance abuse, low self-efficacy, unhealthy relationships, educational deficits, and poverty" (Salisbury et al., 2009, p. 84) are critical to reintegration and reunification success. The latter point is well taken and can aid in the successful completion of probation compliance if services are tailored to address the residual trauma and challenges that women and girls deal with on a daily basis. Probation reporting conditions are traditionally implemented in a way that does not take into account the fact that many women on probation may be the primary caregivers for their child/ren or other family members, may be the sole financial providers for their family, and may be dealing with a dysfunctional relationship and abject poverty. Applied social justice theory and practice takes aim at these factors and seeks to work in concert with a gender-responsive lens to create effective and efficient long-term stability and success.

Summary and Conclusion: Gendered Justice or Injustice?

The degree of civilization in a society can be judged by entering its prisons.
— Fyodor Dostoyevsky, Russian novelist (1821–1881)

Carceral spaces are complex spaces. If prisons and jails measure "success rates" for rehabilitation according to prisoner recidivism, the picture is incomplete. This mode of measurement does not take into account many of the struggles (e.g., poverty, abuse, stigma, unemployment, disconnection from family and friends) that women and girls face both prior to coming into contact with the Canadian criminal justice system and post-release. When women and girls in general, and racialized and minoritized women and girls specifically, do not return to prison, this does not necessarily mean that they have achieved economic and social parity with the mainstream. This chapter has argued for the necessity of a more nuanced focus on the particularities of socio-political experiences of women and girls in contact with the Canadian criminal justice system. There has been a lack of research in the social sciences that has explicitly sought to examine this often overlooked segment of the jail and prison population. Furthermore, the intersectional variables of race, class, gender, and ability are seldom considered when the application of program imperatives is delivered. This chapter has sought to underscore the importance of considering these key intersectional variables when developing community-based justice programming for women and girls in custodial spaces and post-release. It has also argued that community-based resource strategies and programming are more beneficial than a reliance on incarceration to "fix" women and girls in contact with Canadian law. In terms of public policy imperatives, this chapter also calls for mandatory program evaluation that measures the efficacy and effectiveness of community-based programming in order to create an integrative approach that qualitatively includes decision-making processes in the delivery of programming, the results of which can be used for short- and long-term social policy implementation.

Women and girls are located in a variety of class positions, and therefore an investment in *herstories* is important to understand and acknowledge this reality. For many women and girls, post-release hardships will be magnified by the fact that they have a criminal record. Community-based justice programming that equips women and girls with the tools to navigate these dilemmas is a starting point on a journey that may seem uncertain and uneasy for many exiting custodial spaces. Generally, broad implications from this chapter are meant to challenge the prevailing stigma, assumptions, and prejudices that many people with criminal records experience. Specifically, it suggests that for women and girls in contact with the Canadian criminal justice system, applied social justice imperatives and gender-responsive analysis in both theory and practice are a good starting point in a move toward to personal empowerment and navigating that journey.

Discussion Questions

1. Discuss the importance of anti-racist feminist theorizing for community-based justice approaches for women and girls in contact with the Canadian criminal justice system.
2. What are some of the critiques of the risk-needs-responsivity model as it applies to the needs of women and girls in the Canadian criminal justice system? How might a gendered lens address these challenges?
3. Design a community-based program for women and girls exiting custodial spaces. In the design of your program consider the needs of your target population, what social service agencies you might partner with and why, how your program could facilitate family reunification, and what some initial program start-up challenges may be.

Additional Resources

Justice for Children and Youth: http://jfcy.org/en/all-jfcy-videos/.

Justice for Girls: http://www.justiceforgirls.org.

Prison-Justice.ca. (n.d.). Activist links: www.prisonjustice.ca/resources_links/activist_links.html.

Prison State Canada: Resisting the Oppressive Arm of the Canadian State and Seeking Out Human Rights Based Alternatives [Blogspot]: http://prisonstatecanada.blogspot.ca/p/women.html.

The Prison System in Canada—Stories from the Revolving Door [Video]. (2012). Vancouver: Pull Focus: www.youtube.com/watch?v=Eb61P8GJrLc.

Stone, L. (2012, May 25). After an Inmate's Release, the Struggle Begins; More Than One in Three Women Will Eventually Return to Custody: Report. *Calgary Herald*: www.canada.com/news/alberta/after+inmate+release+struggle+begins/5553868/story.html.

Stone, L. (2014, April 6). Canada's Women Prison Plan Includes Rooms for Mothers—and Children. *Global News*: www.globalnews.ca/news/1191486/canadas-women-prison-expansion-includes-rooms-for-mothers-and-children/.

Task Force on Federally Sentenced Women (TFFSW). (1990). *Creating Choices: The Report of the Task Force on Federally Sentenced Women*. Ottawa: Correctional Service Canada: http://www.csc-scc.gc.ca/women/toce-eng.shtml.

Notes

1. As outlined by Henry and Tator (2006), discourses on ethnicity have been central to debates around social class. Scholars have argued that the focus on ethnicity may actually negate processes of racialization and the prevalence of racism that people of colour face on a daily basis. Overemphasis on ethnic relations obscures systemic racism and the social structural factors that marginalize people of colour, because discussions about the workings of White privilege, Whiteness, and institutionalized racism are negated.
2. Drug mules are persons who carry large quantities of illegal narcotics across land borders for a fee. These narcotics are often transported on the person or by ingesting.

3. Howard Sapers's *2013–2014 Annual Report of the Office of the Correctional Investigator* suggested that Correctional Service Canada implement CHILD LINK at all regional women's facilities. CHILD LINK was a pilot project that operated from February to June 2013, which allowed for women approved by a Child and Family Services (CFS) worker and who were the primary caregivers of their child/ren at the time of incarceration to participate in video conferencing with their children at a predetermined location in a large city centre.

4. I am referring here to reunification that is empowering and consensual, and that does not place women and children in physical, emotional, or mental harm.

5. For an in-depth look at the program, see www.justice.gc.ca/eng/rp-pr/aj-ja/fs09-fi09.html.

6. These are government-funded, community-led justice programs for youth that are developed in consultation and partnership with Aboriginal communities. On-the-land programs focus on strength-based approaches to program development (related to employment, education, and life skills training) for youth in their communities and/or on reserves.

7. Stride refers to Community Justice Initiative Program Circles. Volunteers provide support to women who they are matched up with prior to release from prison. The goal is to assist women in their reintegration to the community. A woman works with her circle to find employment, housing, and education.

References

Beiser, M., & Bauder, H. (2014, May 12). Canada's immigration system undergoing quiet, ugly revolution. *Toronto Star.* Retrieved from www.thestar.com/opinion/commentary/2014/05/12/canadas_immigration_system_undergoing_quiet_ugly_revolution.html

Blanchette, K., & Dowden, C. (1998). A profile of federally sentenced women in the community: Addressing needs for successful integration. *Forum on Corrections Research,* (10)1.

Canada. (n.d.). *Canada's Economic Action Plan.* Ottawa: Government of Canada. Retrieved from www.actionplan.gc.ca/en/initiative/aboriginal-justice-strategy (site no longer active)

CBC News. (2015, January 6). Abuse, trauma leads women in prison to cry out for help. *CBC News.* Retrieved from www.cbc.ca/news/health/abuse-trauma-leads-women-in-prison-to-cry-out-for-help-1.2891680

Chesney-Lind, M. (2006). Editorial. *Feminist Criminology, 3*(1), 3–5.

Cohen, S. (1972). *Folk devils and moral panics.* London: MacGibbon and Kee.

Correctional Service Canada (CSC). (2014, December 9). Offender rehabilitation. Retrieved from www.csc-scc.gc.ca/correctional-process/002001-2000-eng.shtml

Correctional Service Canada (CSC). (2015, March 5). A profile of federally sentenced women in the community: Addressing needs for successful integration. *FORUM on Corrections Research.* Retrieved from www.csc-scc.gc.ca/research/forum/e101/e101i-eng.shtml

Correctional Service Canada (CSC). (2015). Research results: Women offenders. Retrieved from http://www.csc-scc.gc.ca/publications/005007-3014-eng.shtml#_ftn1

Daly, K., & Maher, L. (1998). Crossroads and intersections: Building from feminist critique. In K. Daly & L. Maher (Eds.), *Criminology at the crossroads: Feminist readings in crime and justice* (pp. 1–17). New York: Oxford University Press.

Delveaux, K., Blanchette, K., & Wicket, J. (2005, April). *Employment needs, interests, and programming for women offenders.* Research Branch, Correctional Service Canada. Retrieved from www.csc-scc.gc.ca/research/r166-eng.shtml

Department of Justice Canada. (2015, March 12). Government of Canada announces funding for Aboriginal justice programs in Northwest Territories. *Government of Canada.* Retrieved from www.news.gc.ca/web/article-en.do?nid=947649

Dua, E. (1999). Canadian anti-racist feminist thought: Scratching the surface of racism. In E. Dua & A. Robertson (Eds.), *Scratching the surface: Canadian anti-racist feminist thought* (pp. 7–31). Toronto: Women's Press.

Finckenauer, J. (2005). Ruminating about boot camps: Panaceas, paradoxes, and ideology. *Journal of Offender Rehabilitation, 40*(3/4), 199–207.

Henry, F., & Tator, C. (2009). *The color of democracy: Racism in Canadian society* (4th ed.). Toronto: Thomson Nelson.

Looman, J., & Abracen, J. (2013). The risk need responsivity model of offender rehabilitation: Is there really a need for a paradigm shift? *International Journal of Behavioural Consultation and Therapy, 8*(3/4), 30–36.

Mahony, T. H. (2011, April). Women and the criminal justice system. Catalogue no. 89-503-X. Ottawa: Statistics Canada. Retrieved from www.statcan.gc.ca/pub/89-503-x/2010001/article/11416-eng.htm

METRAC. (2008). Women in provincial institutions. *Ontario Women's Justice Network.* Retrieved from www.owjn.org/owjn_2009/component/content/article/41-criminalized-women/60-criminalized-women-women-in-provincial-institutions

Pate, K. (2011, April 26). Best interests of the child: A promise broken. Why are women Canada's fastest growing prison population; and, why should you care? A Defence for Children International—Canada Grant Lowery Lecture. Retrieved from http://www.caefs.ca/wp-content/uploads/2013/05/Why_are_women_Canadas_fastest_growing_prison_population_and_why_should_youcare.pdf

Perreault, S. (2014, March 27). Admissions to youth correctional services in Canada, 2011/2012. *Statistics Canada.* Retrieved from www.statcan.gc.ca/pub/85-002-x/2014001/article/11917-eng.htm

Public Safety Canada Portfolio Corrections Statistics Committee. (2013). *Corrections and conditional release statistical overview, 2013.* Ottawa: Public Works and Government Services Canada. Retrieved from http://www.publicsafety.gc.ca/cnt/rsrcs/pblctns/ccrso-2013/crrctns-cndtnl-rls-2013-eng.pdf

Reece, R. (2010). Caged (no) bodies: Exploring the racialized and gendered politics of incarceration of Black women in the Canadian prison system. Unpublished doctoral dissertation, York University.

Rennie, S. (2014, December 2). Huge increase in number of aboriginal women in Canadian prisons. *Toronto Star*. Retrieved from www.thestar.com/news/canada/2014/12/02/huge_increase_in_number_of_aboriginal_women_in_canadian_prisons.html

Ross. R. R., & Gendreau, P. (1980). Effective correctional treatment. *National Criminal Justice Reference Service*. Retrieved from www.ncjrs.gov/App/Publications/abstract.aspx?ID=73342

Salisbury, E. J., Van Voorhis, P., Wright, E. M., & Bauman, A. (2009). Changing probation experiences for female offenders based on women's needs and risk assessment project findings. *Women, Girls & Criminal Justice, 10*, 81–96.

Sapers, H. (2014, June 27). *Annual report of the Office of the Correctional Investigator 2013–2014*. Catalogue no. PS100-2014E-PDF. Ottawa: The Correctional Investigator Canada. Retrieved from http://www.ocibec.gc.ca/cnt/rpt/annrpt/annrpt20132014-eng.aspx#sV

Statistics Canada. (2015). Police-reported crime statistics, 2014. *Statistics Canada*. Retrieved from http://www.statcan.gc.ca/daily-quotidien/150722/dq150722a-eng.htm

Task Force on Federally Sentenced Women. (1990). *Creating choices: The report of the Task Force on Federally Sentenced Women*. Ottawa: Correctional Service Canada. Retrieved from http://www.csc-scc.gc.ca/women/toce-eng.shtml

Thompson, C. (2015, March 19). Kitchener prison opens new minimum security wing. *Waterloo Region Record*. Retrieved from www.therecord.com/news-story/5516501-kitchener-prison-opens-new-minimum-security-wing/

Van Voorhis, P., Bauman, A., Wright, E. M., & Salisbury, E. J. (2009). Implementing the Women's Risk/Needs Assessment (WRNAs): Early lessons from the field. *Women, Girls & Criminal Justice, 10*(6), 81–96.

CHAPTER 12

Building Healthy Communities and Reducing Crime: Communities of Practice

Beverly-Jean M. Daniel

Chapter Objectives

This chapter will highlight the varying forms of community-based justice initiatives that are being used to create healthier communities and address the varying forms of marginalization that are evidenced in the justice system and society as a whole.

What Are the Markers of a Healthy Community?

As has been argued throughout this book, crime occurs because there is dysfunction in communities. Crime happens when neighbourhoods are unhealthy. The chapters have provided discussions that examine the occurrence of crime in a variety of contexts. The consistent themes that flow through all of the chapters is that there are systemic and institutional practices of injustices that produce unhealthy communities, and unhealthy communities lead to higher levels of crime. This means that there are practices that are implemented and condoned by our governments, supported by our justice systems and authorities, and embedded as visible and invisible practices in all of our societal institutions. The school system and its agents provide a different quality of schooling and education to differently located student populations. Middle-class and rich kids get the best quality of education, while poor children receive a substandard quality of education that ill-prepares them to access good jobs and careers to support their families, thus leading to precarious or unstable employment, underemployment, or unemployment.

The justice system and all too many of its agents—police, lawyers, prosecutors, judges, etc.—engage in highly discriminatory practices that are embedded in their personal biases and prejudices, which lead to miscarriages of justice (Delgado & Stefanic, 2001) that continue to destroy communities. The creed of serving and protecting the public and the investment in statements of inclusion and equity seldom show up in daily practice. Social workers, who are charged with the task of supporting family integrity, play a significant role in the dismantling of families through practices of unjustifiable removal of children from families. Rather than ensuring that families that are already struggling to function are provided with the necessary supports to strengthen their familial bonds, all too many social workers place additional burdens on the family by removing children and getting police and lawyers involved. These practices, which unfairly target Aboriginal, Black (Comack, 2012), and, increasingly, South Asian families, serve to further fragment already tenuous bonds. Teachers, many of whom do not believe in the inherent capacity of all students (Downey, Ainsworth, & Qian, 2009; Haberman, 1991) can limit educational and career outcomes for students. All of these factors lead to familial and community fragmentation and crisis.

Based on the chapters in this book, it is clear that there is no direct connection between crime and race. Those in power, however, structure social relations and interactions in such a manner as to produce this mythical link. The reality is that those members of society who are racialized are exposed to conditions (e.g., poor quality schooling, imprisonment, injustices) that limit opportunities for economic advancement. For example, when crimes are committed by those who are racialized and marginalized, this information is continuously looped in all media outlets, thus producing moral panic and fear (Jewkes, 2011); however, when crime occurs among members of the dominant group, media coverage is minimized, and the crime is explained away and usually marked as a form of individual pathology or sickness. Therefore, the relationship between crime and race emerges because our thoughts and ideas are controlled, and at very unconscious levels we make the association between various racialized groups and crime. The reality in Canada is that the majority of offenders in the system are White. What we continue to critique, however, is the overrepresentation of some groups in the justice system not because they are committing more crimes, but because they are profiled and arrested at a significantly higher level, thus leading to their increased involvement in the justice system. Race cannot simply be replaced by class. A Black man, regardless of his social class, will be judged first by his skin colour (Cole, 2015).

If one were to remove the racialized group from a particular geographical area that is plagued by various forms of social crises and replace it with another racialized group, with the circumstances remaining the same, the outcomes would be the same. This notion has been referred to as *social disorganization*—the idea that disorganized neighbourhoods and environments are the primary factors that lead to crime, rather than individuals themselves (McMurtry & Curling, 2008; Sampson & Wilson, 2005; Shaw & McKay, 1942). This pattern is evident when we look at poverty and crime on a global scale. Within a North American context, Black and Aboriginal men are often regarded as the groups that commit most of the crimes; however, when crime occurs in other parts of the world, such as China or India or even in places like Scandinavia, they are not being committed by either Black or Aboriginal males. If there were a connection between race and crime, in parts of the world where there are no or very few Black or Aboriginal males, crime levels should be non-existent; however, crime occurs everywhere, and places that are plagued by poverty and varying forms of disenfranchisement, regardless of the racial or ethnic group that occupies the space, tend to have higher levels of survival crimes.

Healthy community development requires an investment in developing these spaces and a commitment to equitable funding and programming, as well as engagement with socially just and anti-oppressive practices. This means that the government will refrain from enacting laws such as mandatory minimum sentencing, which history and research show have no positive impacts on society or the community and heavily target already disenfranchised communities. Given that males generate higher incomes than women and that the basic well-being of families in this country requires the investment of two incomes for families to be economically viable, the continued targeting of Aboriginal, Black, and poor males of other racialized, immigrant, or economically impoverished communities is a guaranteed prescription for continued crisis in these communities. War on crime approaches should be renamed the "war on families," because the end result is the continued crisis in families and communities. It is interesting that the government creates these conditions, places multiple obstacles in the way of members of these communities (for example, increasing the cost of having a criminal record cleared), and underfunds support programs, but continues to increase funding for prisons and hiring more police.

Given that we know what leads to unhealthy communities—historical practices of oppression and marginalization, contemporary discrimination, destabilization of families by unjust practices at the institutional level, and the ongoing impact of experiences of injustice—we are also aware of what needs to be done to improve and produce healthy communities.

To ensure the development of healthy communities, some basic necessities have to be in place. These include affordable and safe housing options, spaces that are economically viable and where there are businesses that provide good jobs and opportunities for growth, and financial incentives and stability that allow for the raising of a family. Healthy communities also require the presence of schools and educational options that can lead to long-term personal, intellectual, and career-related growth. The teachers and other agents who staff the school have to believe and invest in the development potential of the children in those schools and be willing to identify strategies that can allow them to learn in spite of challenges. A basic example is recognizing that some of the projects outlined in the curriculum can be adapted to meet the needs of the local community, and that each child does not have to, for example, build a castle or have homework, particularly if parents or supports are not in place to help them with it. Instead, the classroom should be the place where the work and business of schooling is conducted. If children are supported in completing their work in school, their sense of accomplishment and reduction in levels of frustration is significantly enhanced. Small steps such as these can go a long way to supporting development and growth in communities.

Another requirement for developing healthy communities is that the neighbourhood must be safe. Most people, even in the most challenging circumstances, want to be able to rely on local police and authorities to keep them safe; however, the frayed relationships between community members and authorities and the practices that all too many officers engage in are counterproductive to community policing and healthy community development. Carding, stop-and-frisk, the assumption of guilt until proven innocent, and the ongoing harassment of members of racialized and marginalized communities by officers, simply because they have the power to do so, undermines public trust in the police.[1] This creates a dangerous cycle in which crimes occur, but the lack of trust in the police and/ or the justice system results in people's unwillingness to co-operate with the police, thus resulting in higher levels of crime because the offenders are never caught. Carding does not help to solve crimes (Tardiel, 2015), and if by chance it does solve some petty crimes, the resulting lack of trust in the police leads to more silence, more distrust, and higher levels of crime in already fragmented neighbourhoods. True community policing is about respect, understanding, and caring for the citizens of the space, rather than going in with the explicit and implicit assumption that the people who reside in these neighbourhoods are less deserving of the respect and service of the police than those in other neighbourhoods (Gans, 1995).

Reducing levels of crime in neighbourhoods requires a commitment from all stakeholders, starting with the government, local politicians, various justice systems, and members of the community (Warner, Beck, & Ohmer, 2010). Community-based justice approaches provide a platform and guide for supporting the development of healthy communities. They focus on relationship building, prevention, advocacy, and recognizing that simply because someone has committed a crime, it does not mean that person cannot be a contributing member of society. Therefore, providing opportunities for rehabilitation, reintegration, and supports to ensure that people can rebuild their lives, their families, and their communities is foundational to community justice practices. Community justice practices do not seek to completely replace the existing criminal justice system, rather they seek to provide options for reframing concepts and practices of justice that lead to positive outcomes for society as a whole rather than the continued development of practices and policies that lead to further dismantling of communities.

Although community justice programs have primarily been used to address minor crimes such as theft, family violence, youth crimes, and petty drug crimes, some consideration should be given to their use in relation to more significant crimes and cases, including gun possession, drug dealing charges, and gang involvement. The continued imprisonment of youth for drug-, gun-, and gang-related charges is counterproductive. Imprisonment essentially becomes a death sentence given that the options for building a viable future are almost non-existent when a person has a criminal record. Recognizing this, a youth with a criminal record sees few options for supporting their family other than continued involvement in criminal activities. Employing community justice options can serve to provide these youths with options that support their future development, rather than simply deploying reactionary responses to irrational fears of crime when, in reality, crime rates continue to drop.

What Are the Benefits of a Healthy Community?

Canada finds itself in a situation where it has now become, at least in its urban centres, one of the most diverse nations in the world. The level of diversity, although accompanied by some challenges, offers our best opportunities for moving forward, if harnessed and managed effectively. Each immigrant group brings with it a host of knowledges, insights, and opportunities that can provide Canadian businesses, colleges, and universities with access to global communities and resources. The increase in the Aboriginal population, which is a testament to their strength and resilience as a people, and the increasing number of members of LGBTQQ2 communities that feel safe enough to live their true identities in public, are also important factors to consider as we develop diversity policies and practices. When including emerging and growing populations, we must also remain aware that all groups do not experience oppression in the same way, and that we cannot erase some sites of oppression in favour of others. Race, for example, is an area in which Canadians continue to experience significant discomfort addressing and, as such, there has been an increasing unwillingness to explore the complexities of race-based oppression by subscribing to colour-blindness and the imaginings of a post-racial society.

The diversity in Canadian society can be harnessed within institutions and organizations to foster multiple viewpoints that can lead to expansive growth, development, and innovation. The recognition that the Canadian population demographic has experienced significant shifts and growth requires that we as a society become much more innovative in the ways in which we address the needs and wants of varying groups. Rather than stifling the growth in diversity, we should, as a society, harness the knowledge that accompanies these changes.

With that said, however, it should also be recognized that there must be realistic guidelines and rules that are applicable to all members of the society regardless of their origins. As much as Canada subscribes to an ethic of multiculturalism, which allows for people to maintain the languages, cultures, and religions of their homeland, the unrestrained and uncritical adoption of those practices can ultimately result in higher levels of crisis and involvement in the criminal justice system for some of these groups. An example of this would be the practice of having child brides, which is common in some Asian and African cultures;

however, in Canada, the age of consent is between 16 and 18. As such, if some groups maintain the practice of child brides, which would be considered illegal here, it would increase the possibility that men in these groups could be charged as child sex offenders and be put on the sex offender registry. Ensuring that there are clear guidelines put in place to explain such differences in legal, cultural, and religious norms can increase compliance with relevant laws and reduce criminal justice involvement because the laws are unclear. This level of clarity would support the development of healthy communities, limit the involvement of justice authorities, and lead to increased citizen involvement in the system.

Citizen involvement is another benefit of healthy communities. As the population has diversified, the level of political involvement, as evidenced by voting, has decreased in many neighbourhoods. When people do not experience a sense of inclusion and integration in the system or society, or believe that the society is not truly committed to their full participation, their level of investment and involvement declines. This can be seen in terms of conflictual relationships with police, limited participation in the political agenda, limited involvement in volunteer activities, and an adherence to the beliefs and practices of their parents' homeland, as evidenced in the increasing number of what have been termed "homegrown terrorists" (Haque, 2010; Philipupillai, 2013). Many of these youth are exposed to highly problematic versions of religion and beliefs that are often manifested as violence. The reality is that many of these youth are searching for a place of belonging and identity that they are not finding in Canada, which is often their place of birth or where they have lived since their formative years. Negative experiences with justice on the ground level in their everyday interactions, and with the criminal justice system, compounds these problems.

As Canadians, we must pay attention to these factors and enact practices that can help these youth develop their identities as Canadian citizens. The effective development and implementation of community justice initiatives requires representation from a broad stakeholder base in order to be truly inclusive and to produce outcomes that are beneficial to the community and its citizens. It is only when people are made to feel included that the true benefits of diversity will be realized in Canada, which can establish this country as a leader in fostering relationships across cultural, religious, and racial boundaries.

Community-Based Justice Initiatives on the Front Lines

In the following section, I will provide a brief discussion of some of the community justice initiatives that are in place in Canada. It is not within the scope of this chapter to provide a comprehensive interrogation of the projects.

Restorative justice, which is often used interchangeably with community justice, is actually a form of community justice. The four key values of the restorative justice paradigm are encounter, making amends, reintegration, and inclusion. The encounter is where the offender and the victim meet and a discussion of the events take place. This encounter aspect is not a central aspect of community justice initiatives. The second value of restorative justice is that the offender must be willing to make amends for the harm that has been caused to the victim and the community. Depending on the nature of the crime, and the input of the victim and community members, the action required by the offender will look different and can include community work or volunteer activity, for example.

The third value of restorative justice is reintegration, which seeks to restore the victim and offender and whole members of the community. This is a central idea because in mainstream dialogues, when people are labelled in a particular way, that label often sticks, thus limiting their full return to the community as a whole person, rather than as simply a criminal or offender. The final value of the restorative justice model, which is also central to community justice initiatives, is the involvement of the community and other stakeholders in deciding upon a resolution. The victim, offender, community members, and stakeholders such as business owners are the ones who are most affected by the outcomes of improper administration of justice. True community justice models require that those who are most affected have a say in how the issue is managed.

Most lawyers, judges, court workers, police officers, and so on do not live in the communities in which they work. As such, their investment in the outcomes of criminal justice issues can be minimal at best simply because they do not have to live with the consequences of the decisions they make. That is a very narrow and limiting view of the impact of their decisions given that all members of society are affected when some members of the society are disenfranchised. I would argue that the impact of disenfranchisement, marginalization, and oppression are experienced at a global level. The World Trade Center bombings that occurred in America in 2001, the subway attacks in Britain in 2005, and the attack on the offices of Charlie Hebdo in Paris in 2015 were all experienced by the populace in Canada. The shootings on Parliament Hill in Ottawa in 2014 were felt across the entire nation. The rise in religious and racist fundamentalist individuals and groups reverberates in Canada. On June 19, 2015, a 22-year-old White male went into a Black church in South Carolina, sat and prayed with the parishioners for over an hour, and then shot and killed nine of them. His intention, according to news reports, was to shoot Black people in order to start a race war. The result instead was that members of the community came together to support each other. This is an example of what happens when communities and neighbourhoods decide to focus on what they have in common, rather than their superficial differences. The rise in anti-Muslim sentiments and the increased killings of Christians in predominantly Muslim countries are all based on flawed interpretations of doctrines and practices. It is important to understand, therefore, that social justice and anti-oppression practices are the responsibility of every citizen of our society and our world.

Community Justice Initiatives (www.cjiwr.com) in the Waterloo Region of Ontario offers a restorative justice program called Revive that provides support to men and women affected by sexual abuse and trauma. This program also provides support for those who have committed sexual offences. Its youth reintegration program, BackHome, provides youth with a mentor who can support their transition back into the community. Each of these programs recognizes the benefits of providing people with second chances.

Another example of community justice on the front lines is the Stride program, which provides reintegration supports for women returning to the community from federal prison, in addition to support circles and mediation services. The program provides responsive community supports and partnerships that work to empower women to improve their quality of life. This is an example of a program that provides an intersectional analysis of the issues that affect female offenders. The multiple factors at play for these women—their experience of victim turned offender, the collateral trauma they experience when forced to leave their children and the trauma of the separation imposed on their children, and their limited options for viable employment—would all be recognized and taken into consideration when providing reintegration programming. In contrast, simply focusing on one aspect of their life challenges would ensure a continuation of the revolving door cycle that would almost certainly guarantee their re-entry into prison.

Sentencing circles is a practice that has been adopted by the Lanark County Community Justice Program (www.commjustice.org/node/2). This is a court-approved diversion program for youths and adults, to which cases are referred both pre- and post-charge meaning that in some circumstances, if the offender follows through on the agreement, no charges will be laid. In cases where charges have already been laid, they can be dropped or withdrawn. The program is run by trained volunteers who discuss specifics of the case with the offender and develop a written agreement, which becomes a legally binding agreement once the document is signed by all of the parties involved. The agreement outlines what the offender will do to make restitution, or to make things right and repair the harm they have caused. Failure to comply means that the case can be referred back to the police or the Crown and that charges can be laid or sentencing can be applied at that time.

Diversion programs, as the name implies, are programs that have been designed to divert cases away from the formal justice system. They can include youth crimes such as vandalism, threats and minor assaults, and drug charges. The organization Peacebuilders provides restorative youth circles for youth 13 to 20 years of age who are involved with the courts under the Youth Criminal Justice Act (Peacebuilders, 2015). In the case of adults, diversion programs can also include assaults and domestic violence cases. The benefit of diversion programs is that they try to put supports in place to reduce rates of recidivism by addressing the criminogenic factors that led to the criminal act. For example, as indicated, many people commit crimes as a form of survival—stealing clothing and food or breaking and entering to support a drug habit. Providing supports to help individuals access employment or drug addiction treatment programs eliminates the initial crisis that led to the commission of the crime. When these needs are met, the need for continued criminal involvement is significantly curtailed and/or eliminated.

Drug courts and mental health courts are also examples of community justice initiatives. These court-approved programs try to divert these types of cases away from the regular criminal justice system based on the recognition that crimes of this nature require different modes of intervention. There tends to be a correlation between people who have mental health challenges and the misuse of drugs. The workers in these courts often have some level of specialization or heightened understanding of these issues, as well as an awareness of the various community-based options and supports available to people who are dealing with these issues; therefore, referrals can be made and recommendations can be implemented to best support the offender even in situations where they may not qualify for a diversion program. According to research conducted by the Centre for Addiction and Mental Health, which is a central site for mental health and drug treatment programming in Toronto, the rates of recidivism for people who are involved in their programs is very low—approximately 3 percent of participants recidivate. In addition to the low rates of recidivism for the "graduates" of the centre's programs, the cost is significantly lower than the cost of warehousing offenders (Centre for Addiction and Mental Health, n.d.).

In response to the overrepresentation of Aboriginal offenders in the criminal justice system, *Gladue* courts were first implemented in 2001. The courts were developed based on the Supreme Court of Canada recommendation that strategies other than incarceration be put in place to address the needs of Aboriginal offenders. These courts pay particular attention to the circumstances faced by

Aboriginal offenders and factor these issues into their decision-making and sentencing procedures. In their report, April and Magrinelli Orsi (2013) stated that at the time of their research there were 19 *Gladue* courts in Canada, and that education and training had been provided for the majority of staff who worked in those courts to familiarize them with issues related to Aboriginal peoples. The authors indicate that although the situation is not perfect, the existence of these types of community justice initiatives in most provinces is a step in the right direction.

The John Howard Society–Toronto Reintegration Centre, which opened its doors across the street from the Toronto South Detention Centre in 2014, is another example of a community justice initiative aimed at effective reintegration of offenders into the community. Based on research conducted by Daniel, Webber, and the John Howard Society of Toronto (2013), the rationale was developed for the establishment of the centre. The premise behind the development of the centre was to ensure that services are made available to releasees as soon as they exit the detention centre. These services include providing money for transportation, information on housing and job opportunities (including identifying organizations that provide job options to people with criminal records), and referrals to programs including treatment programs and individual and family support services. The research identified the multiple potential benefits of providing such services in a one-stop-shop format, including ensuring that releasees had the necessary resources to facilitate a timely return to their home community, the implementation of a wrap-around case management approach, and early intervention options. In addition, stakeholders in the community where the detention centre is located would not be made to feel uncomfortable because of the presumption that released offenders would remain in their community, thus possibly increasing the crime rates. (It is important to note that the research did not identify any relationship between the presence of a prison and increased crime rates in a community.)

The final example of a community-based justice initiative is the Rexdale Hub, which is located in the northwest part of Toronto in one of the city's 13 priority neighbourhoods. A priority neighbourhood an area that has a number of risk factors, such as high rates of poverty, high numbers of immigrant families, and high population density, which can increase the possibility of the occurrence of crime. In an attempt to increase the equitable distribution of resources, the Ontario government identified 31 neighbourhoods that required additional resources to increase economic opportunities, improve physical surroundings, and encourage healthy lifestyles to reduce the levels of crisis in those areas (City of Toronto, 2014). The Rexdale Hub is highly collaborative in its approach and works closely with local police, social workers, children's aid services, probation, and parole to provide services in the local community. If a member of the community is experiencing some type of crisis, the partner agencies convene a case management meeting to identify the immediate needs and options for resolving the crisis. If, for example, an assault occurs in a family, the police may be called in, but they may not be the ones to take the lead in the case. Instead, a social worker may be the lead partner in this particular situation because it may have emerged during the case conference that the assault was a misunderstanding rather than an actual physical assault. In most cases, once the police are involved, the family is brought into the criminal justice system if charges are laid and the courts may be involved for years before the situation is resolved. The benefit of the Hub's involvement is that the case conference becomes a place where the specifics of the case can be discussed, and the support agencies can analyze it to identify the best course of action, rather than simply engaging in reactionary options. The anecdotal results of the outcomes for clients who have made use of the services offered through the Hub indicate that there is a significant reduction in the number of incidences of future involvement with the law for families and individuals. In addition to this, fewer criminal charges are laid and families develop strategies for seeking supports prior to an actual crisis.

Conclusion

This chapter has provided a discussion of the many benefits of developing healthy communities through the application of community justice principles. The implications of the existing research and the anecdotal patterns are that our systems of justice, offenders, victims, and all community stakeholders would experience significant benefits if society as a whole were changed to centralize community justice values. The benefits of advocacy, early intervention, effective reintegration, and support services are immeasurable. And the impact for all of us as members of Canadian society is both immediate and long term. The only way in which people can make a commitment to social justice is by laying bare the devastation of injustice. This volume has attempted to provide a brief look into the realities of life for members of our society who are affected by multiple and longstanding experiences of unjust social practices and criminal justice procedures. It is hoped that by examining these realities, those of you who have read these pieces will have developed an enhanced sensitivity to the issues and will revisit this text to help you reaffirm your commitment to developing a socially, morally, and ethically just, equitable, and anti-oppressive society.

Discussion Questions

1. Identify something (characteristic, practice, behaviour, etc.) that is present in one community or racial group that absolutely *does not* exist in any other community or group. (Note: you cannot choose religious practices, because they are culturally determined).
2. Identify one pattern of crime or criminality that exists in *only one* group on earth and that has never occurred amongst the members of another group. If you are able to identify one, please discuss what accounts for that difference. If you are not able to, please also discuss why you were unable to do so.
3. Discuss some of the community-based strategies that can be adopted when working with marginalized groups in society.

Additional Resources

Alberta Restorative Justice Association. (2011). Research and Articles: http://www.arjassoc.ca/index.php/resources/research.

Public Safety Canada. (2015). Restorative Justice: http://www.publicsafety.gc.ca/cnt/cntrng-crm/crrctns/rstrtv-jstc-eng.aspx.

Royal Canadian Mounted Police (RCMP). (2008). Community Justice Forums: http://www.rcmp-grc.gc.ca/pubs/ccaps-spcca/cjf-fjc-eng.htm.

Note

1. See documentary *Crisis of Distrust: Police and Community in Toronto*, available at https://www.youtube.com/watch?v=u627BsqA5BM.

References

April, S., & Magrinelli Orsi, M. (2013). Gladue *practices in the provinces and territories*. Ottawa: Department of Justice Canada.

Centre for Addiction and Mental Health. (n.d.). About drug treatment courts. Retrieved from http://www.tdtc.ca/about

City of Toronto. (2014, March 4). Toronto Strong Neighbourhoods Strategy 2020: Recommended neighbourhood improvement areas. Retrieved from http://www.toronto.ca/legdocs/mmis/2014/cd/bgrd/backgroundfile-67382.pdf

Cole, D. (2015, April 21). The skin I'm in: I've been interrogated by police more than 50 times — all because I'm Black. *Toronto Life*.

Comack, E. (2012). *Racialized policing: Aboriginal people's encounters with the police*. Black Point, NS: Fernwood.

Daniel, B.-J., Webber, J., & the John Howard Society of Toronto. (2013). *The impact of "prison sitting" on host communities in Toronto*. Toronto: Humber College & the John Howard Society.

Delgado, R. A., & Stefanic, J. (2001). *Critical race theory: An introduction*. New York: New York University Press.

Downey, D. B., Ainsworth, J. W., & Qian, Z. (2009). Rethinking the attitude-achievement paradox among Blacks. *Sociology of Education*, 82(1), 1–19.

Gans, H. J. (1995). *The war against the poor*. New York: Basic Books.

Haberman, M. (1991). The pedagogy of poverty versus good teaching. *Phi Delta Kappan*, 73(4), 290–294.

Haque, E. (2010). Homegrown, Muslim and other: Tolerance, secularism and the limits of multiculturalism. *Social Identities*, 16(1), 79–101.

Jewkes, Y. (2011). *Media and crime*. Los Angeles: Sage.

Lanark County Community Justice Program. (n.d.). History. Retrieved from www.commjustice.org/node/2.

McMurtry, R., & Curling, A. (2008). *The review of the roots of youth violence*. Toronto: Service Ontario Publications.

Peacebuilders. (2015). Restorative youth circles. Retrieved from http://peacebuilders.ca/programs/restorative-youth-circles/

Philipupillai, G. G. (2013). *The marking of Tamil youth and the making of Canada as a White settler society*. Master of Arts thesis, University of Toronto.

Sampson, R. J., & Wilson, W. J. (2005). Towards a theory of race, crime and urban inequality. In S. L. Gabbidon & H. T. Greene (Eds.), *Crime and justice: A reader*. New York: Routledge.

Shaw, C. R., & McKay, H. D. (1942). *Juvenile delinquency and urban areas: A study of rates of delinquents in relation to differential characteristics of local communities in American cities*. Chicago: University of Chicago Press.

Tardiel, C. (2015). Racial profiling: The unintended outcomes of street checks. Vaughan, ON: The Association of Black Law Enforcers.

Warner, B. D., Beck, E., & Ohmer, M. L. (2010). Linking infomal sector control and restorative justice: Moving social disorganization theory beyond community policing. *Contemporary Justice Review: Issues in Criminal, Social and Restorative Justice*, 13(4), 355–369.

AUTHOR BIOGRAPHIES

Beverly-Jean M. Daniel holds a PhD in Sociology and Equity Studies in Education (OISE/University of Toronto) with a combined focus on Women and Gender Studies. For more than 20 years her academic work has investigated and conceptualized race, racism, and equity. She currently holds the position of Professor in the Community and Justice Studies Program at Humber College in Toronto. In 2012, she founded and developed a groundbreaking student intervention program, The Bridge, at Humber College. This program, the first of its kind in any Canadian college or university, identifies the types of programming and strategies needed to foster and enhance academic success in post-secondary institutions among students who self-identify as African, Black, and Caribbean.

Sabra Desai is Administrator and Faculty Member at Humber Institute of Technology and Advanced Learning/Polytechnic. She currently works with internal and external partners to co-create and deliver programs facilitating access to post-secondary education and employment for marginalized and vulnerable youth and adults.

Marty Fink works in archives, zines, and digital media to bridge activist histories of resistance with contemporary queer/trans cultures. His work has appeared in journals including *Science Fiction Studies*, *Television and New Media*, *Jump Cut*, and *The Journal of Fat Studies*, and in the recent book *Disrupting Queer Inclusion: Canadian Homonationalisms and the Politics of Belonging* (2015). He is Assistant Professor in the School of Professional Communication at Ryerson University and works with Montreal's Prisoner Correspondence Project.

Jennifer Fraser is a decolonial feminist who received her PhD in Criminology from the University of Ottawa in 2014. She conducts social justice research and is active in community work on violence against women and Indigenous history. Currently, she is Assistant Professor of Sociology at Bishop's University in Lennoxville, Quebec.

Mia Hershkowitz is a fourth-year student in the Criminal Justice Degree Program and a Research Assistant with the Female Gang Research Project at Humber College in Toronto.

Ahmed Ali Ilmi is Lecturer in the Department of Historical Studies, University of Toronto Mississauga. He teaches courses in diaspora studies, sociology of education, and culture philosophies. He is the author of *The "Say Walahi" Generation: Identity, Profiling, Tradition and Survival from a Somali Canadian Perspective* (2013), and co-editor (with Njoki Wane and Francis Adyanga) of *Spiritual Discourse in the Academy: A Globalized Indigenous Perspective* (2014). His current research interests include African/Black diaspora identities, cultural knowledges, and the history of social movements in Somalia.

Greg McElligott is Professor of Community and Justice Services/Criminal Justice at Humber College. He is the author of *Beyond Service: State Workers, Public Policy, and the Prospects for Democratic Administration* (2001) and several articles on corrections officers and other frontline workers. His current research focuses on the role of prisons in neoconservative labour market policy and alternative work arrangements in prison and beyond.

Rai Reece has published in the areas of race and racism, Canadian Black feminist criminology, and social justice education, and has coordinated project initiatives focusing on eradicating violence against women and children. She has a PhD in Women's Studies from York University and was formerly employed as the Women's Prison Program Coordinator for the Prisoners' HIV/AIDS Support Action Network (PASAN) and the Toronto District School Board. She is currently Professor in the Community Justice Services program at Humber College.

Aqeel Saeid is Professor of Criminal Justice in the School of Social and Community Services at Humber Institute of Technology and Advanced Learning. He has been an educator of sociology and criminology since 1995. He is a past President of the United Nations Association–Toronto Regional Branch (UNACTO) and a former board member of the Children's Aid Society of Toronto (CAST). He has been involved in research that addresses a variety of issues related to sociology of religion, settlement, problem gambling, addiction, and immigration. He has authored three books and articles of several academic journals.

Emily Stroebel is a graduate of the Criminal Justice Degree Program and Coordinator of the Female Gang Research Project at Humber College in Toronto.

Mark Totten is Professor in the Criminal Justice Degree Program at Humber College in Toronto. As a registered social worker and researcher, he has worked with groups across Canada in the areas of gangs, mental health, violence, and corrections for many years. His fifth book, which focuses on female gangs, will be released in late 2017.

Copyright Acknowledgements